GUARD… of the GALAXY

M… ENTROPY

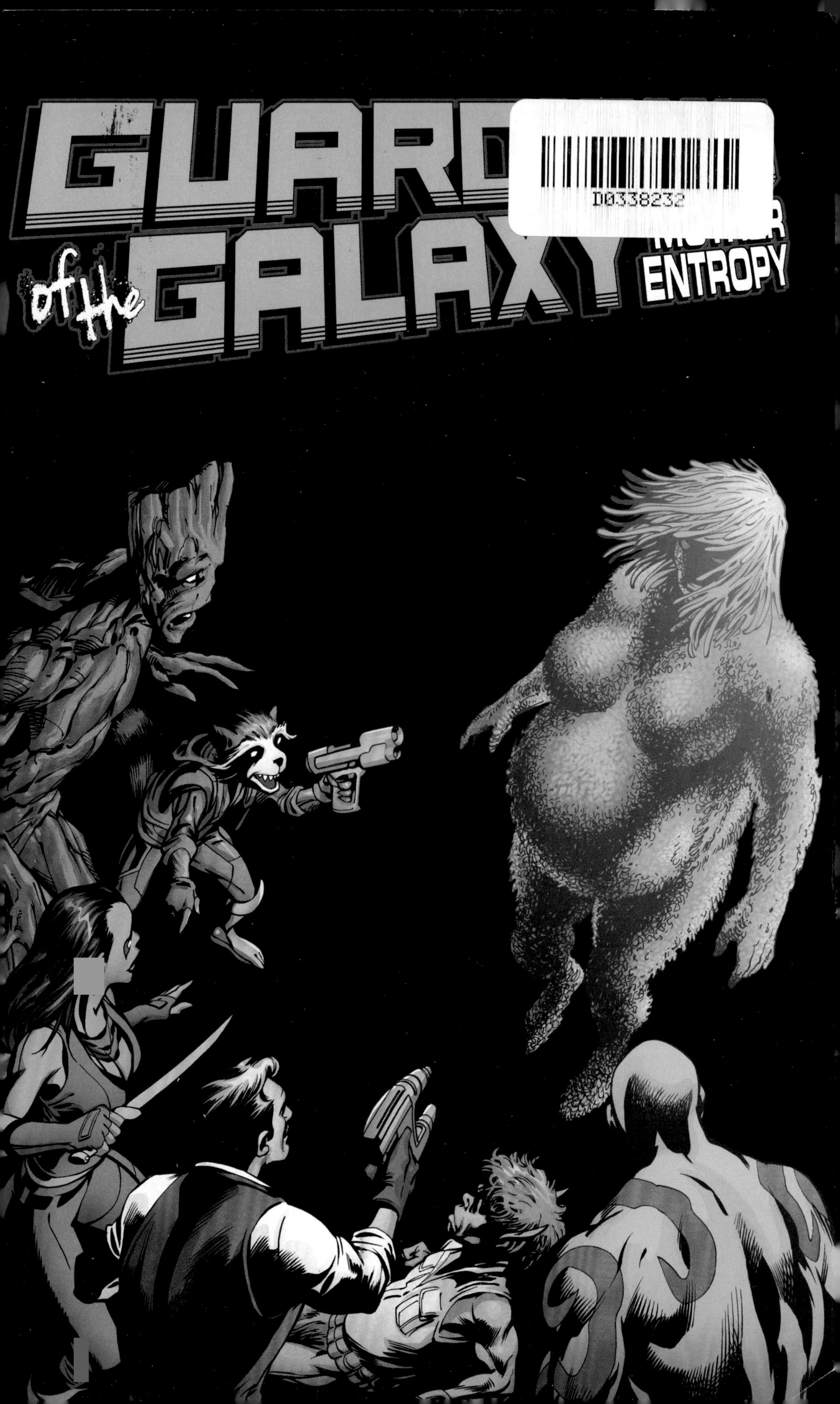

COLLECTION EDITOR **MARK D. BEAZLEY**
ASSISTANT EDITOR **CAITLIN O´CONNELL**
ASSOCIATE MANAGING EDITOR **KATERI WOODY**
ASSOCIATE MANAGER, DIGITAL ASSETS **JOE HOCHSTEIN**
SENIOR EDITOR, SPECIAL PROJECTS **JENNIFER GRÜNWALD**
VP PRODUCTION & SPECIAL PROJECTS **JEFF YOUNGQUIST**
SVP PRINT, SALES & MARKETING **DAVID GABRIEL**
BOOK DESIGNER **JAY BOWEN**

EDITOR IN CHIEF **AXEL ALONSO**
CHIEF CREATIVE OFFICER **JOE QUESADA**
PRESIDENT **DAN BUCKLEY**
EXECUTIVE PRODUCER **ALAN FINE**

GUARDIANS OF THE GALAXY: MOTHER ENTROPY. Contains material originally published in magazine form as GUARDIANS OF THE GALAXY: MOTHER ENTROPY #1-5. First printing 2017. ISBN# 978-1-302-90488-3. Published by MARVEL WORLDWIDE, INC., a subsidiary of MARVEL ENTERTAINMENT, LLC. OFFICE OF PUBLICATION: 135 West 50th Street, New York, NY 10020. Copyright © 2017 MARVEL No similarity between any of the names, characters, persons, and/or institutions in this magazine with those of any living or dead person or institution is intended, and any such similarity which may exist is purely coincidental. **Printed in Canada.** DAN BUCKLEY, President, Marvel Entertainment; JOE QUESADA, Chief Creative Officer; TOM BREVOORT, SVP of Publishing; DAVID BOGART, SVP of Business Affairs & Operations, Publishing & Partnership; C.B. CEBULSKI, VP of Brand Management & Development, Asia; DAVID GABRIEL, SVP of Sales & Marketing, Publishing; JEFF YOUNGQUIST, VP of Production & Special Projects; DAN CARR, Executive Director of Publishing Technology; ALEX MORALES, Director of Publishing Operations; SUSAN CRESPI, Production Manager; STAN LEE, Chairman Emeritus. For information regarding advertising in Marvel Comics or on Marvel.com. please contact Vit DeBellis, Integrated Sales Manager, at vdebellis@marvel.com. For Marvel subscription inquiries, please call 888-511-5480. **Manufactured between 6/23/2017 and 7/25/2017 by SOLISCO PRINTERS, SCOTT, QC, CANADA.**

10 9 8 7 6 5 4 3 2 1

GUARDIANS of the GALAXY
MOTHER ENTROPY

JIM STARLIN
WRITER

ALAN DAVIS
PENCILER

MARK FARMER
INKER

MATT YACKEY
COLORIST

VC'S CORY PETIT
LETTERER

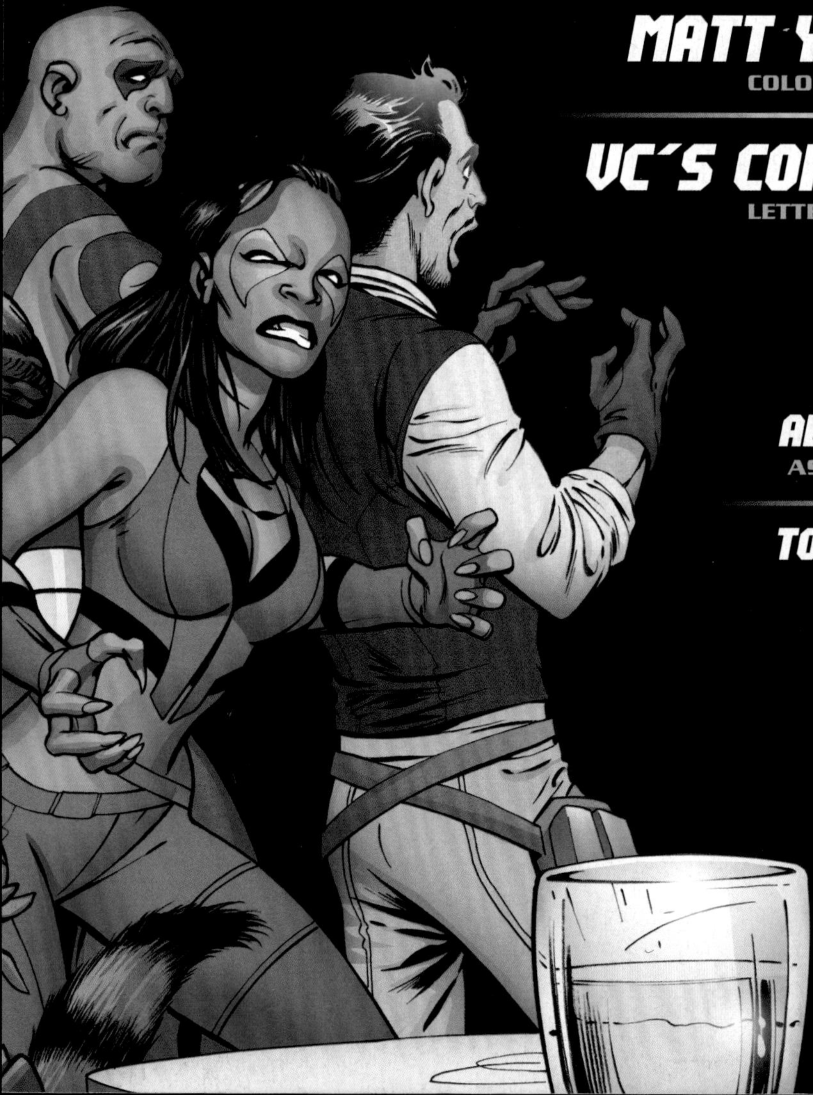

ALANNA SMITH
ASSISTANT EDITOR

TOM BREVOORT
EDITOR

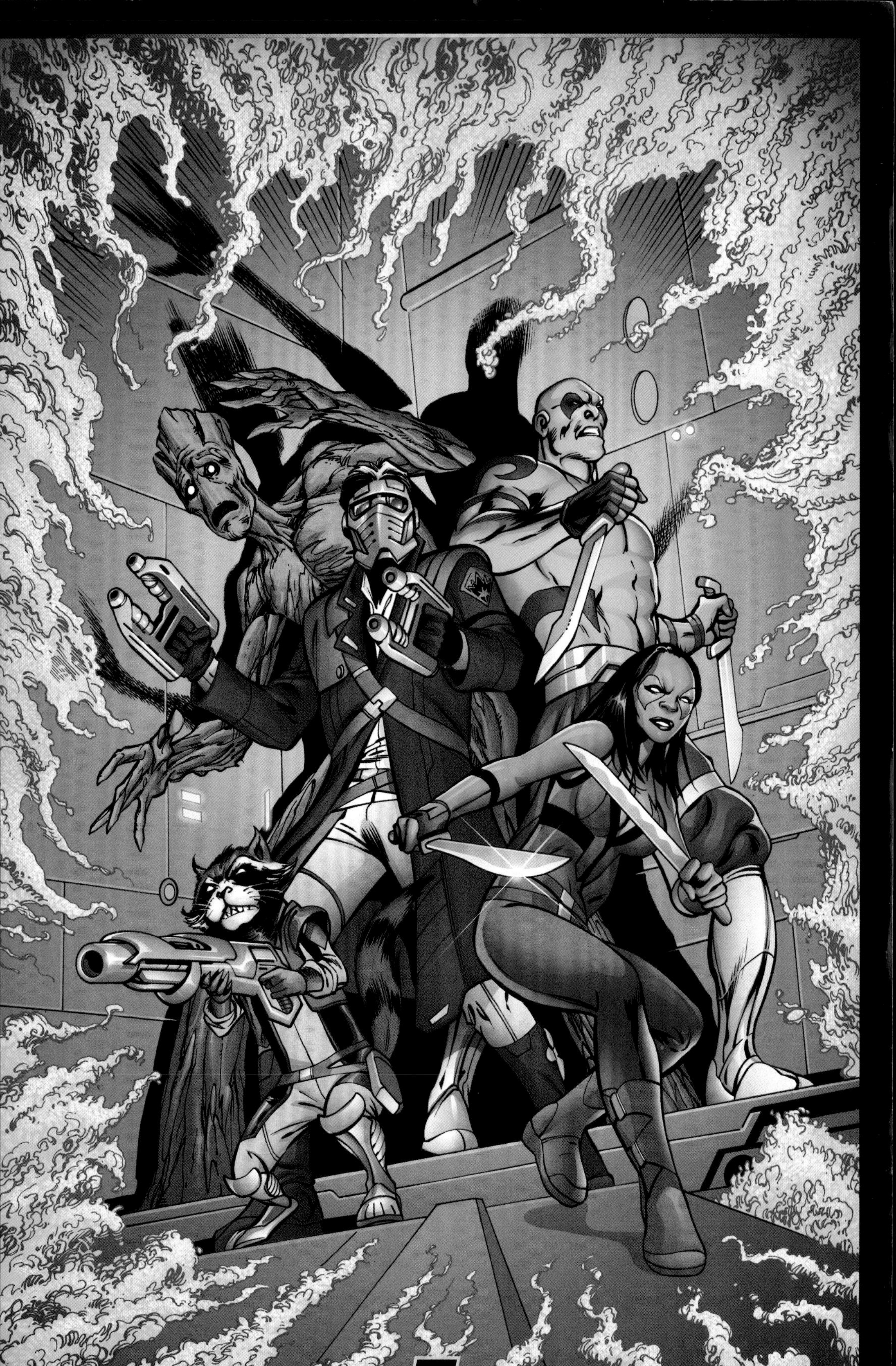

1

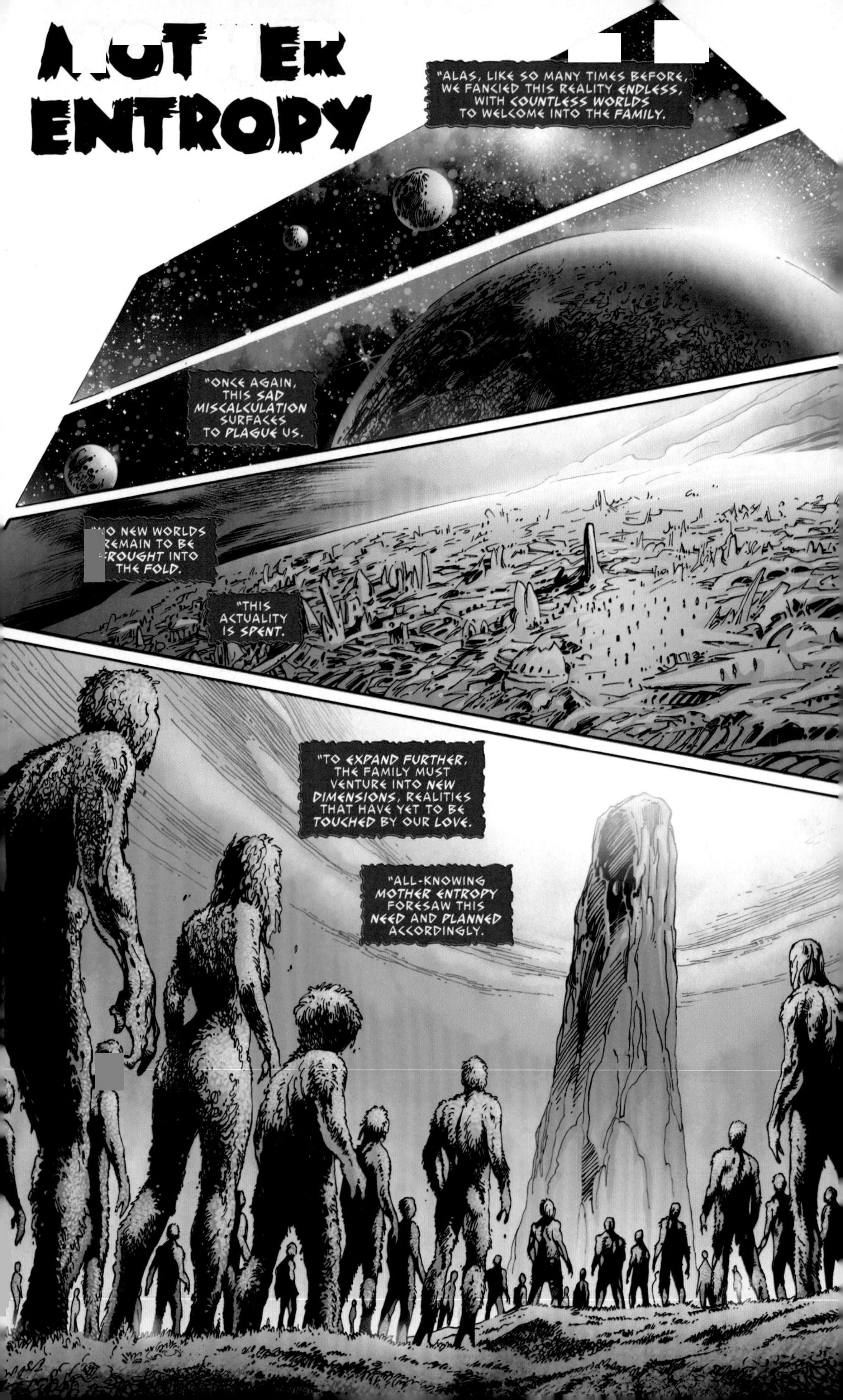
ENTROPY
"ALAS, LIKE SO MANY TIMES BEFORE, WE FANCIED THIS REALITY ENDLESS, WITH COUNTLESS WORLDS TO WELCOME INTO THE FAMILY.
"ONCE AGAIN, THIS SAD MISCALCULATION SURFACES TO PLAGUE US.
O NEW WORLDS EMAIN TO BE ROUGHT INTO THE FOLD.
"THIS ACTUALITY IS SPENT.
"TO EXPAND FURTHER, THE FAMILY MUST VENTURE INTO NEW DIMENSIONS, REALITIES THAT HAVE YET TO BE TOUCHED BY OUR LOVE.
"ALL-KNOWING MOTHER ENTROPY FORESAW THIS NEED AND PLANNED ACCORDINGLY.

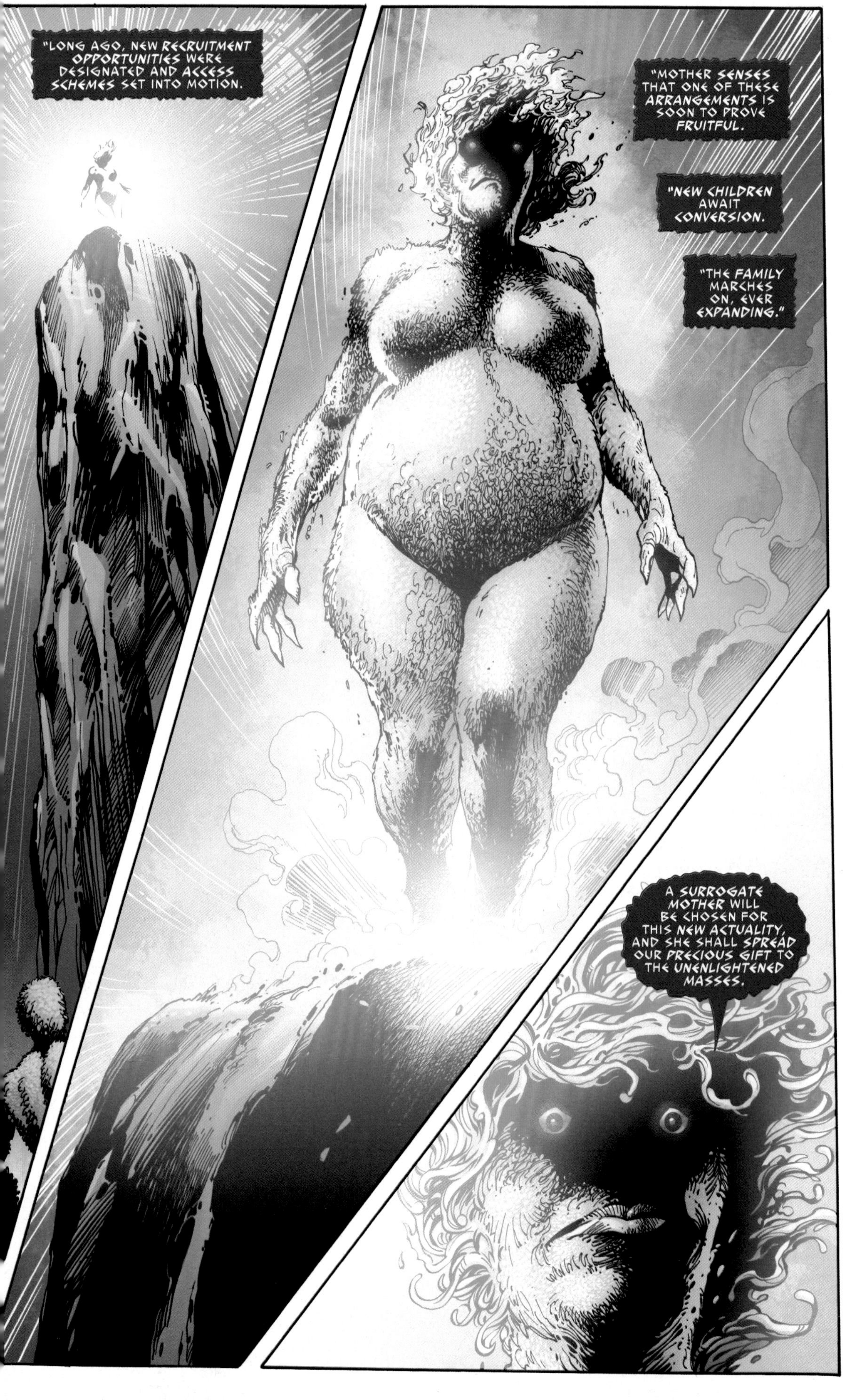
"LONG AGO, NEW RECRUITMENT OPPORTUNITIES WERE DESIGNATED AND ACCESS SCHEMES SET INTO MOTION.
"MOTHER SENSES THAT ONE OF THESE ARRANGEMENTS IS SOON TO PROVE FRUITFUL.
"NEW CHILDREN AWAIT CONVERSION.
"THE FAMILY MARCHES ON, EVER EXPANDING."
A SURROGATE MOTHER WILL BE CHOSEN FOR THIS NEW ACTUALITY, AND SHE SHALL SPREAD OUR PRECIOUS GIFT TO THE UNENLIGHTENED MASSES.

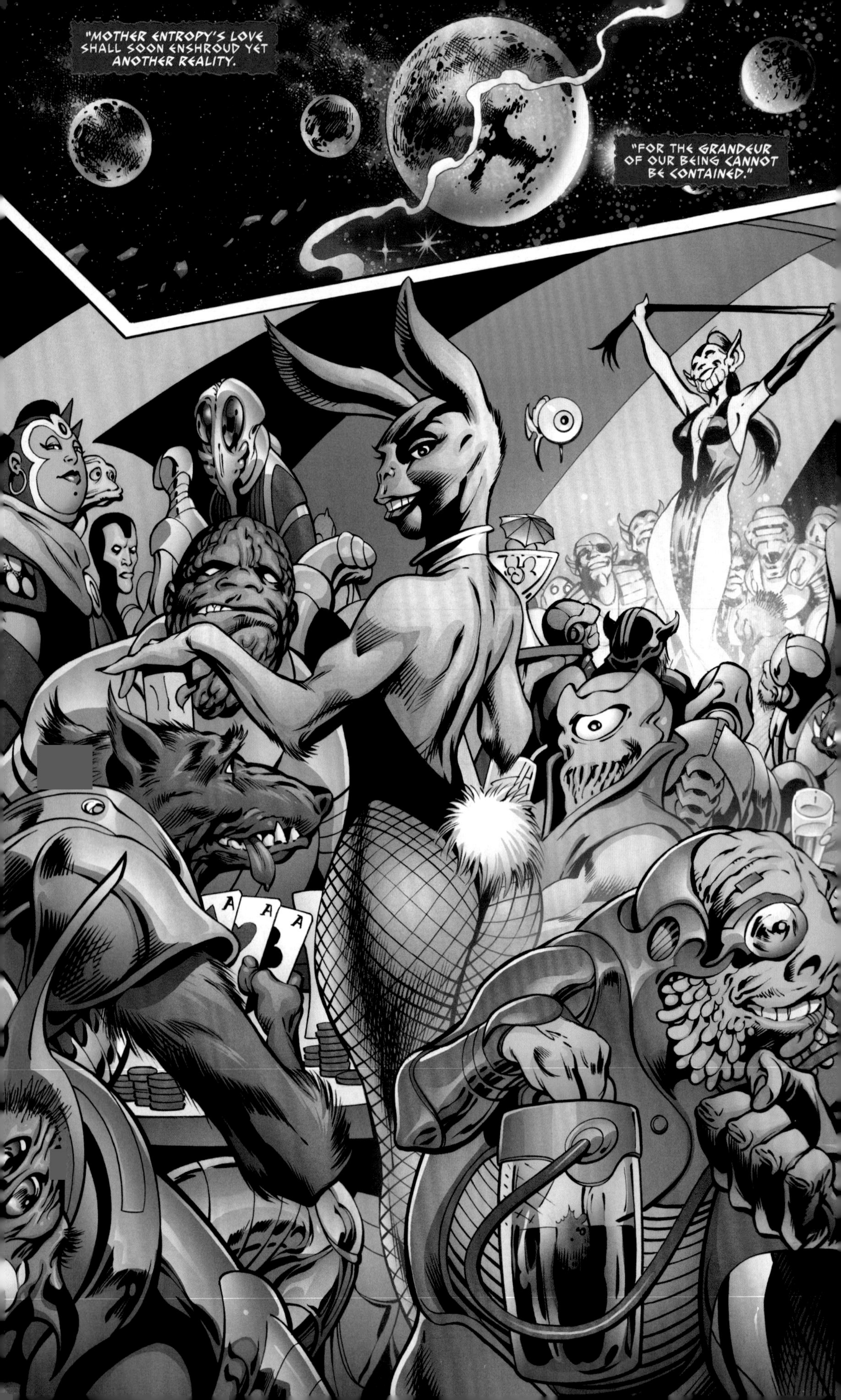
"MOTHER ENTROPY'S LOVE SHALL SOON ENSHROUD YET ANOTHER REALITY.
"FOR THE GRANDEUR OF OUR BEING CANNOT BE CONTAINED."

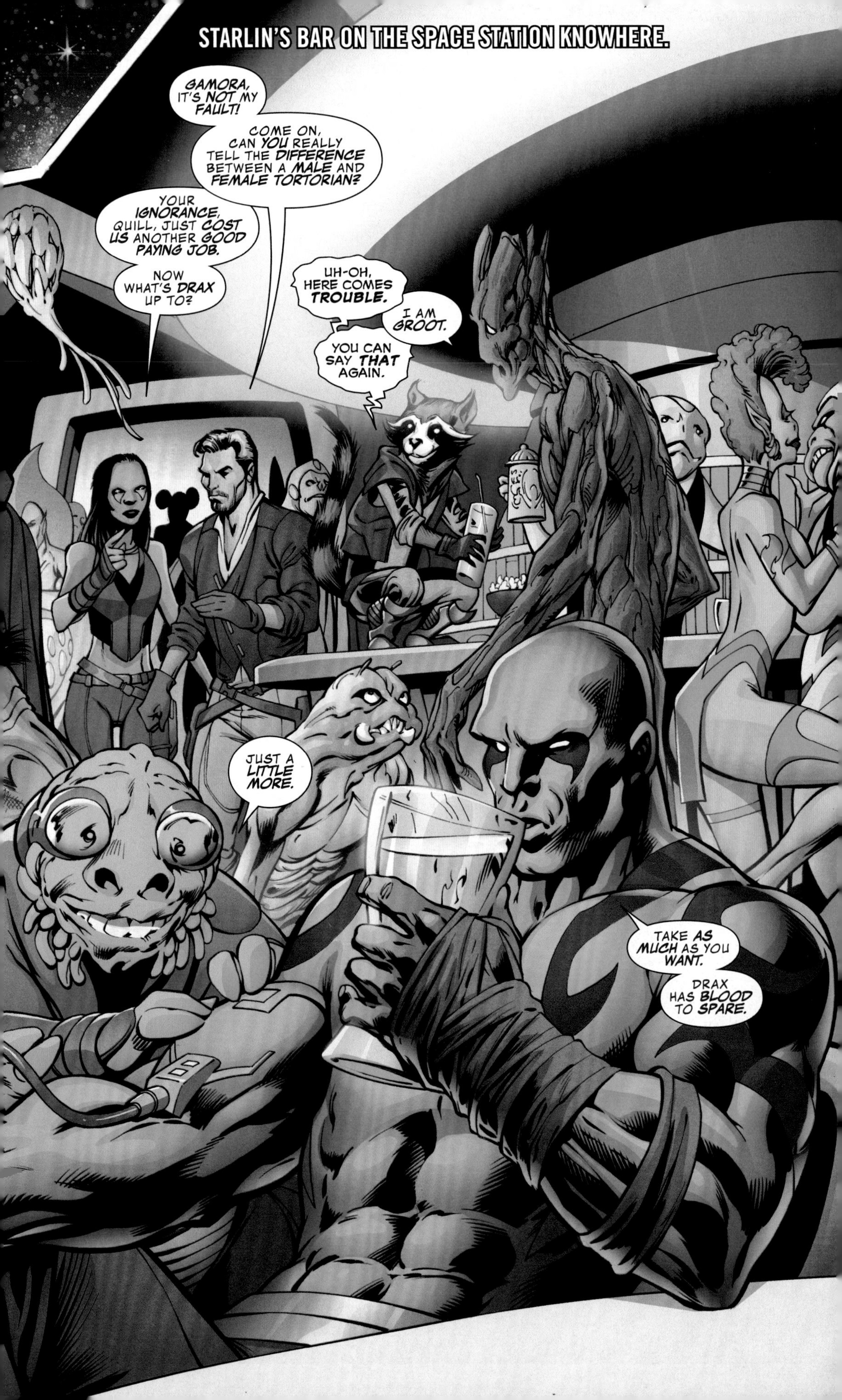
STARLIN'S BAR ON THE SPACE STATION KNOWHERE.
GAMORA, IT'S NOT MY FAULT!
COME ON, CAN YOU REALLY TELL THE DIFFERENCE BETWEEN A MALE AND FEMALE TORTORIAN?
YOUR IGNORANCE, QUILL, JUST COST US ANOTHER GOOD PAYING JOB.
NOW WHAT'S DRAX UP TO?
UH-OH, HERE COMES TROUBLE.
I AM GROOT.
YOU CAN SAY THAT AGAIN.
JUST A LITTLE MORE.
TAKE AS MUCH AS YOU WANT.
DRAX HAS BLOOD TO SPARE.

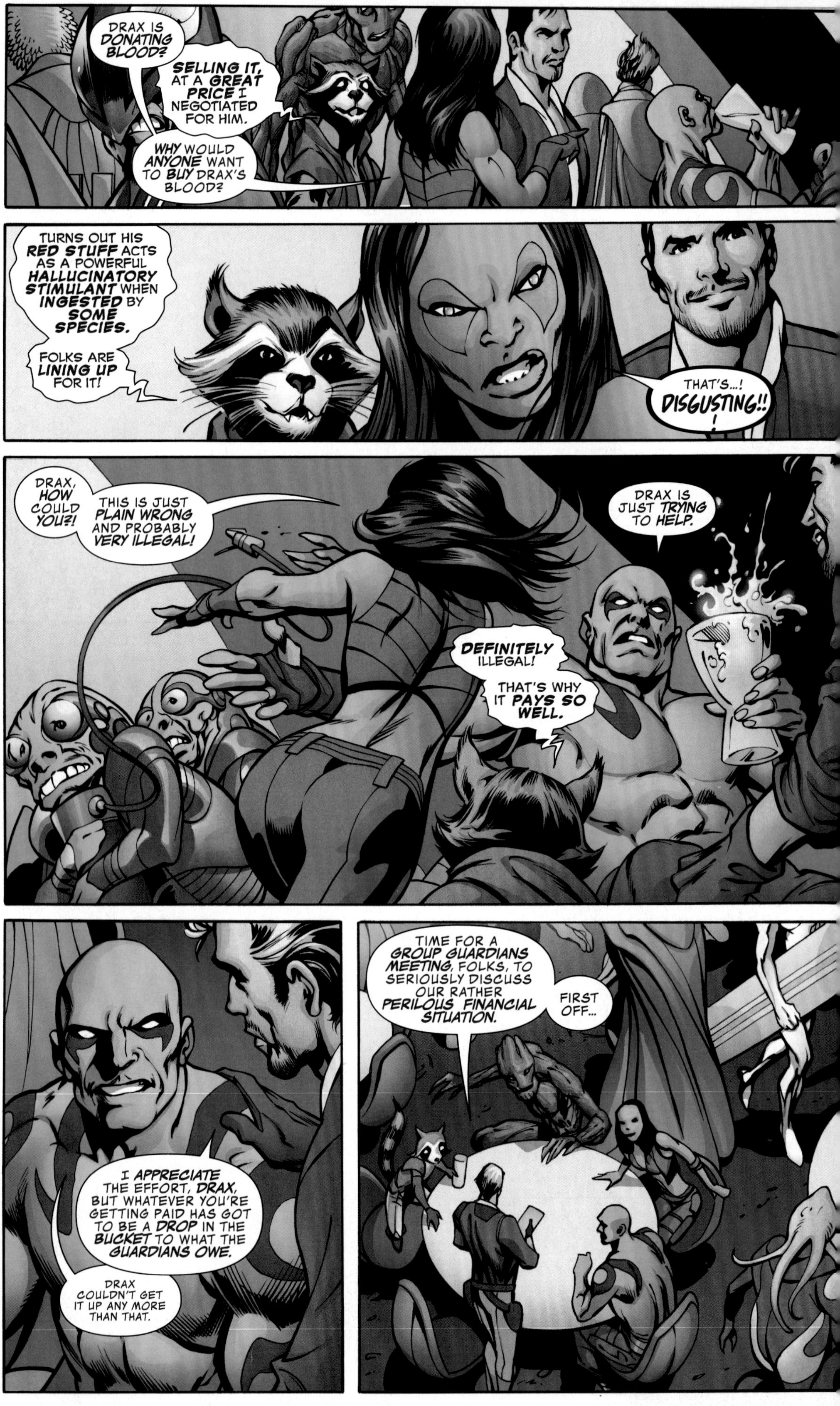
DRAX IS DONATING BLOOD?
SELLING IT, AT A GREAT PRICE I NEGOTIATED FOR HIM.
WHY WOULD ANYONE WANT TO BUY DRAX'S BLOOD?
TURNS OUT HIS RED STUFF ACTS AS A POWERFUL HALLUCINATORY STIMULANT WHEN INGESTED BY SOME SPECIES.
FOLKS ARE LINING UP FOR IT!
THAT'S...! DISGUSTING!!!
DRAX, HOW COULD YOU?!
THIS IS JUST PLAIN WRONG AND PROBABLY VERY ILLEGAL!
DRAX IS JUST TRYING TO HELP.
DEFINITELY ILLEGAL!
THAT'S WHY IT PAYS SO WELL.
I APPRECIATE THE EFFORT, DRAX, BUT WHATEVER YOU'RE GETTING PAID HAS GOT TO BE A DROP IN THE BUCKET TO WHAT THE GUARDIANS OWE.
DRAX COULDN'T GET IT UP ANY MORE THAN THAT.
TIME FOR A GROUP GUARDIANS MEETING, FOLKS, TO SERIOUSLY DISCUSS OUR RATHER PERILOUS FINANCIAL SITUATION.
FIRST OFF...

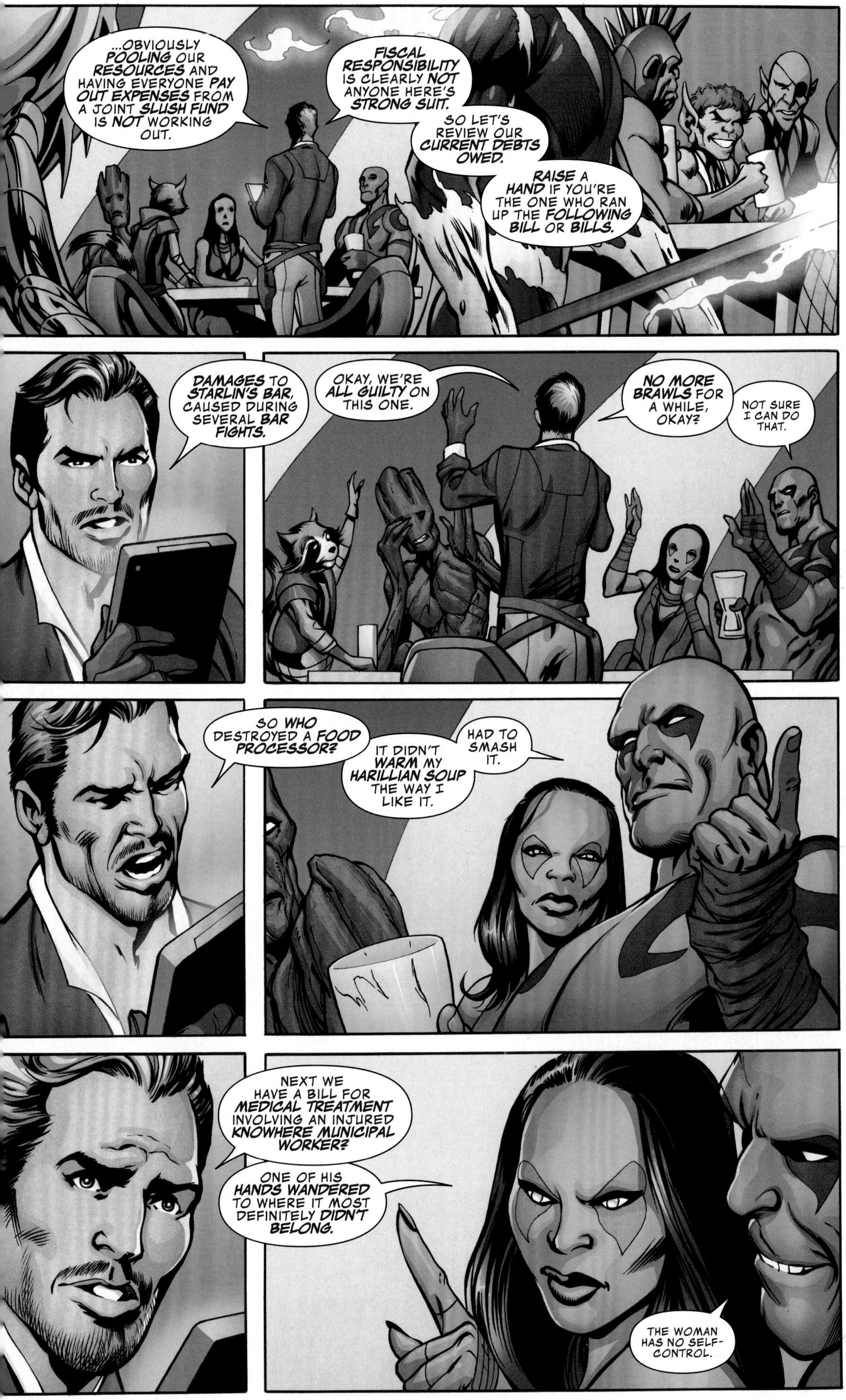
...OBVIOUSLY POOLING OUR RESOURCES AND HAVING EVERYONE PAY OUT EXPENSES FROM A JOINT SLUSH FUND IS NOT WORKING OUT.
FISCAL RESPONSIBILITY IS CLEARLY NOT ANYONE HERE'S STRONG SUIT.
SO LET'S REVIEW OUR CURRENT DEBTS OWED.
RAISE A HAND IF YOU'RE THE ONE WHO RAN UP THE FOLLOWING BILL OR BILLS.
DAMAGES TO STARLIN'S BAR, CAUSED DURING SEVERAL BAR FIGHTS.
OKAY, WE'RE ALL GUILTY ON THIS ONE.
NO MORE BRAWLS FOR A WHILE, OKAY?
NOT SURE I CAN DO THAT.
SO WHO DESTROYED A FOOD PROCESSOR?
IT DIDN'T WARM MY HARILLIAN SOUP THE WAY I LIKE IT.
HAD TO SMASH IT.
NEXT WE HAVE A BILL FOR MEDICAL TREATMENT INVOLVING AN INJURED KNOWHERE MUNICIPAL WORKER?
ONE OF HIS HANDS WANDERED TO WHERE IT MOST DEFINITELY DIDN'T BELONG.
THE WOMAN HAS NO SELF-CONTROL.

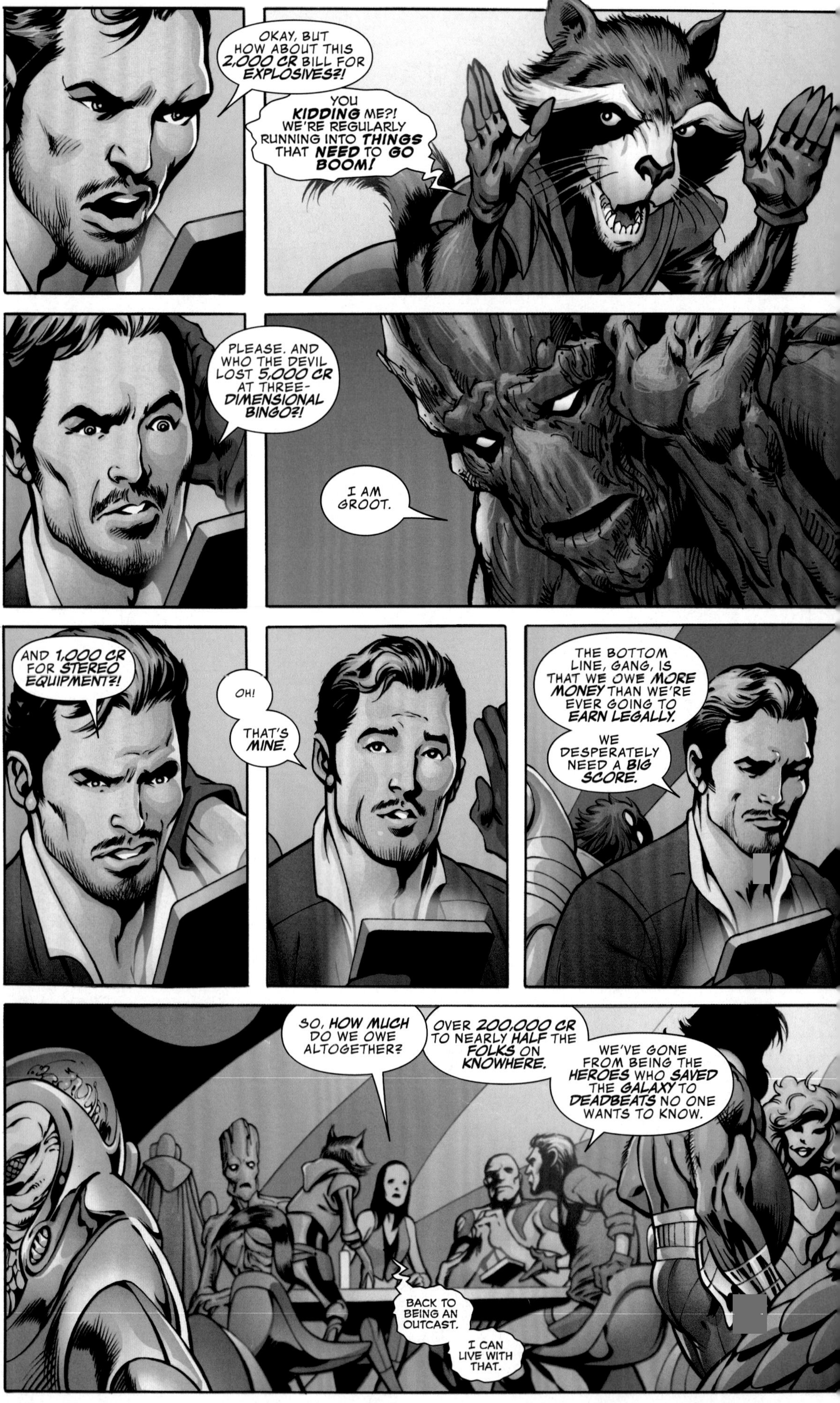
OKAY, BUT HOW ABOUT THIS 2,000 CR BILL FOR EXPLOSIVES?!
YOU KIDDING ME?! WE'RE REGULARLY RUNNING INTO THINGS THAT NEED TO GO BOOM!
PLEASE. AND WHO THE DEVIL LOST 5,000 CR AT THREE-DIMENSIONAL BINGO?!
I AM GROOT.
AND 1,000 CR FOR STEREO EQUIPMENT?!
OH!
THAT'S MINE.
THE BOTTOM LINE, GANG, IS THAT WE OWE MORE MONEY THAN WE'RE EVER GOING TO EARN LEGALLY.
WE DESPERATELY NEED A BIG SCORE.
SO, HOW MUCH DO WE OWE ALTOGETHER?
OVER 200,000 CR TO NEARLY HALF THE FOLKS ON KNOWHERE.
WE'VE GONE FROM BEING THE HEROES WHO SAVED THE GALAXY TO DEADBEATS NO ONE WANTS TO KNOW.
BACK TO BEING AN OUTCAST.
I CAN LIVE WITH THAT.

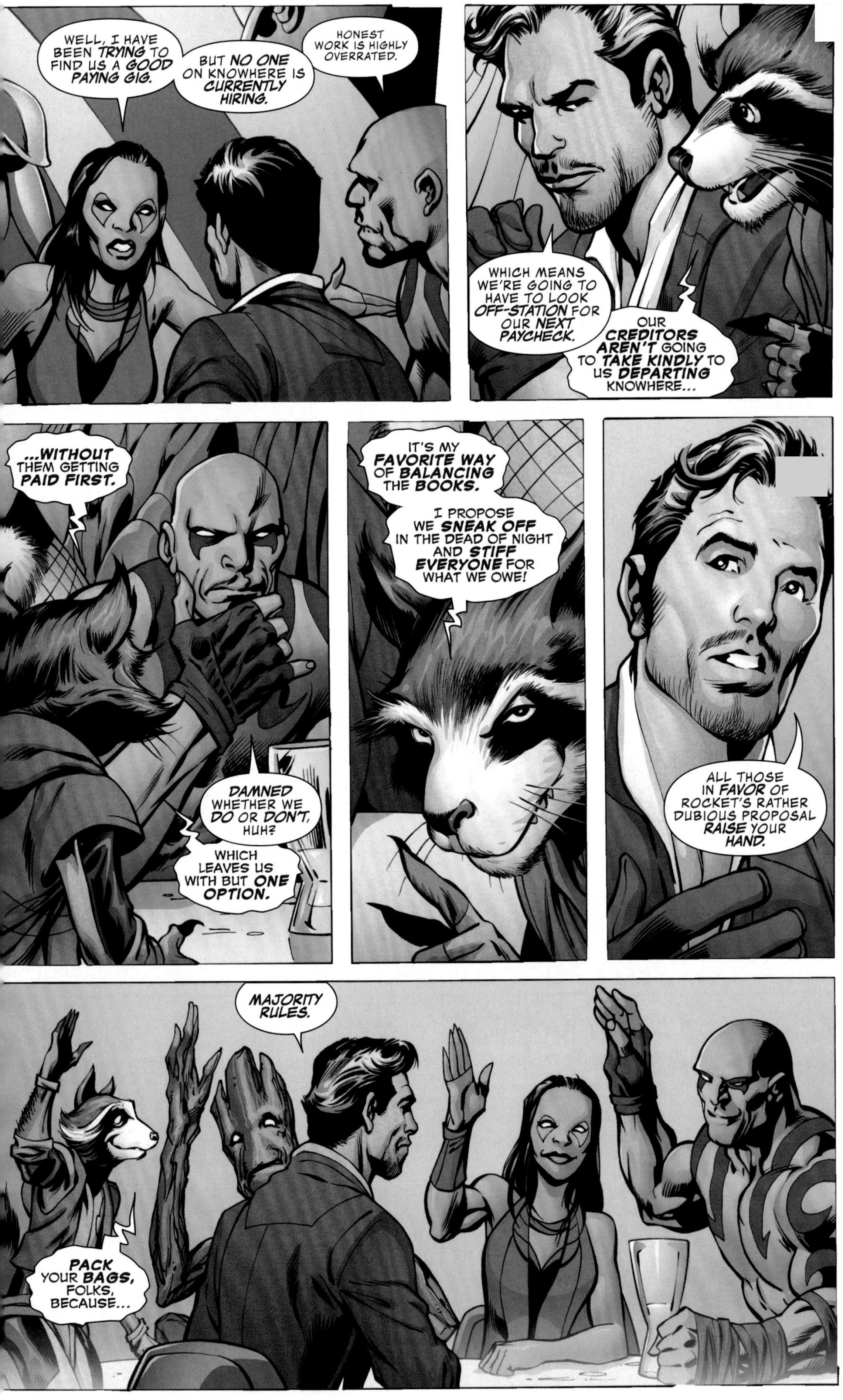
WELL, I HAVE BEEN TRYING TO FIND US A GOOD PAYING GIG.
BUT NO ONE ON KNOWHERE IS CURRENTLY HIRING.
HONEST WORK IS HIGHLY OVERRATED.
WHICH MEANS WE'RE GOING TO HAVE TO LOOK OFF-STATION FOR OUR NEXT PAYCHECK.
OUR CREDITORS AREN'T GOING TO TAKE KINDLY TO US DEPARTING KNOWHERE...
...WITHOUT THEM GETTING PAID FIRST.
DAMNED WHETHER WE DO OR DON'T, HUH?
WHICH LEAVES US WITH BUT ONE OPTION.
IT'S MY FAVORITE WAY OF BALANCING THE BOOKS.
I PROPOSE WE SNEAK OFF IN THE DEAD OF NIGHT AND STIFF EVERYONE FOR WHAT WE OWE!
ALL THOSE IN FAVOR OF ROCKET'S RATHER DUBIOUS PROPOSAL RAISE YOUR HAND.
MAJORITY RULES.
PACK YOUR BAGS, FOLKS, BECAUSE...

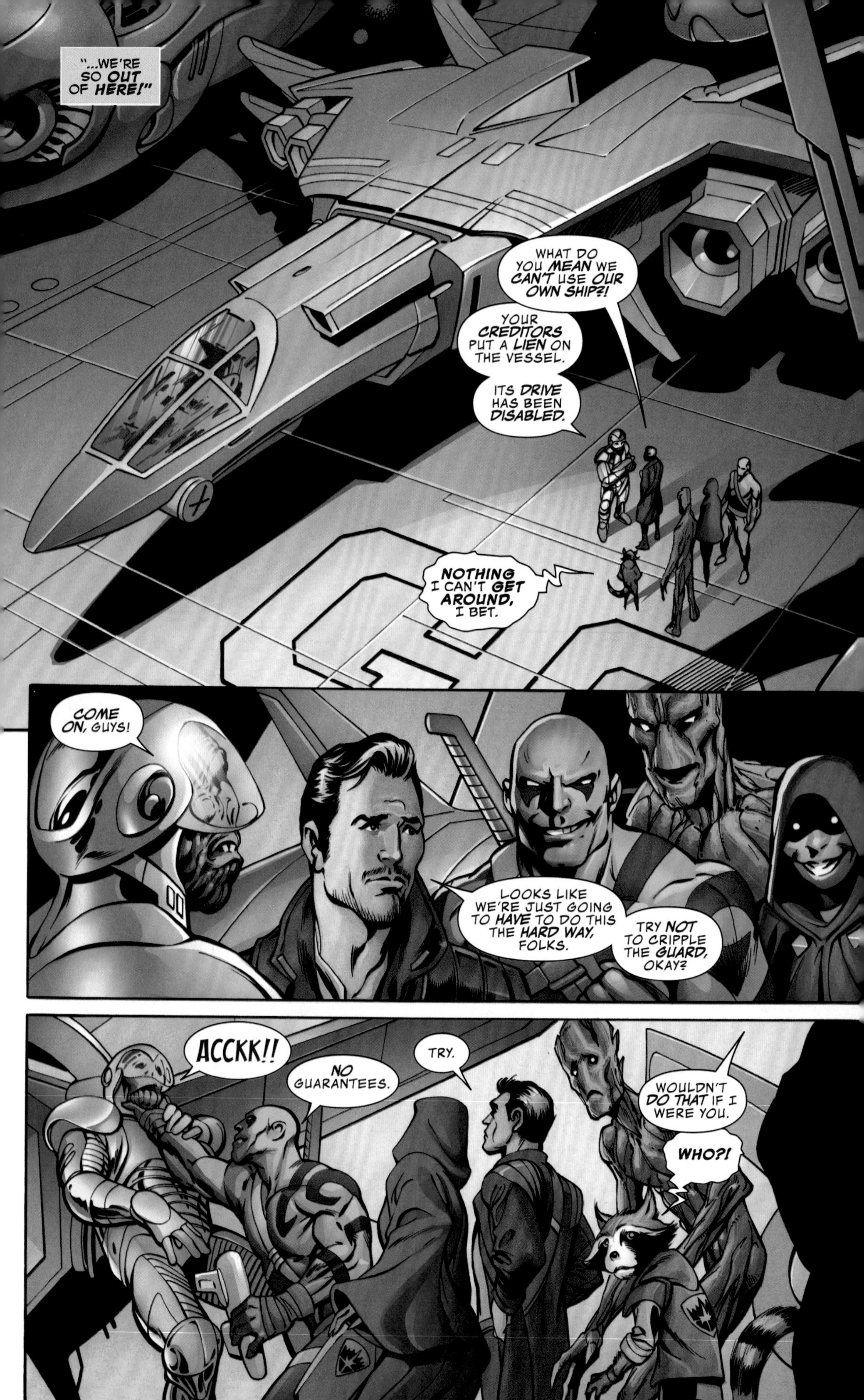
"...WE'RE SO OUT OF HERE!"
WHAT DO YOU MEAN WE CAN'T USE OUR OWN SHIP?!
YOUR CREDITORS PUT A LIEN ON THE VESSEL.
ITS DRIVE HAS BEEN DISABLED.
NOTHING I CAN'T GET AROUND, I BET.
COME ON, GUYS!
LOOKS LIKE WE'RE JUST GOING TO HAVE TO DO THIS THE HARD WAY, FOLKS.
TRY NOT TO CRIPPLE THE GUARD, OKAY?
ACCKK!!
NO GUARANTEES.
TRY.
WOULDN'T DO THAT IF I WERE YOU.
WHO?!

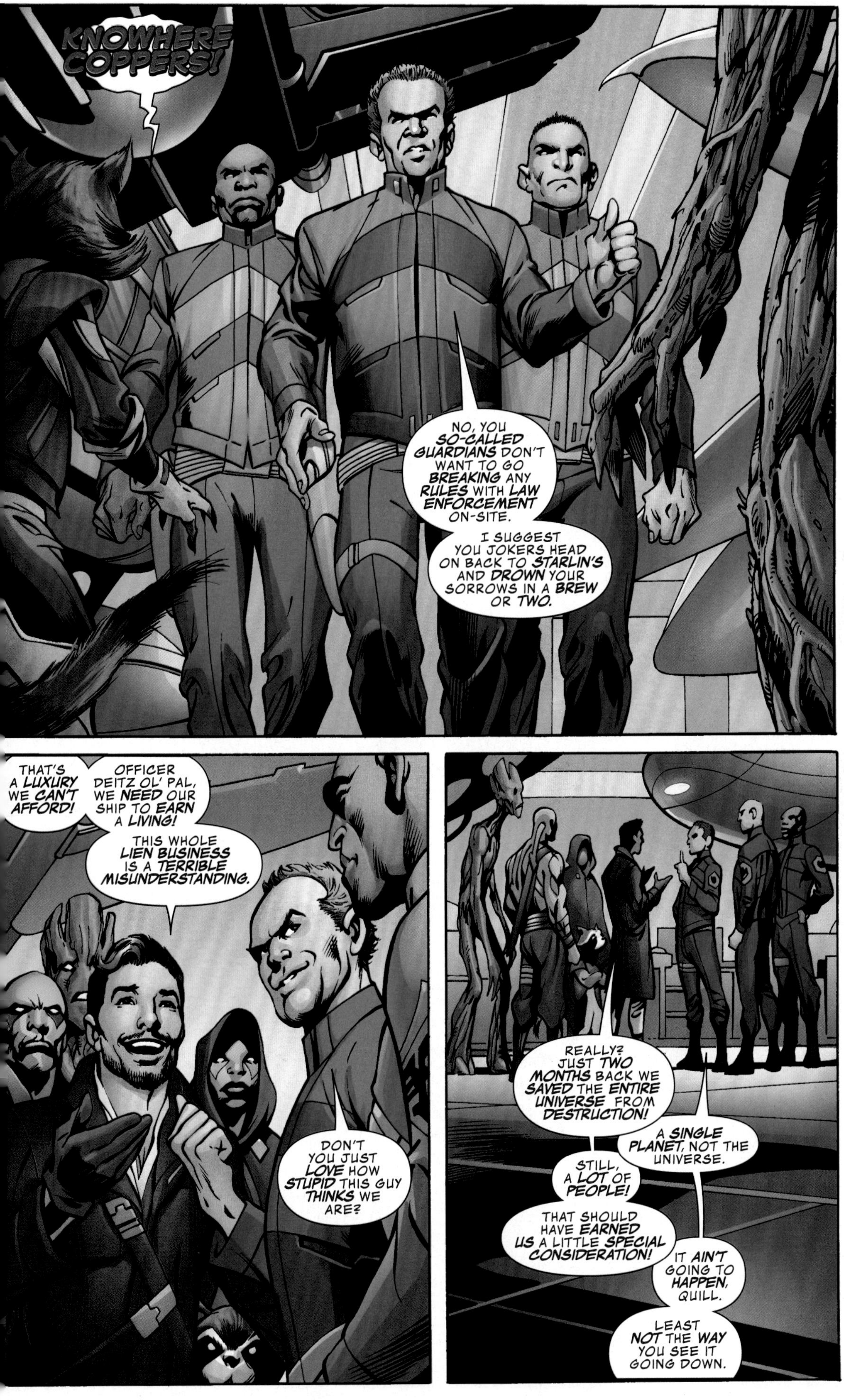
KNOWHERE COPPERS!
NO, YOU SO-CALLED GUARDIANS DON'T WANT TO GO BREAKING ANY RULES WITH LAW ENFORCEMENT ON-SITE.
I SUGGEST YOU JOKERS HEAD ON BACK TO STARLIN'S AND DROWN YOUR SORROWS IN A BREW OR TWO.
THAT'S A LUXURY WE CAN'T AFFORD!
OFFICER DEITZ OL' PAL, WE NEED OUR SHIP TO EARN A LIVING!
THIS WHOLE LIEN BUSINESS IS A TERRIBLE MISUNDERSTANDING.
DON'T YOU JUST LOVE HOW STUPID THIS GUY THINKS WE ARE?
REALLY? JUST TWO MONTHS BACK WE SAVED THE ENTIRE UNIVERSE FROM DESTRUCTION!
A SINGLE PLANET, NOT THE UNIVERSE.
STILL, A LOT OF PEOPLE!
THAT SHOULD HAVE EARNED US A LITTLE SPECIAL CONSIDERATION!
IT AIN'T GOING TO HAPPEN, QUILL.
LEAST NOT THE WAY YOU SEE IT GOING DOWN.

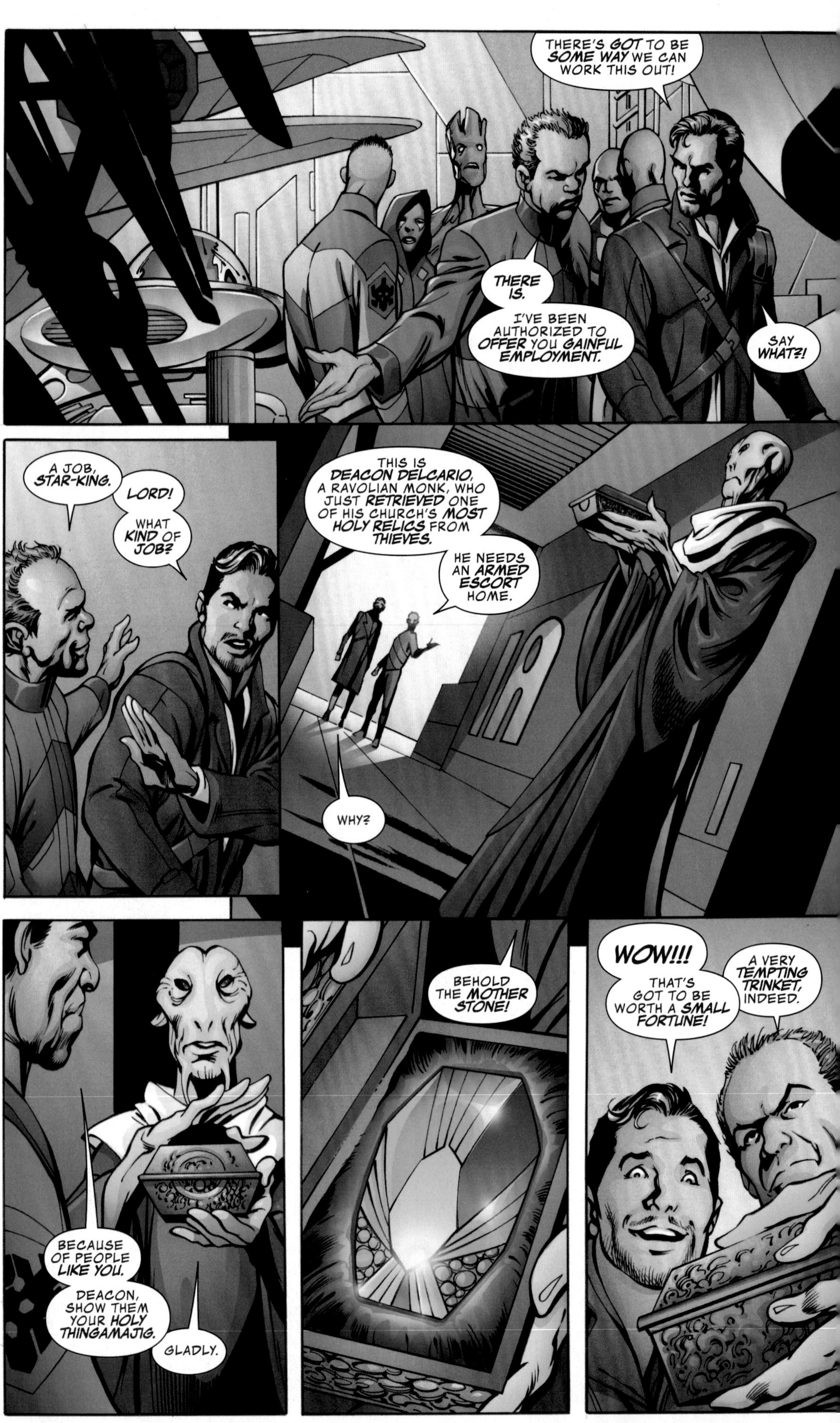

THERE'S GOT TO BE SOME WAY WE CAN WORK THIS OUT!
THERE IS.
I'VE BEEN AUTHORIZED TO OFFER YOU GAINFUL EMPLOYMENT.
SAY WHAT?!
A JOB, STAR-KING.
LORD!
WHAT KIND OF JOB?
THIS IS DEACON DELCARIO, A RAVOLIAN MONK, WHO JUST RETRIEVED ONE OF HIS CHURCH'S MOST HOLY RELICS FROM THIEVES.
HE NEEDS AN ARMED ESCORT HOME.
WHY?
BECAUSE OF PEOPLE LIKE YOU.
DEACON, SHOW THEM YOUR HOLY THINGAMAJIG.
GLADLY.
BEHOLD THE MOTHER STONE!
WOW!!!
THAT'S GOT TO BE WORTH A SMALL FORTUNE!
A VERY TEMPTING TRINKET, INDEED.

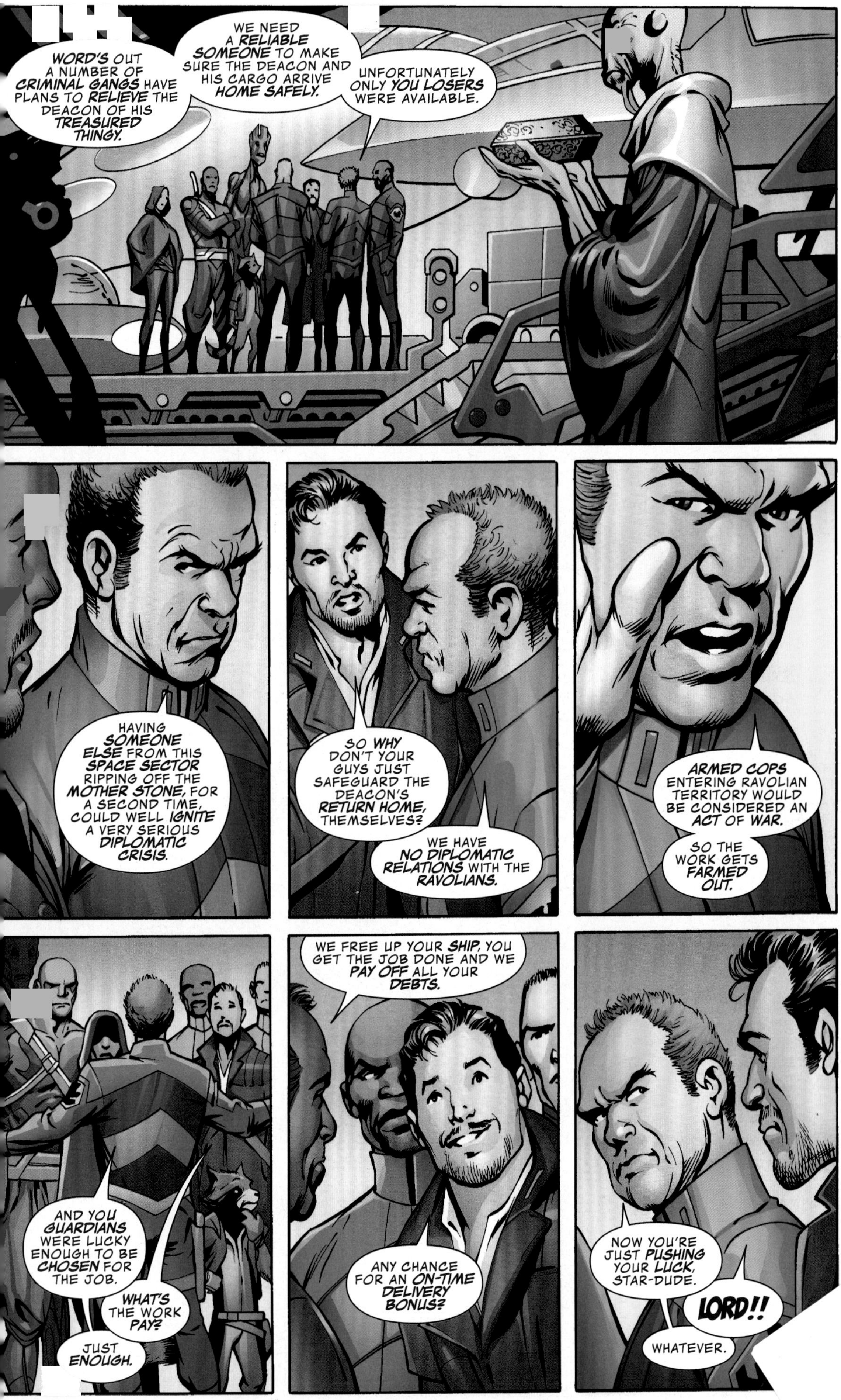
WORD'S OUT A NUMBER OF CRIMINAL GANGS HAVE PLANS TO RELIEVE THE DEACON OF HIS TREASURED THINGY.
WE NEED A RELIABLE SOMEONE TO MAKE SURE THE DEACON AND HIS CARGO ARRIVE HOME SAFELY.
UNFORTUNATELY ONLY YOU LOSERS WERE AVAILABLE.
HAVING SOMEONE ELSE FROM THIS SPACE SECTOR RIPPING OFF THE MOTHER STONE, FOR A SECOND TIME, COULD WELL IGNITE A VERY SERIOUS DIPLOMATIC CRISIS.
SO WHY DON'T YOUR GUYS JUST SAFEGUARD THE DEACON'S RETURN HOME, THEMSELVES?
WE HAVE NO DIPLOMATIC RELATIONS WITH THE RAVOLIANS.
ARMED COPS ENTERING RAVOLIAN TERRITORY WOULD BE CONSIDERED AN ACT OF WAR.
SO THE WORK GETS FARMED OUT.
AND YOU GUARDIANS WERE LUCKY ENOUGH TO BE CHOSEN FOR THE JOB.
WHAT'S THE WORK PAY?
JUST ENOUGH.
WE FREE UP YOUR SHIP, YOU GET THE JOB DONE AND WE PAY OFF ALL YOUR DEBTS.
ANY CHANCE FOR AN ON-TIME DELIVERY BONUS?
NOW YOU'RE JUST PUSHING YOUR LUCK, STAR-DUDE.
LORD!!
WHATEVER.

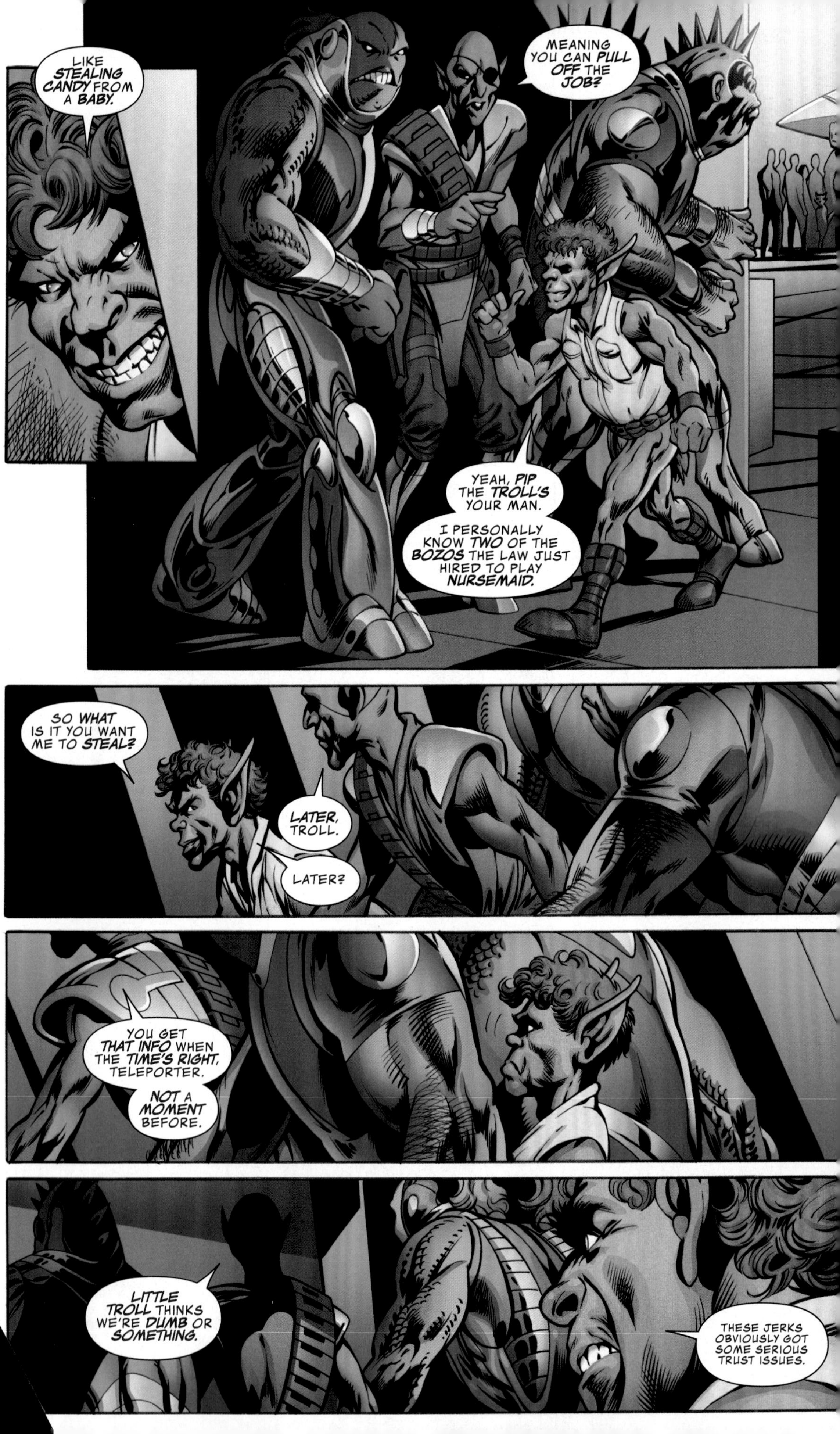
LIKE STEALING CANDY FROM A BABY.
MEANING YOU CAN PULL OFF THE JOB?
YEAH, PIP THE TROLL'S YOUR MAN.
I PERSONALLY KNOW TWO OF THE BOZOS THE LAW JUST HIRED TO PLAY NURSEMAID.
SO WHAT IS IT YOU WANT ME TO STEAL?
LATER, TROLL.
LATER?
YOU GET THAT INFO WHEN THE TIME'S RIGHT, TELEPORTER.
NOT A MOMENT BEFORE.
LITTLE TROLL THINKS WE'RE DUMB OR SOMETHING.
THESE JERKS OBVIOUSLY GOT SOME SERIOUS TRUST ISSUES.

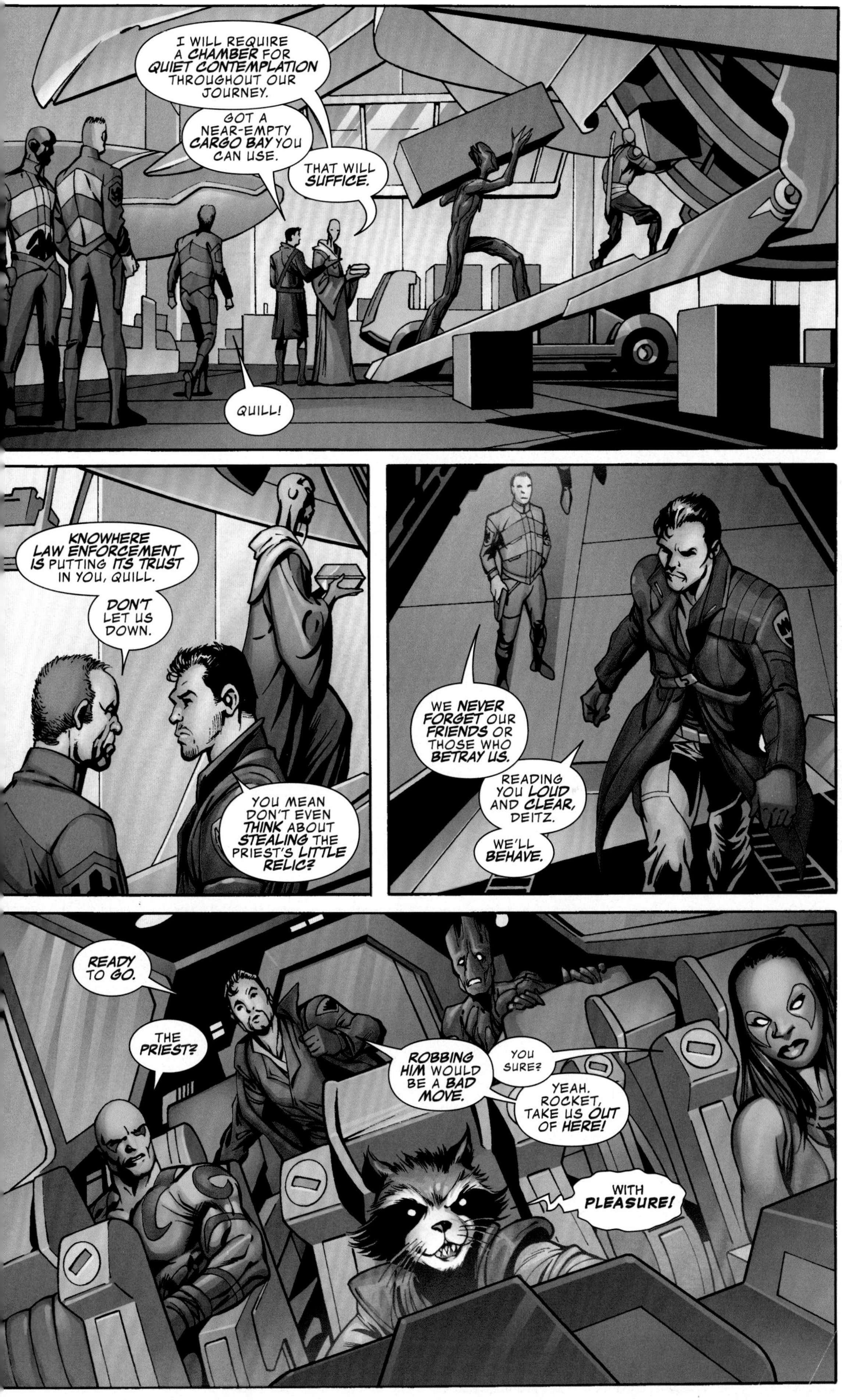
I WILL REQUIRE A CHAMBER FOR QUIET CONTEMPLATION THROUGHOUT OUR JOURNEY.
GOT A NEAR-EMPTY CARGO BAY YOU CAN USE.
THAT WILL SUFFICE.
QUILL!
KNOWHERE LAW ENFORCEMENT IS PUTTING ITS TRUST IN YOU, QUILL.
DON'T LET US DOWN.
YOU MEAN DON'T EVEN THINK ABOUT STEALING THE PRIEST'S LITTLE RELIC?
WE NEVER FORGET OUR FRIENDS OR THOSE WHO BETRAY US.
READING YOU LOUD AND CLEAR, DEITZ.
WE'LL BEHAVE.
READY TO GO.
THE PRIEST?
ROBBING HIM WOULD BE A BAD MOVE.
YOU SURE?
YEAH. ROCKET, TAKE US OUT OF HERE!
WITH PLEASURE!

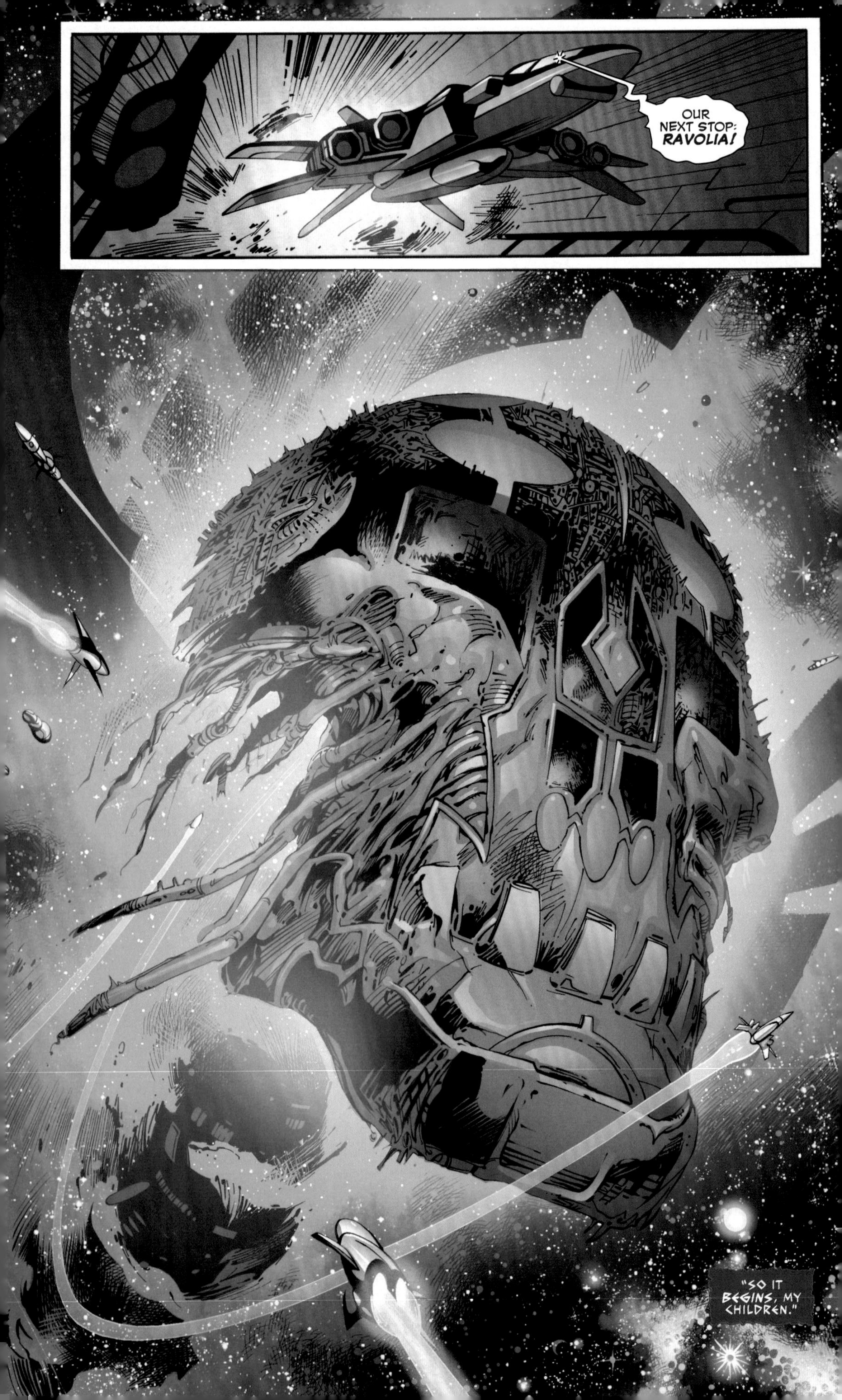
OUR NEXT STOP: RAVOLIA!
"SO IT BEGINS, MY CHILDREN."

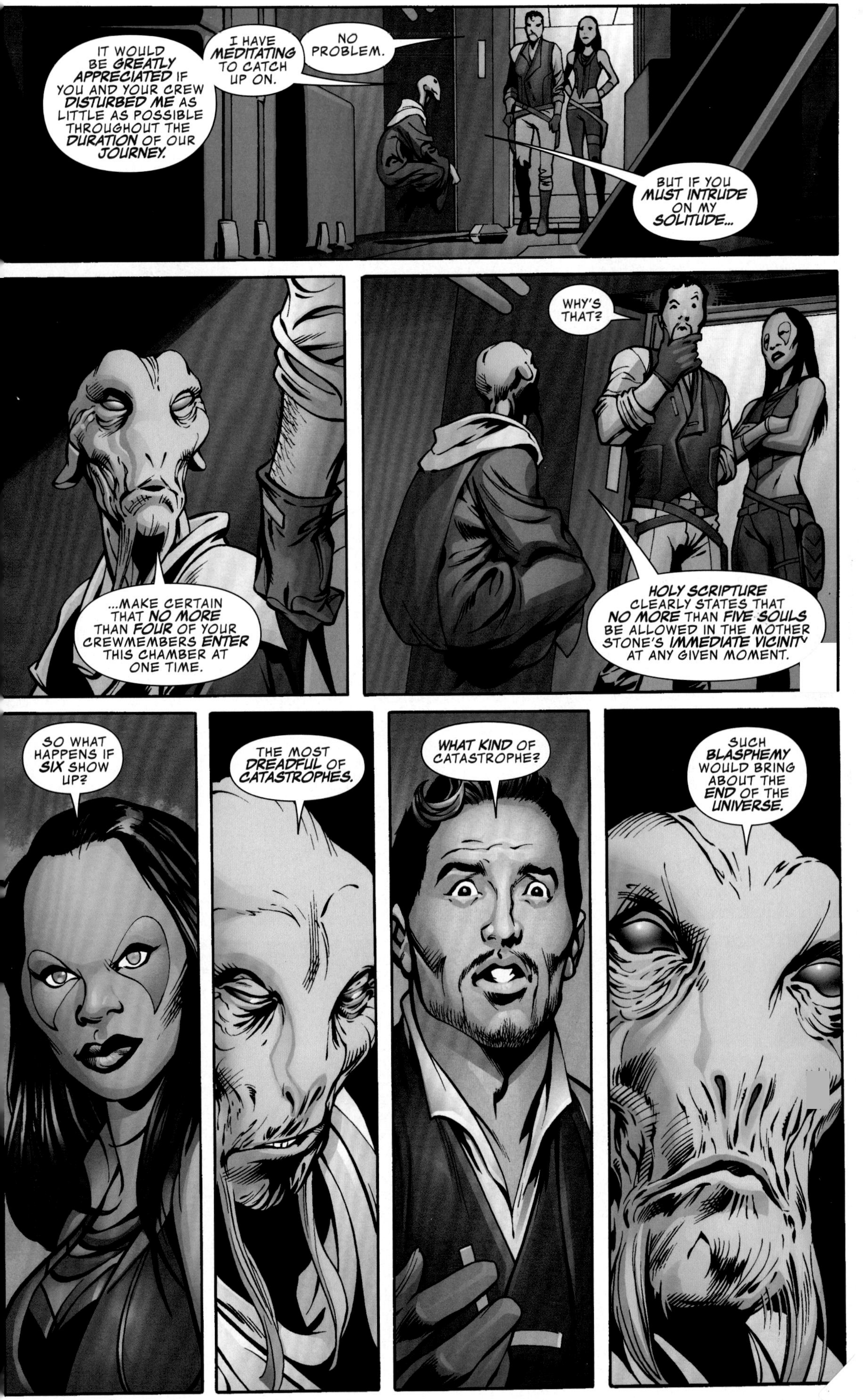

IT WOULD BE GREATLY APPRECIATED IF YOU AND YOUR CREW DISTURBED ME AS LITTLE AS POSSIBLE THROUGHOUT THE DURATION OF OUR JOURNEY.
I HAVE MEDITATING TO CATCH UP ON.
NO PROBLEM.
BUT IF YOU MUST INTRUDE ON MY SOLITUDE...
...MAKE CERTAIN THAT NO MORE THAN FOUR OF YOUR CREWMEMBERS ENTER THIS CHAMBER AT ONE TIME.
WHY'S THAT?
HOLY SCRIPTURE CLEARLY STATES THAT NO MORE THAN FIVE SOULS BE ALLOWED IN THE MOTHER STONE'S IMMEDIATE VICINITY AT ANY GIVEN MOMENT.
SO WHAT HAPPENS IF SIX SHOW UP?
THE MOST DREADFUL OF CATASTROPHES.
WHAT KIND OF CATASTROPHE?
SUCH BLASPHEMY WOULD BRING ABOUT THE END OF THE UNIVERSE.

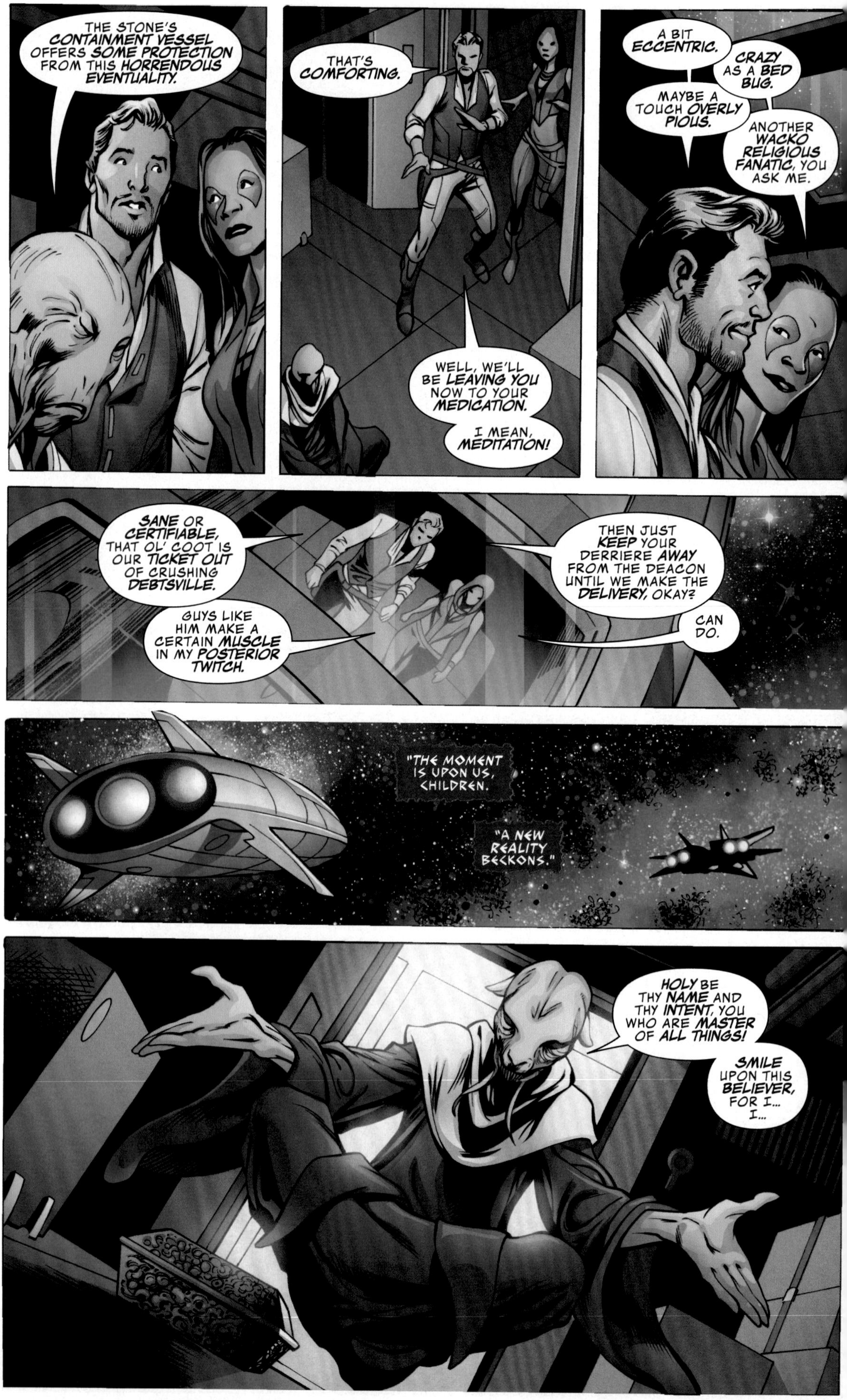
THE STONE'S CONTAINMENT VESSEL OFFERS SOME PROTECTION FROM THIS HORRENDOUS EVENTUALITY.
THAT'S COMFORTING.
WELL, WE'LL BE LEAVING YOU NOW TO YOUR MEDICATION.
I MEAN, MEDITATION!
A BIT ECCENTRIC.
MAYBE A TOUCH OVERLY PIOUS.
CRAZY AS A BED BUG.
ANOTHER WACKO RELIGIOUS FANATIC, YOU ASK ME.
SANE OR CERTIFIABLE, THAT OL' COOT IS OUR TICKET OUT OF CRUSHING DEBTSVILLE.
GUYS LIKE HIM MAKE A CERTAIN MUSCLE IN MY POSTERIOR TWITCH.
THEN JUST KEEP YOUR DERRIERE AWAY FROM THE DEACON UNTIL WE MAKE THE DELIVERY, OKAY?
CAN DO.
"THE MOMENT IS UPON US, CHILDREN.
"A NEW REALITY BECKONS."
HOLY BE THY NAME AND THY INTENT, YOU WHO ARE MASTER OF ALL THINGS!
SMILE UPON THIS BELIEVER, FOR I... I...

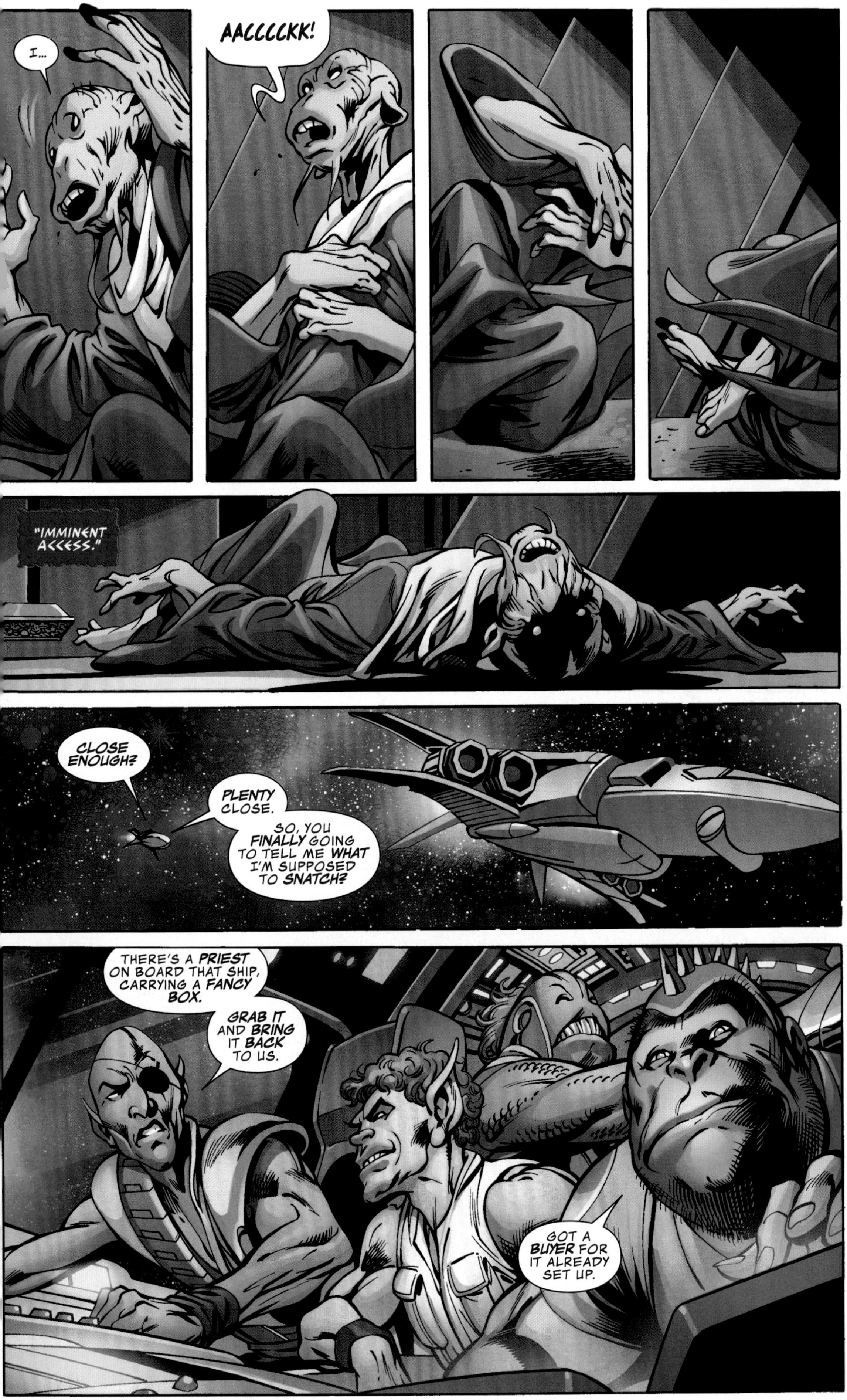
I...
AACCCCKK!
"IMMINENT ACCESS."
CLOSE ENOUGH?
PLENTY CLOSE.
SO, YOU FINALLY GOING TO TELL ME WHAT I'M SUPPOSED TO SNATCH?
THERE'S A PRIEST ON BOARD THAT SHIP, CARRYING A FANCY BOX.
GRAB IT AND BRING IT BACK TO US.
GOT A BUYER FOR IT ALREADY SET UP.

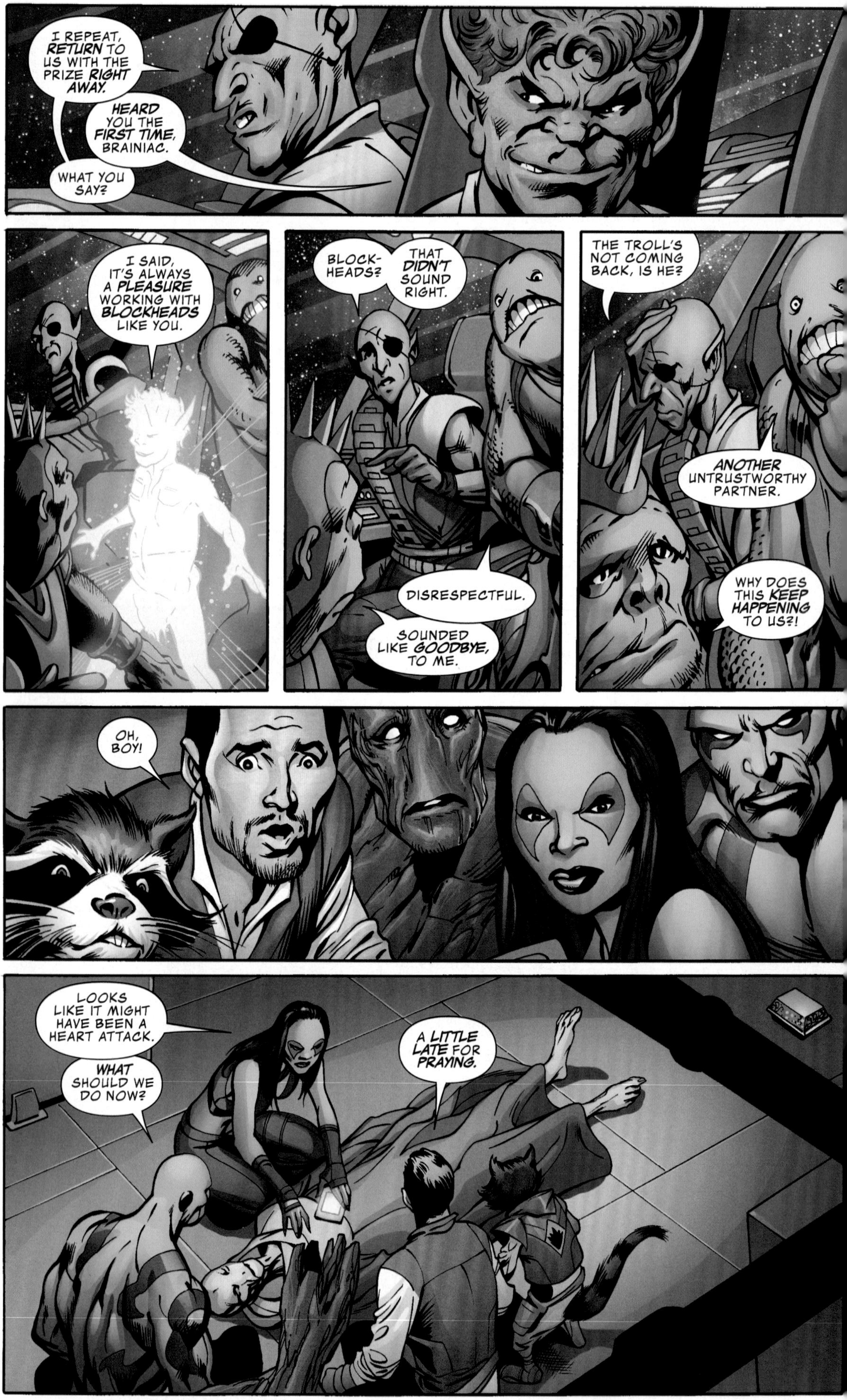
I REPEAT, RETURN TO US WITH THE PRIZE RIGHT AWAY.
HEARD YOU THE FIRST TIME, BRAINIAC.
WHAT YOU SAY?
I SAID, IT'S ALWAYS A PLEASURE WORKING WITH BLOCKHEADS LIKE YOU.
BLOCK-HEADS?
THAT DIDN'T SOUND RIGHT.
DISRESPECTFUL.
SOUNDED LIKE GOODBYE, TO ME.
THE TROLL'S NOT COMING BACK, IS HE?
ANOTHER UNTRUSTWORTHY PARTNER.
WHY DOES THIS KEEP HAPPENING TO US?!
OH, BOY!
LOOKS LIKE IT MIGHT HAVE BEEN A HEART ATTACK.
WHAT SHOULD WE DO NOW?
A LITTLE LATE FOR PRAYING.

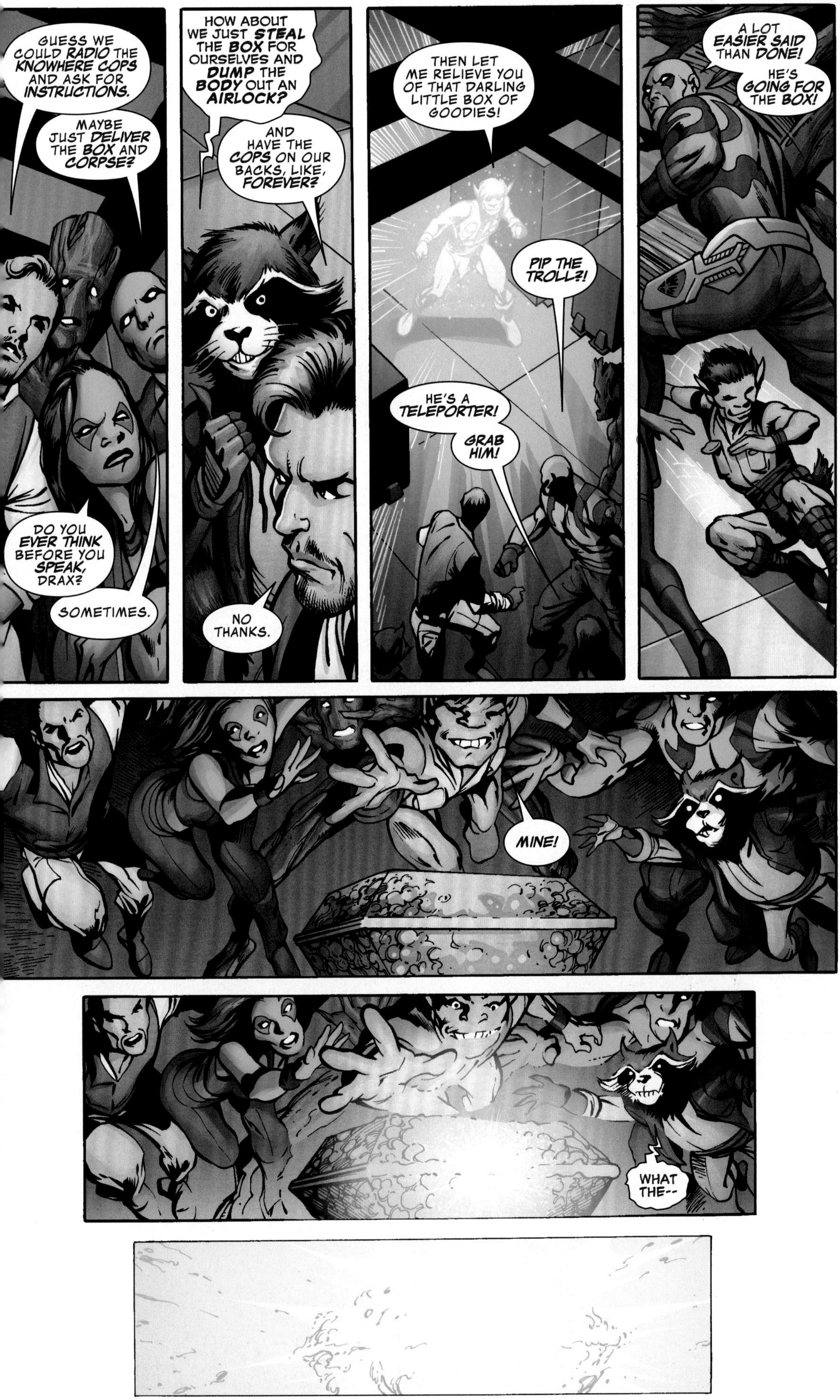
GUESS WE COULD RADIO THE KNOWHERE COPS AND ASK FOR INSTRUCTIONS.
MAYBE JUST DELIVER THE BOX AND CORPSE?
DO YOU EVER THINK BEFORE YOU SPEAK, DRAX?
SOMETIMES.
HOW ABOUT WE JUST STEAL THE BOX FOR OURSELVES AND DUMP THE BODY OUT AN AIRLOCK?
AND HAVE THE COPS ON OUR BACKS, LIKE, FOREVER?
NO THANKS.
THEN LET ME RELIEVE YOU OF THAT DARLING LITTLE BOX OF GOODIES!
PIP THE TROLL?!
HE'S A TELEPORTER!
GRAB HIM!
A LOT EASIER SAID THAN DONE!
HE'S GOING FOR THE BOX!
MINE!
WHAT THE--

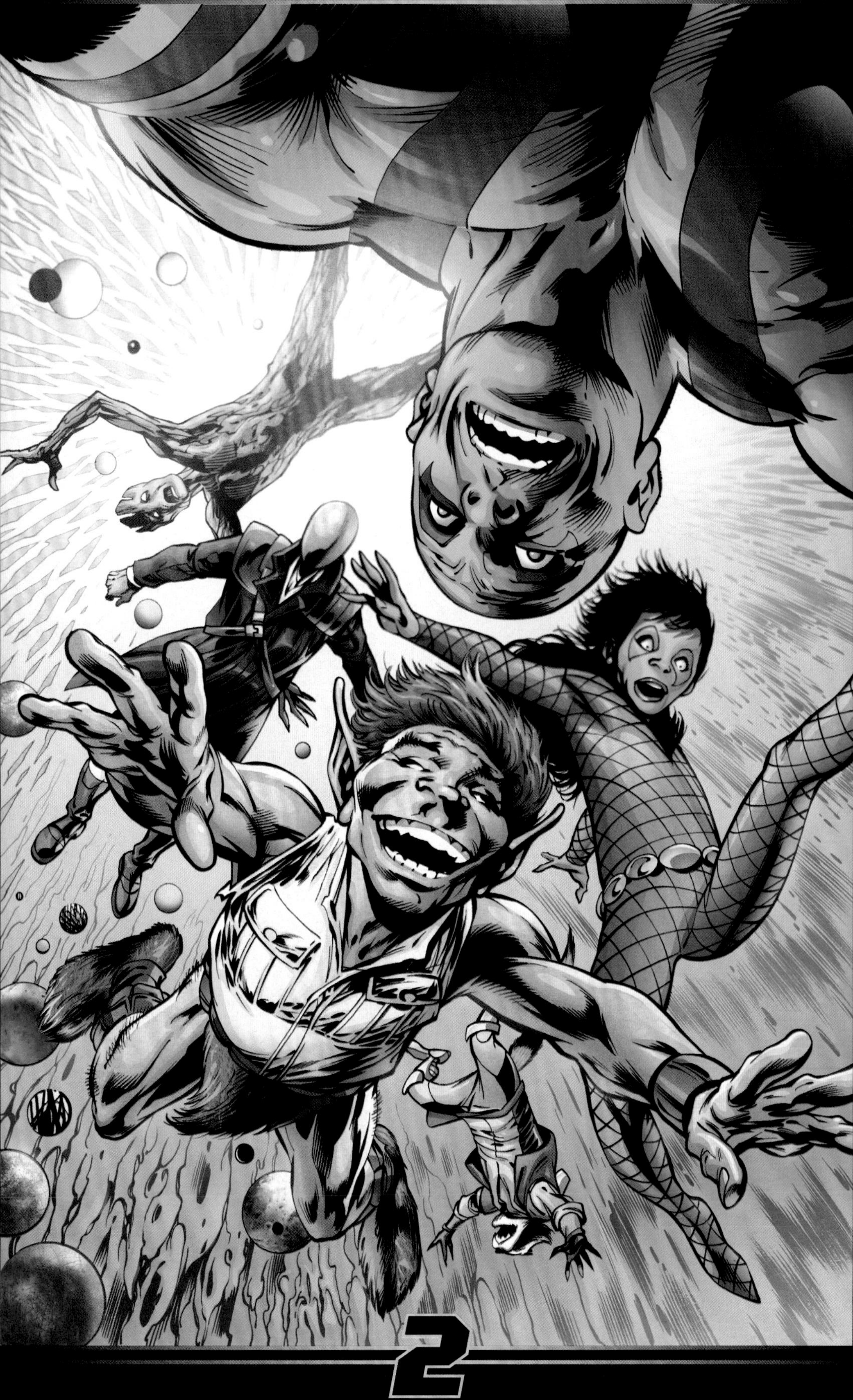
2

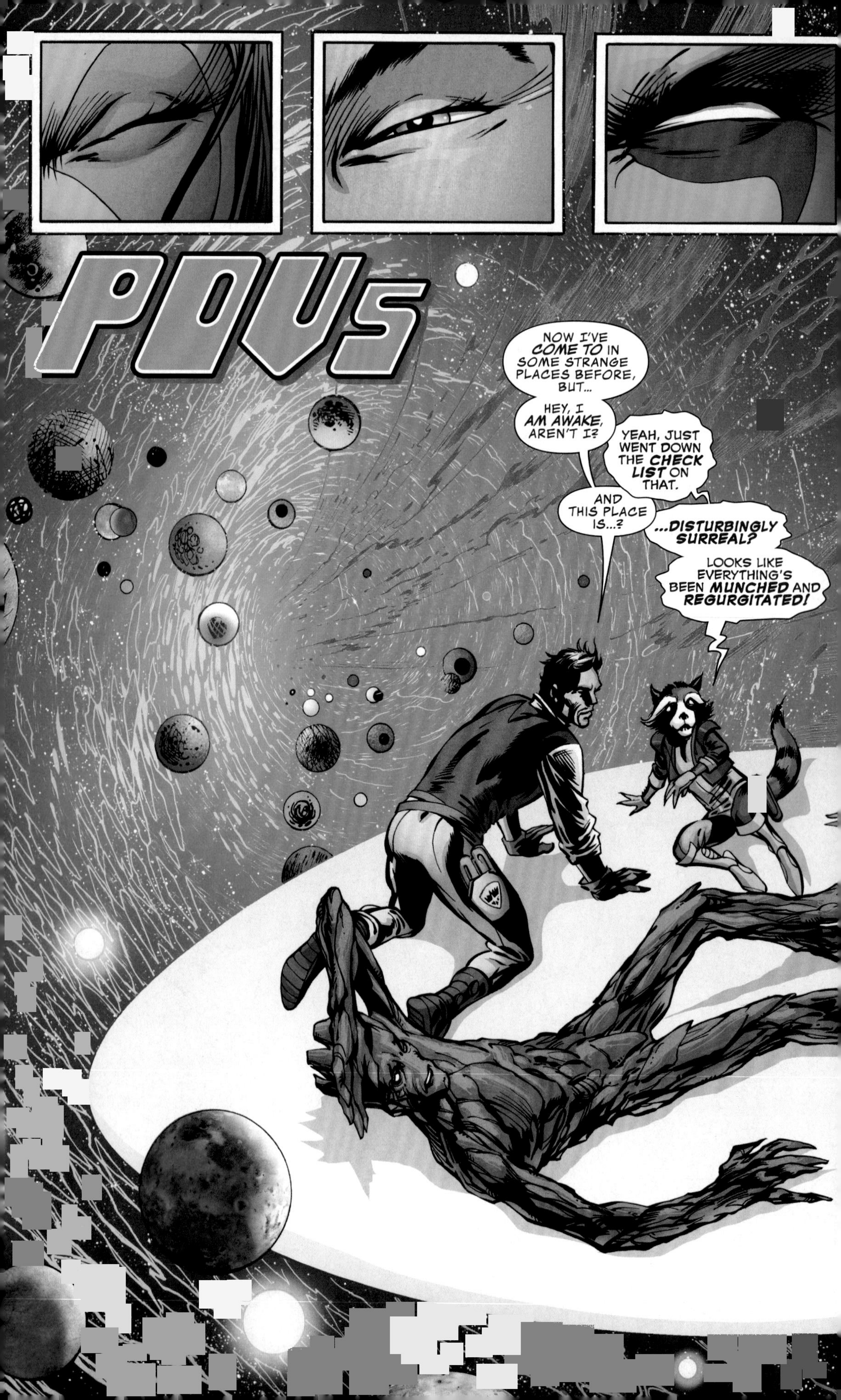
PDVs
NOW I'VE COME TO IN SOME STRANGE PLACES BEFORE, BUT...
HEY, I AM AWAKE, AREN'T I?
YEAH, JUST WENT DOWN THE CHECK LIST ON THAT.
AND THIS PLACE IS...?
...DISTURBINGLY SURREAL?
LOOKS LIKE EVERYTHING'S BEEN MUNCHED AND REGURGITATED!

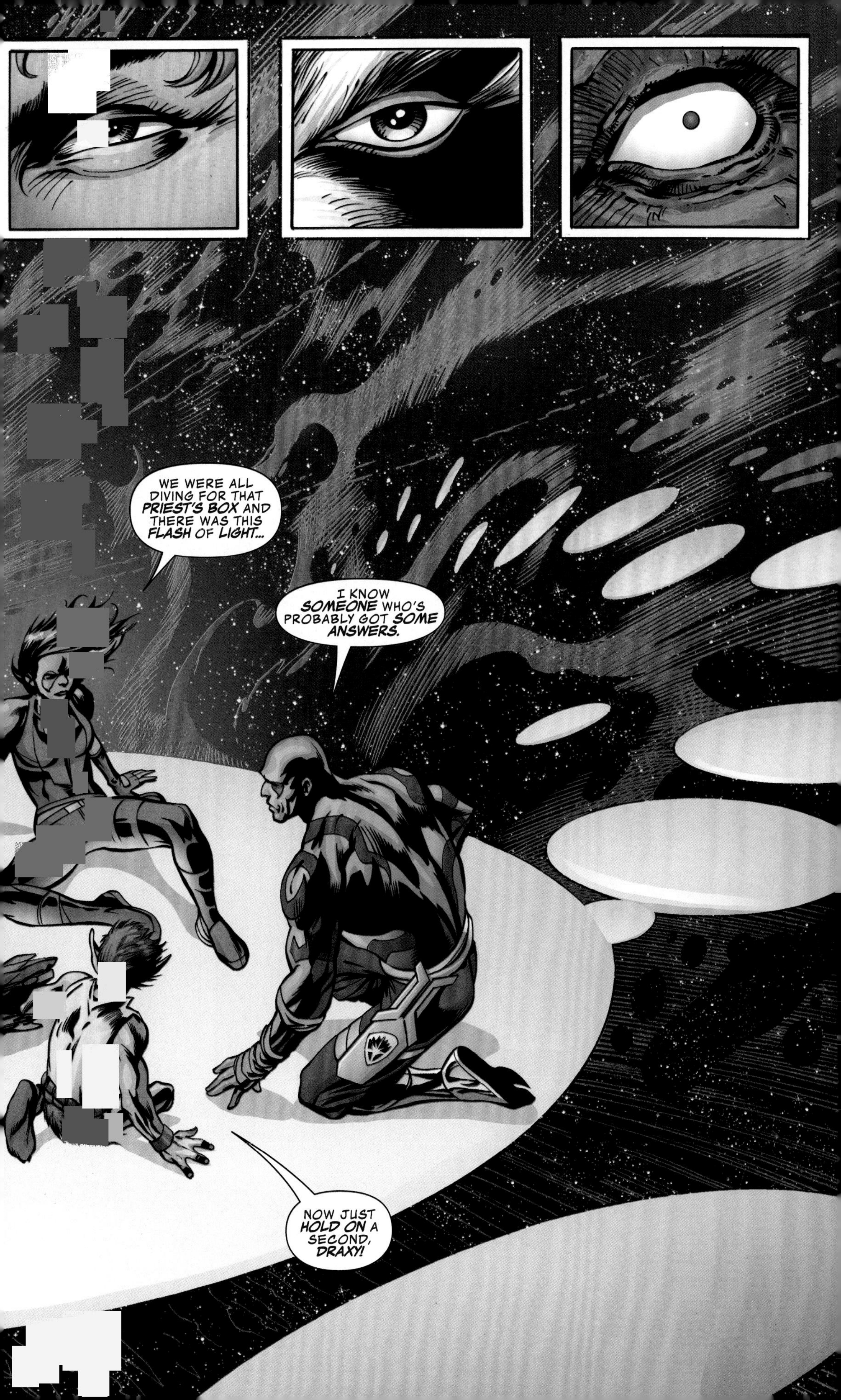
WE WERE ALL DIVING FOR THAT PRIEST'S BOX AND THERE WAS THIS FLASH OF LIGHT...
I KNOW SOMEONE WHO'S PROBABLY GOT SOME ANSWERS.
NOW JUST HOLD ON A SECOND, DRAXY!

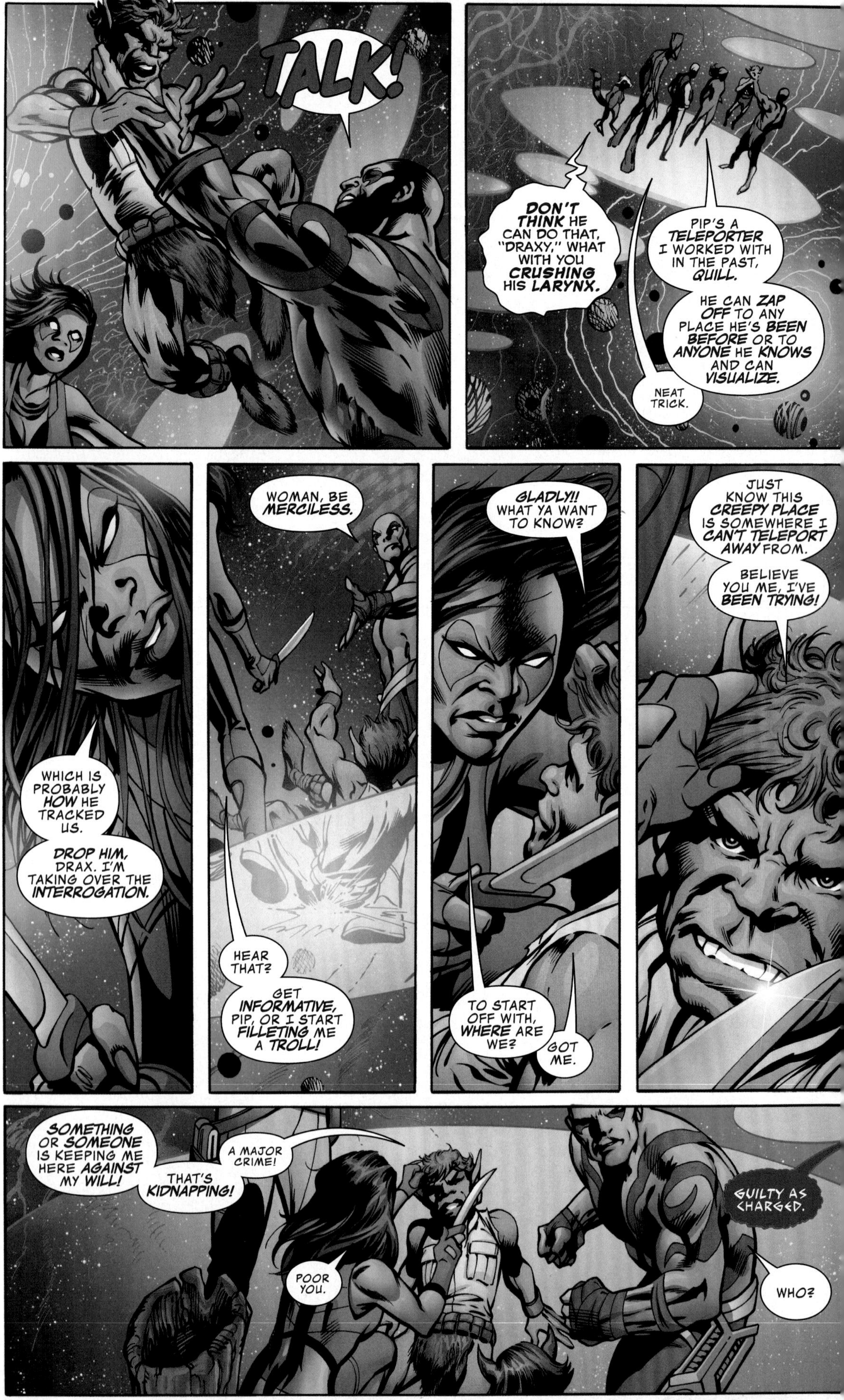
TALK!
DON'T THINK HE CAN DO THAT, "DRAXY," WHAT WITH YOU CRUSHING HIS LARYNX.
PIP'S A TELEPORTER I WORKED WITH IN THE PAST, QUILL.
HE CAN ZAP OFF TO ANY PLACE HE'S BEEN BEFORE OR TO ANYONE HE KNOWS AND CAN VISUALIZE.
NEAT TRICK.
WHICH IS PROBABLY HOW HE TRACKED US.
DROP HIM, DRAX. I'M TAKING OVER THE INTERROGATION.
WOMAN, BE MERCILESS.
HEAR THAT?
GET INFORMATIVE, PIP, OR I START FILLETING ME A TROLL!
GLADLY!! WHAT YA WANT TO KNOW?
TO START OFF WITH, WHERE ARE WE?
GOT ME.
JUST KNOW THIS CREEPY PLACE IS SOMEWHERE I CAN'T TELEPORT AWAY FROM.
BELIEVE YOU ME, I'VE BEEN TRYING!
SOMETHING OR SOMEONE IS KEEPING ME HERE AGAINST MY WILL!
THAT'S KIDNAPPING!
A MAJOR CRIME!
POOR YOU.
GUILTY AS CHARGED.
WHO?

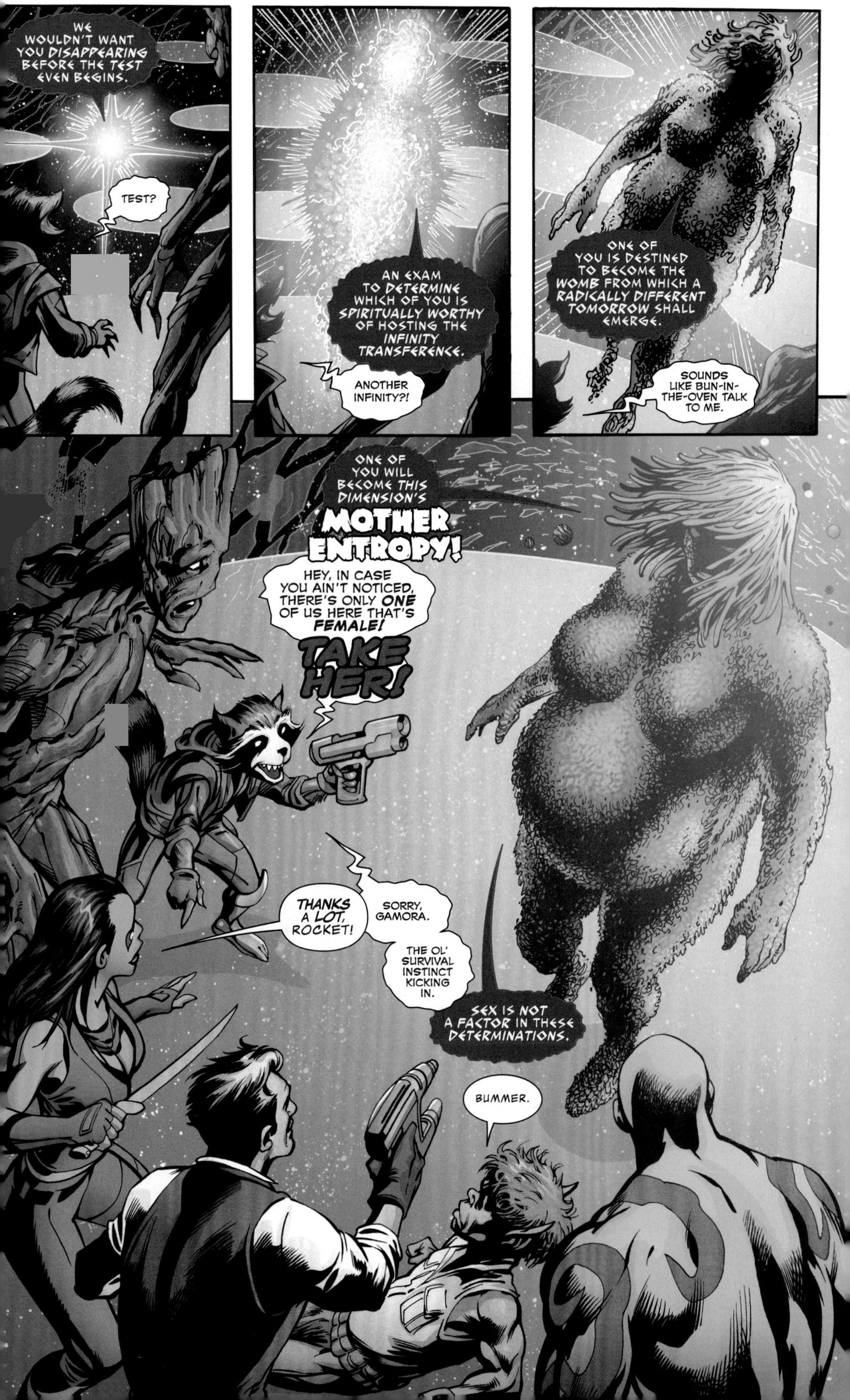
WE WOULDN'T WANT YOU DISAPPEARING BEFORE THE TEST EVEN BEGINS.
TEST?
AN EXAM TO DETERMINE WHICH OF YOU IS SPIRITUALLY WORTHY OF HOSTING THE INFINITY TRANSFERENCE.
ANOTHER INFINITY?!
ONE OF YOU IS DESTINED TO BECOME THE WOMB FROM WHICH A RADICALLY DIFFERENT TOMORROW SHALL EMERGE.
SOUNDS LIKE BUN-IN-THE-OVEN TALK TO ME.
ONE OF YOU WILL BECOME THIS DIMENSION'S MOTHER ENTROPY!
HEY, IN CASE YOU AIN'T NOTICED, THERE'S ONLY ONE OF US HERE THAT'S FEMALE!
TAKE HER!
THANKS A LOT, ROCKET!
SORRY, GAMORA.
THE OL' SURVIVAL INSTINCT KICKING IN.
SEX IS NOT A FACTOR IN THESE DETERMINATIONS.
BUMMER.

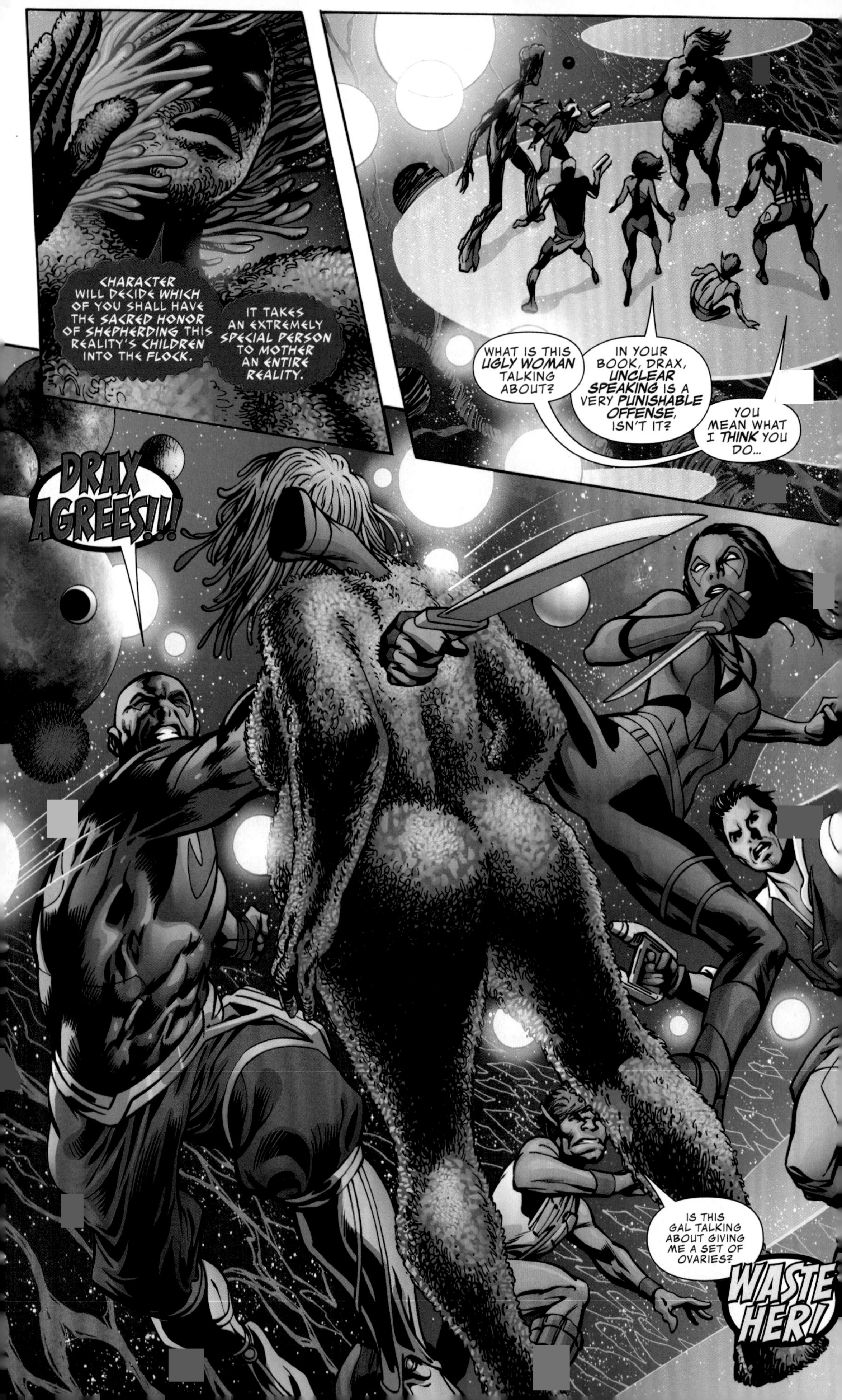
CHARACTER WILL DECIDE WHICH OF YOU SHALL HAVE THE SACRED HONOR OF SHEPHERDING THIS REALITY'S CHILDREN INTO THE FLOCK.
IT TAKES AN EXTREMELY SPECIAL PERSON TO MOTHER AN ENTIRE REALITY.
WHAT IS THIS UGLY WOMAN TALKING ABOUT?
IN YOUR BOOK, DRAX, UNCLEAR SPEAKING IS A VERY PUNISHABLE OFFENSE, ISN'T IT?
YOU MEAN WHAT I THINK YOU DO...
DRAX AGREES!!!
IS THIS GAL TALKING ABOUT GIVING ME A SET OF OVARIES?
WASTE HER!

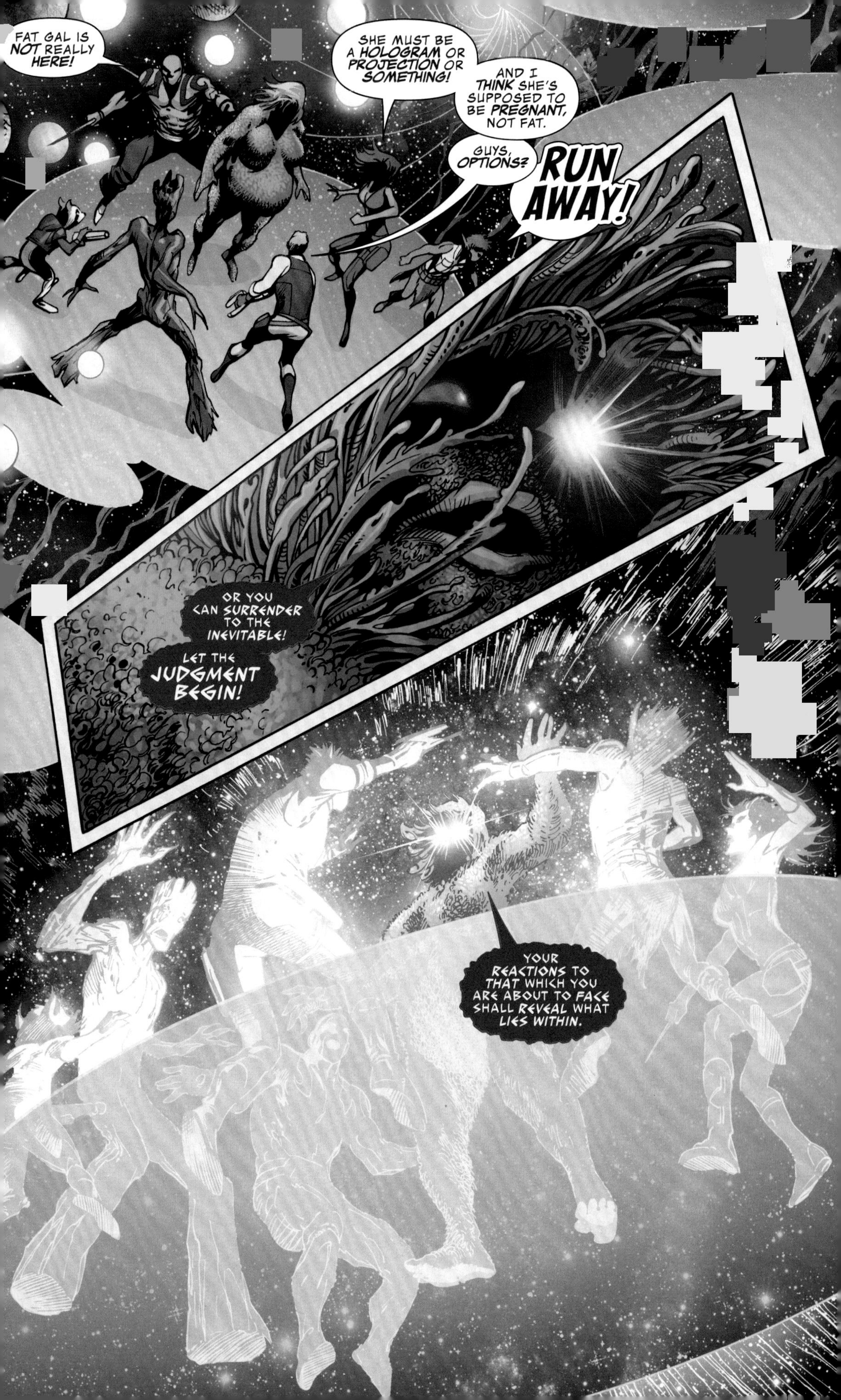
FAT GAL IS NOT REALLY HERE!
SHE MUST BE A HOLOGRAM OR PROJECTION OR SOMETHING!
AND I THINK SHE'S SUPPOSED TO BE PREGNANT, NOT FAT.
GUYS, OPTIONS?
RUN AWAY!
OR YOU CAN SURRENDER TO THE INEVITABLE!
LET THE JUDGMENT BEGIN!
YOUR REACTIONS TO THAT WHICH YOU ARE ABOUT TO FACE SHALL REVEAL WHAT LIES WITHIN.

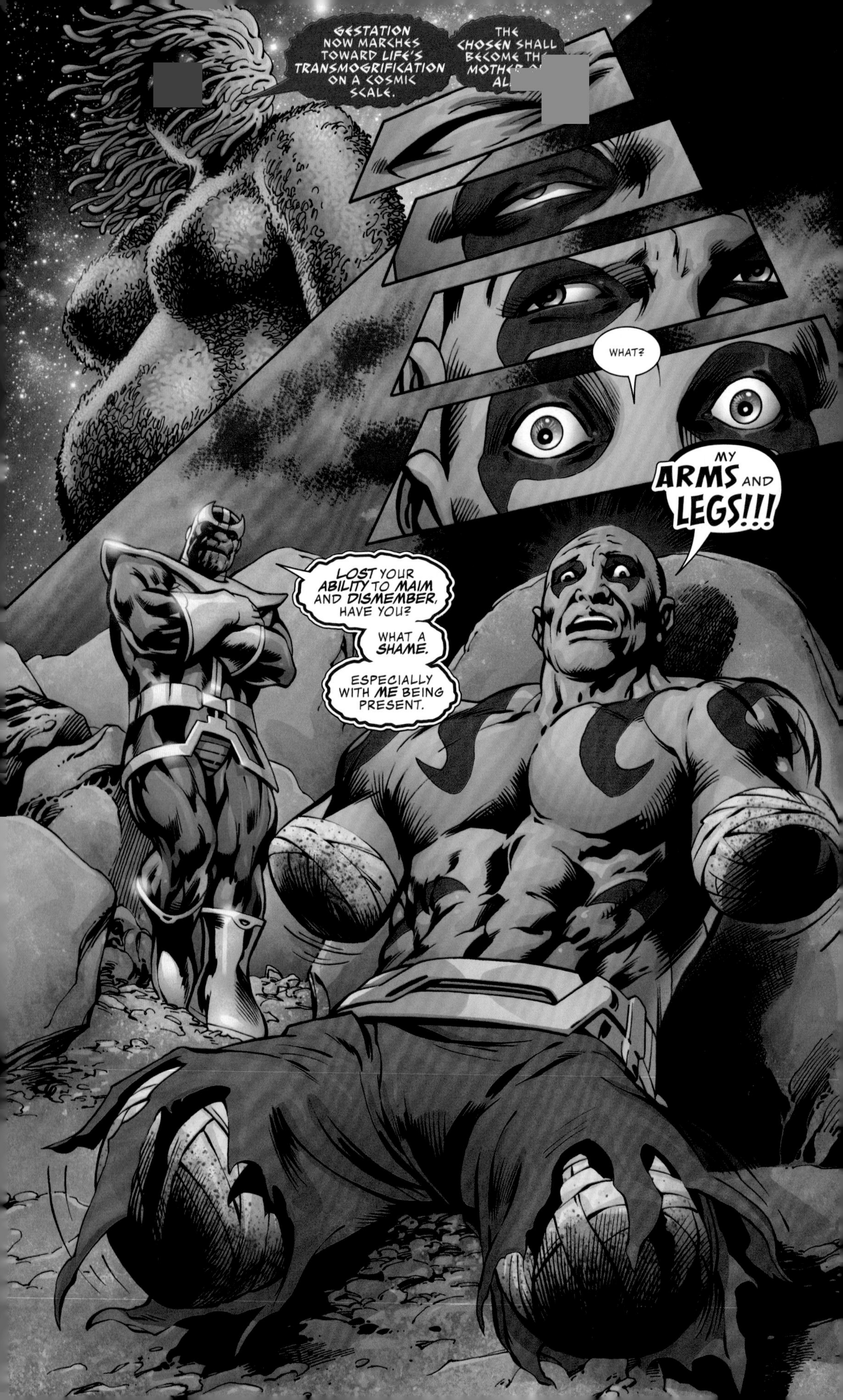

GESTATION NOW MARCHES TOWARD LIFE'S TRANSMOGRIFICATION ON A COSMIC SCALE.
THE CHOSEN SHALL BECOME THE MOTHER OF ALL.
WHAT?
MY ARMS AND LEGS!!!
LOST YOUR ABILITY TO MAIM AND DISMEMBER, HAVE YOU?
WHAT A SHAME.
ESPECIALLY WITH ME BEING PRESENT.

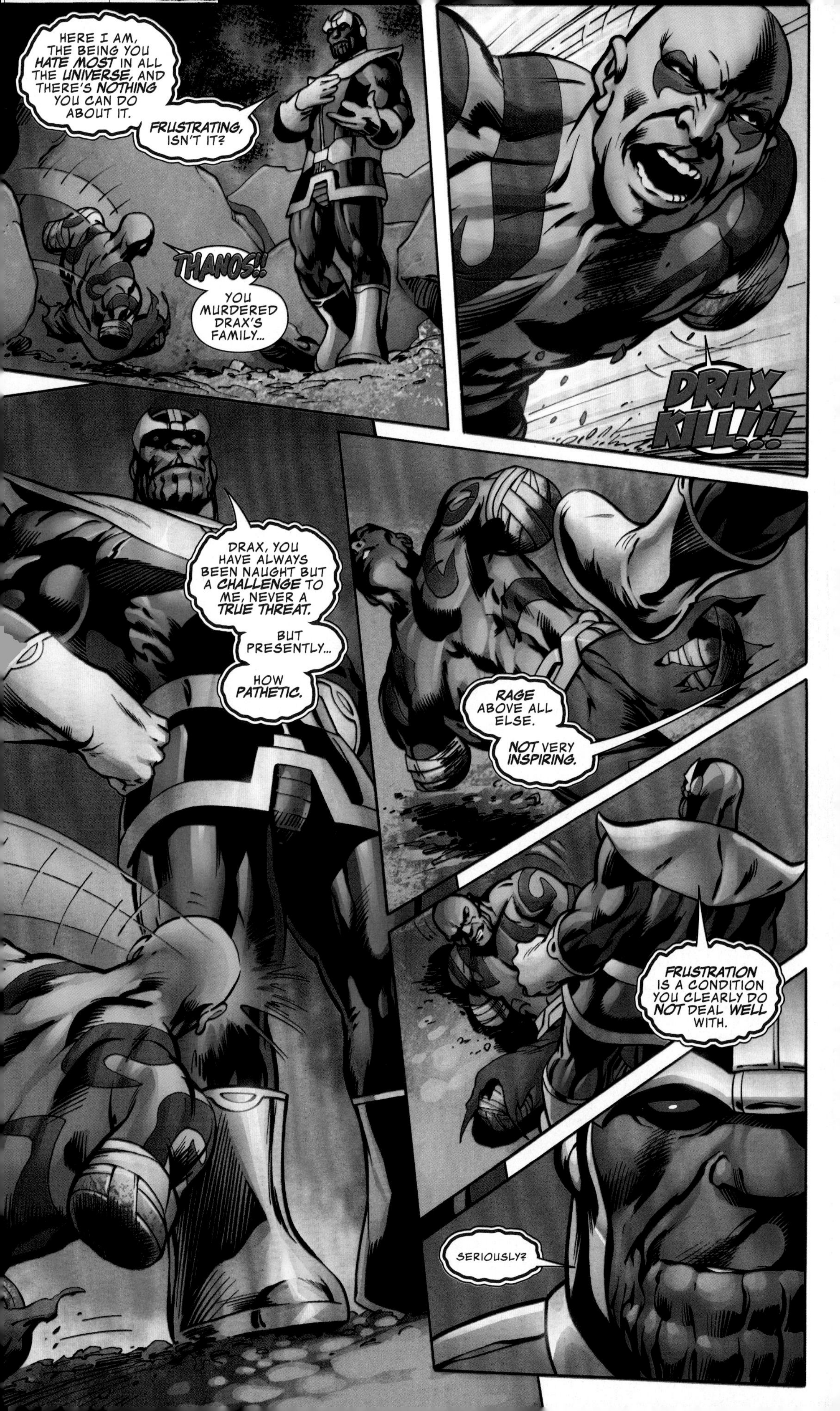

HERE I AM, THE BEING YOU HATE MOST IN ALL THE UNIVERSE, AND THERE'S NOTHING YOU CAN DO ABOUT IT.
FRUSTRATING, ISN'T IT?
THANOS!!
YOU MURDERED DRAX'S FAMILY...
DRAX KILL!!!
DRAX, YOU HAVE ALWAYS BEEN NAUGHT BUT A CHALLENGE TO ME, NEVER A TRUE THREAT.
BUT PRESENTLY...
HOW PATHETIC.
RAGE ABOVE ALL ELSE.
NOT VERY INSPIRING.
FRUSTRATION IS A CONDITION YOU CLEARLY DO NOT DEAL WELL WITH.
SERIOUSLY?

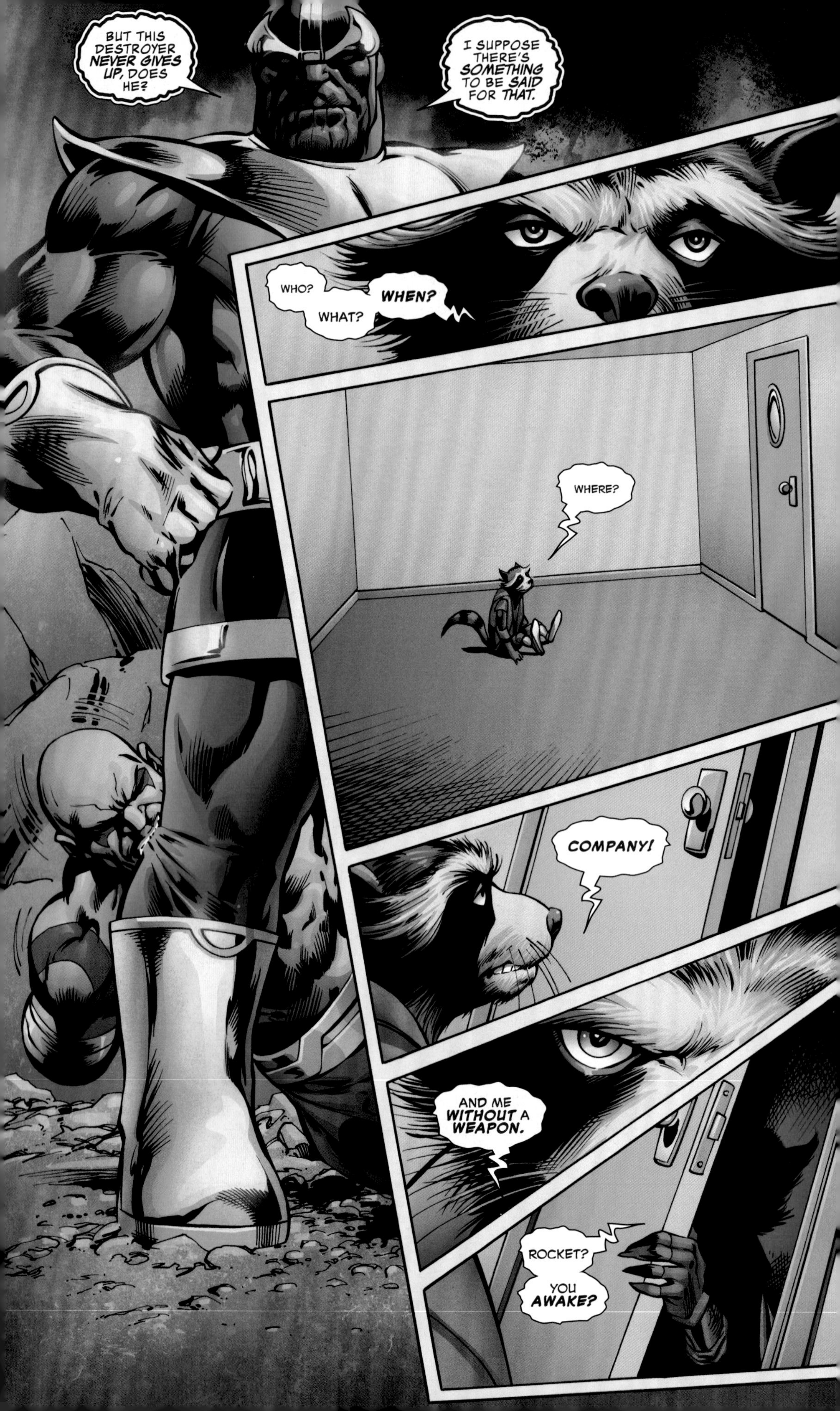

BUT THIS DESTROYER NEVER GIVES UP, DOES HE?
I SUPPOSE THERE'S SOMETHING TO BE SAID FOR THAT.
WHO?
WHAT?
WHEN?
WHERE?
COMPANY!
AND ME WITHOUT A WEAPON.
ROCKET?
YOU AWAKE?

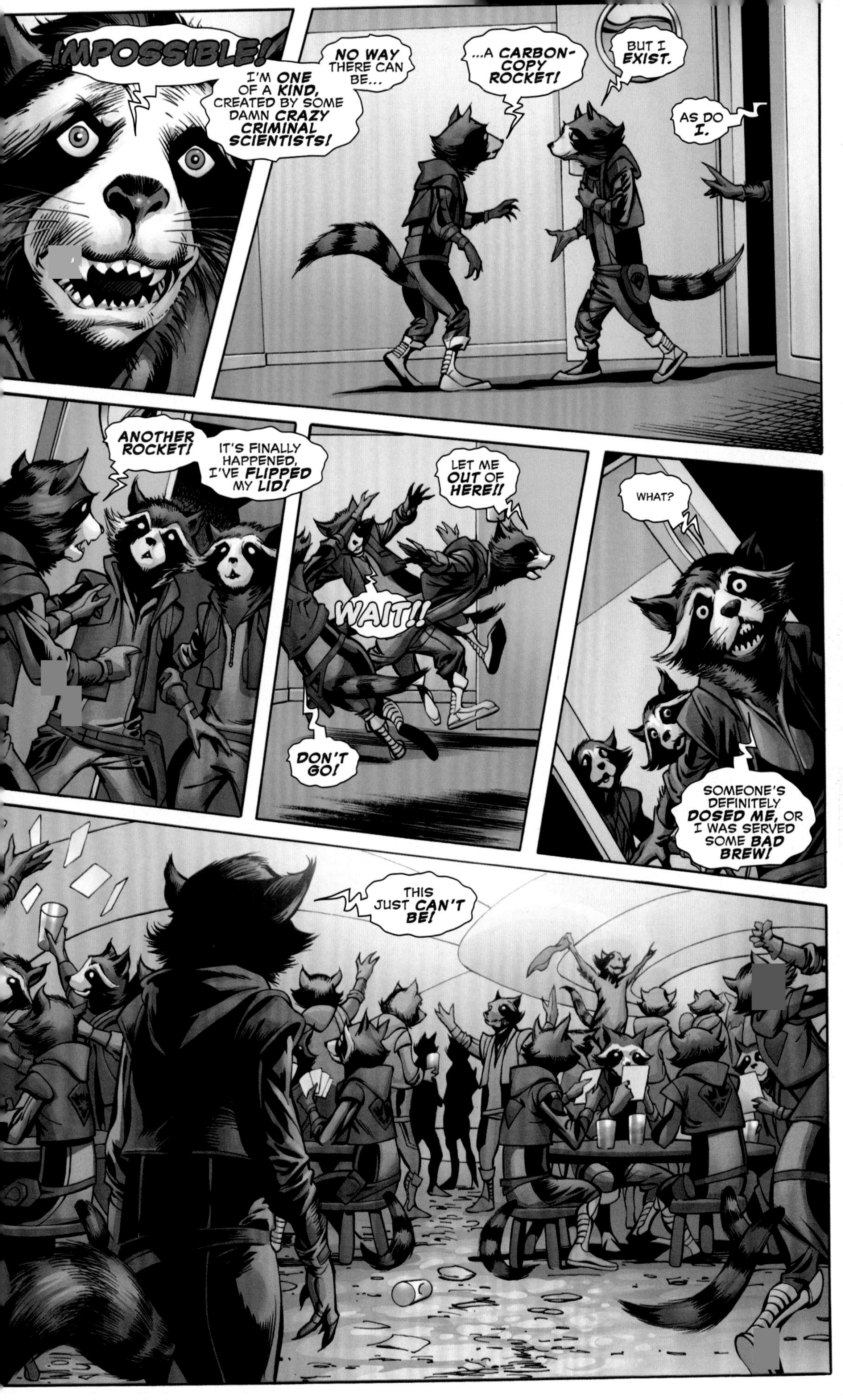

IMPOSSIBLE!
I'M ONE OF A KIND, CREATED BY SOME DAMN CRAZY CRIMINAL SCIENTISTS!
NO WAY THERE CAN BE...
...A CARBON-COPY ROCKET!
BUT I EXIST.
AS DO I.
ANOTHER ROCKET!
IT'S FINALLY HAPPENED, I'VE FLIPPED MY LID!
LET ME OUT OF HERE!!
WAIT!!
DON'T GO!
WHAT?
SOMEONE'S DEFINITELY DOSED ME, OR I WAS SERVED SOME BAD BREW!
THIS JUST CAN'T BE!

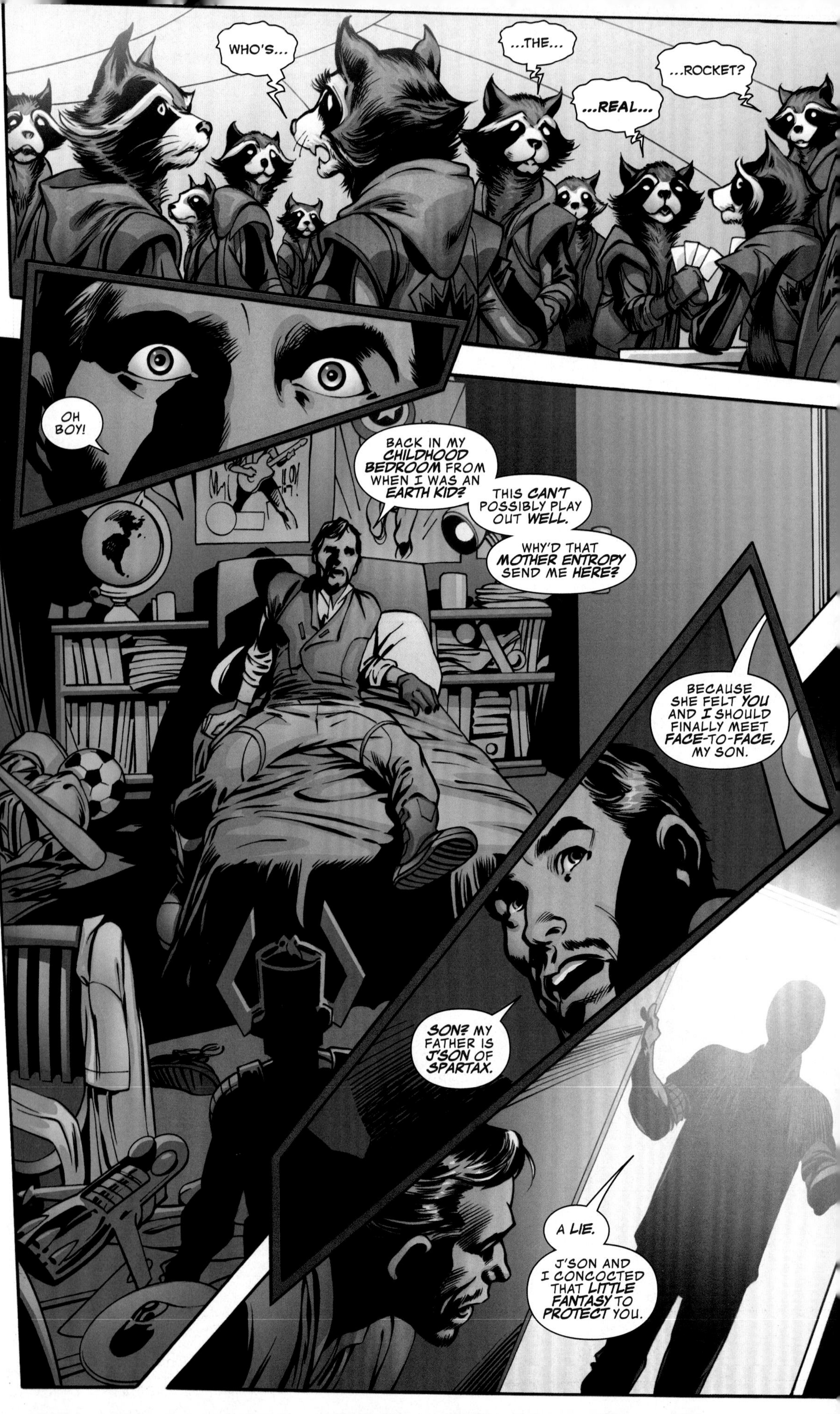

WHO'S...
...THE...
...REAL...
...ROCKET?
OH BOY!
BACK IN MY CHILDHOOD BEDROOM FROM WHEN I WAS AN EARTH KID?
THIS CAN'T POSSIBLY PLAY OUT WELL.
WHY'D THAT MOTHER ENTROPY SEND ME HERE?
BECAUSE SHE FELT YOU AND I SHOULD FINALLY MEET FACE-TO-FACE, MY SON.
SON? MY FATHER IS J'SON OF SPARTAX.
A LIE.
J'SON AND I CONCOCTED THAT LITTLE FANTASY TO PROTECT YOU.

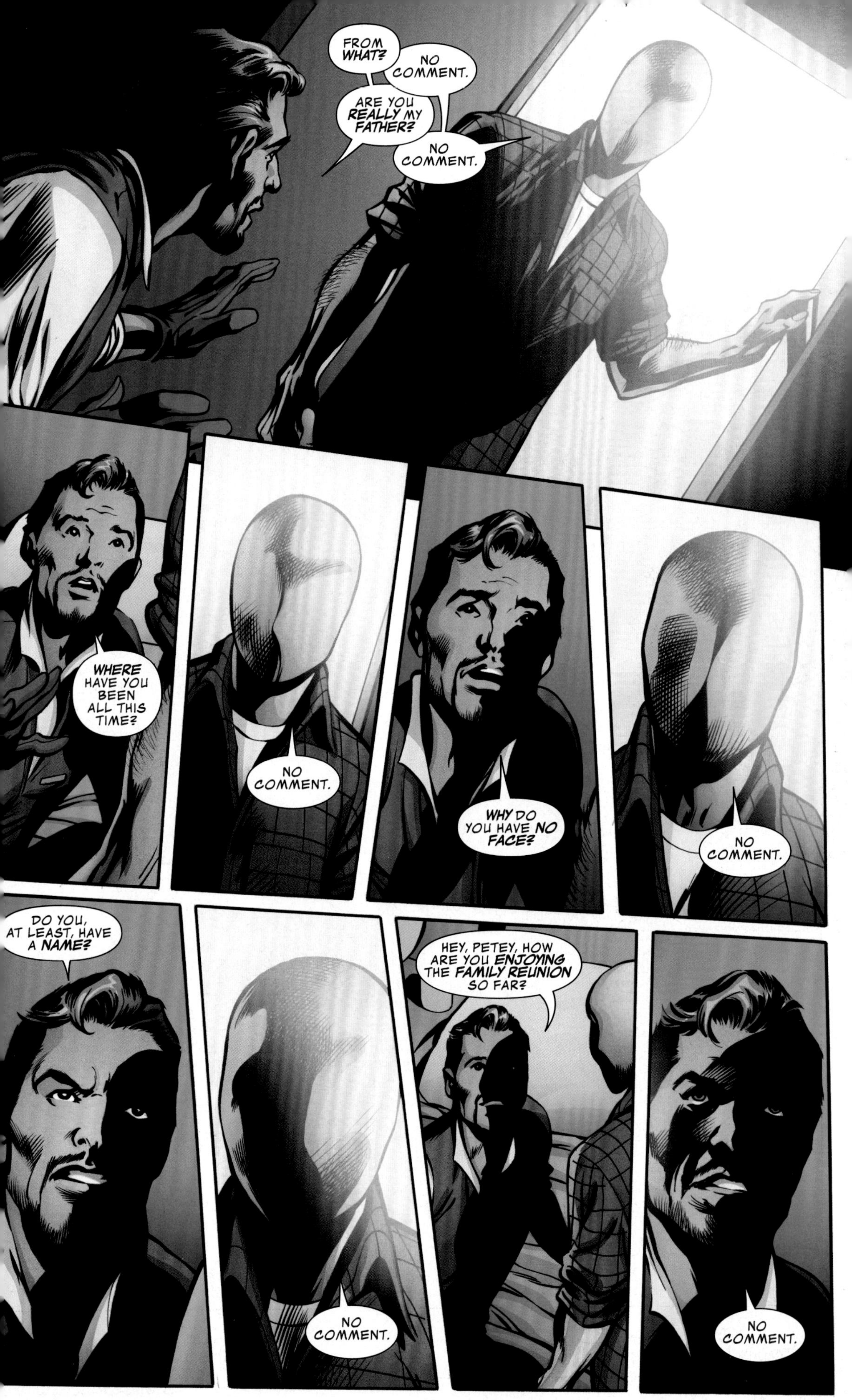

FROM WHAT?
NO COMMENT.
ARE YOU REALLY MY FATHER?
NO COMMENT.
WHERE HAVE YOU BEEN ALL THIS TIME?
NO COMMENT.
WHY DO YOU HAVE NO FACE?
NO COMMENT.
DO YOU, AT LEAST, HAVE A NAME?
NO COMMENT.
HEY, PETEY, HOW ARE YOU ENJOYING THE FAMILY REUNION SO FAR?
NO COMMENT.

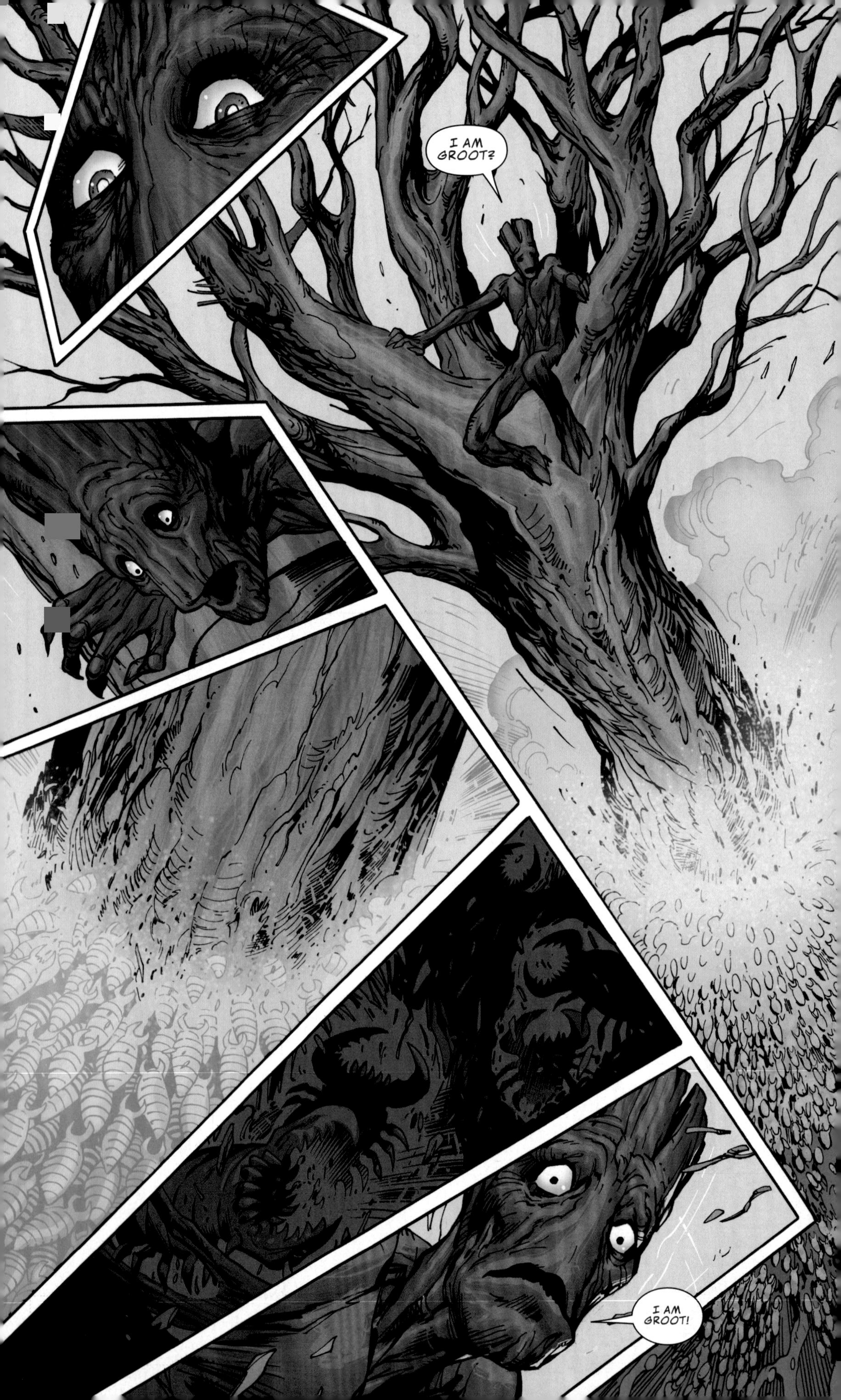
I AM GROOT?
I AM GROOT!

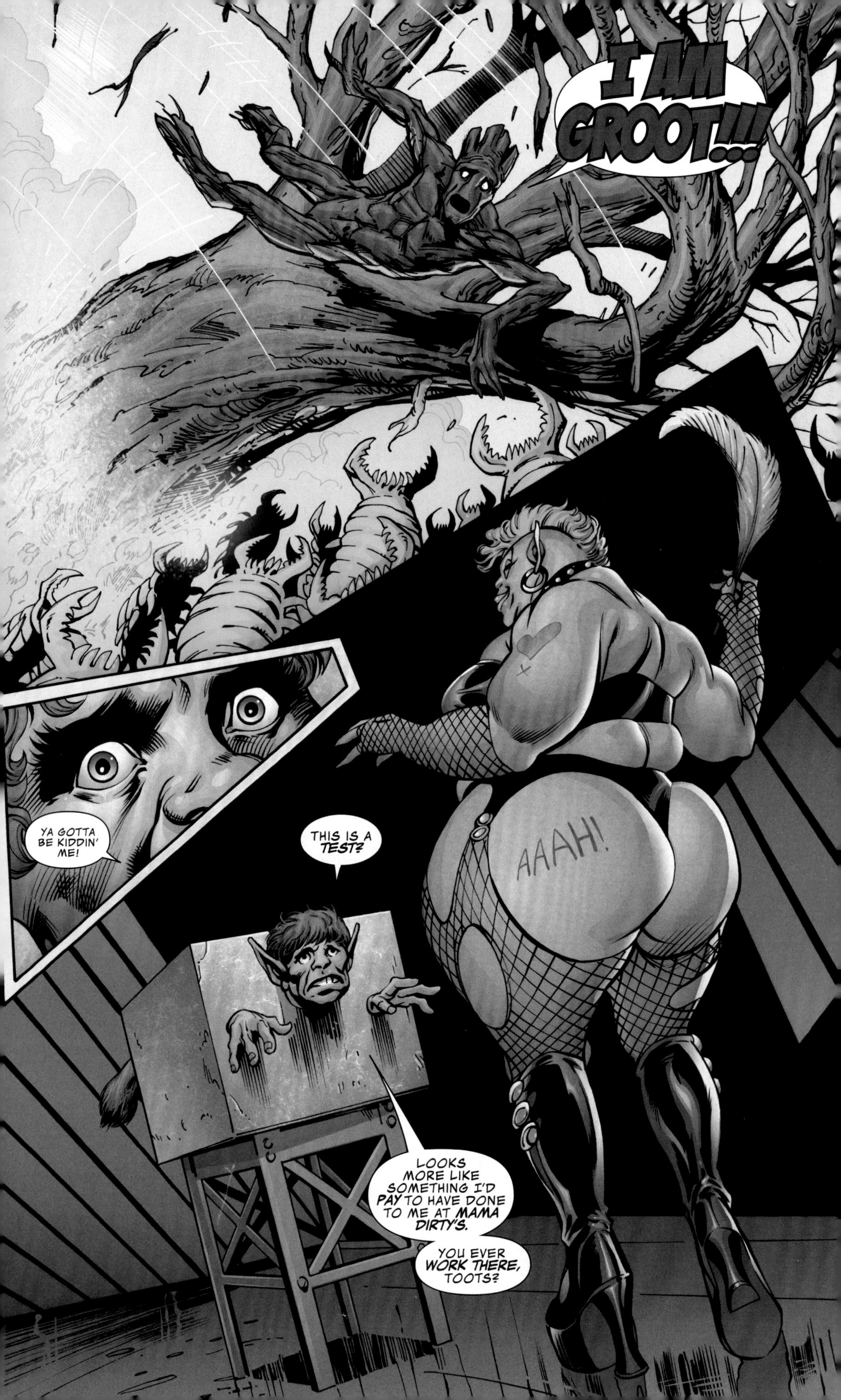
I AM GROOT!!!
YA GOTTA BE KIDDIN' ME!
THIS IS A TEST?
AAAH!
LOOKS MORE LIKE SOMETHING I'D PAY TO HAVE DONE TO ME AT MAMA DIRTY'S.
YOU EVER WORK THERE, TOOTS?

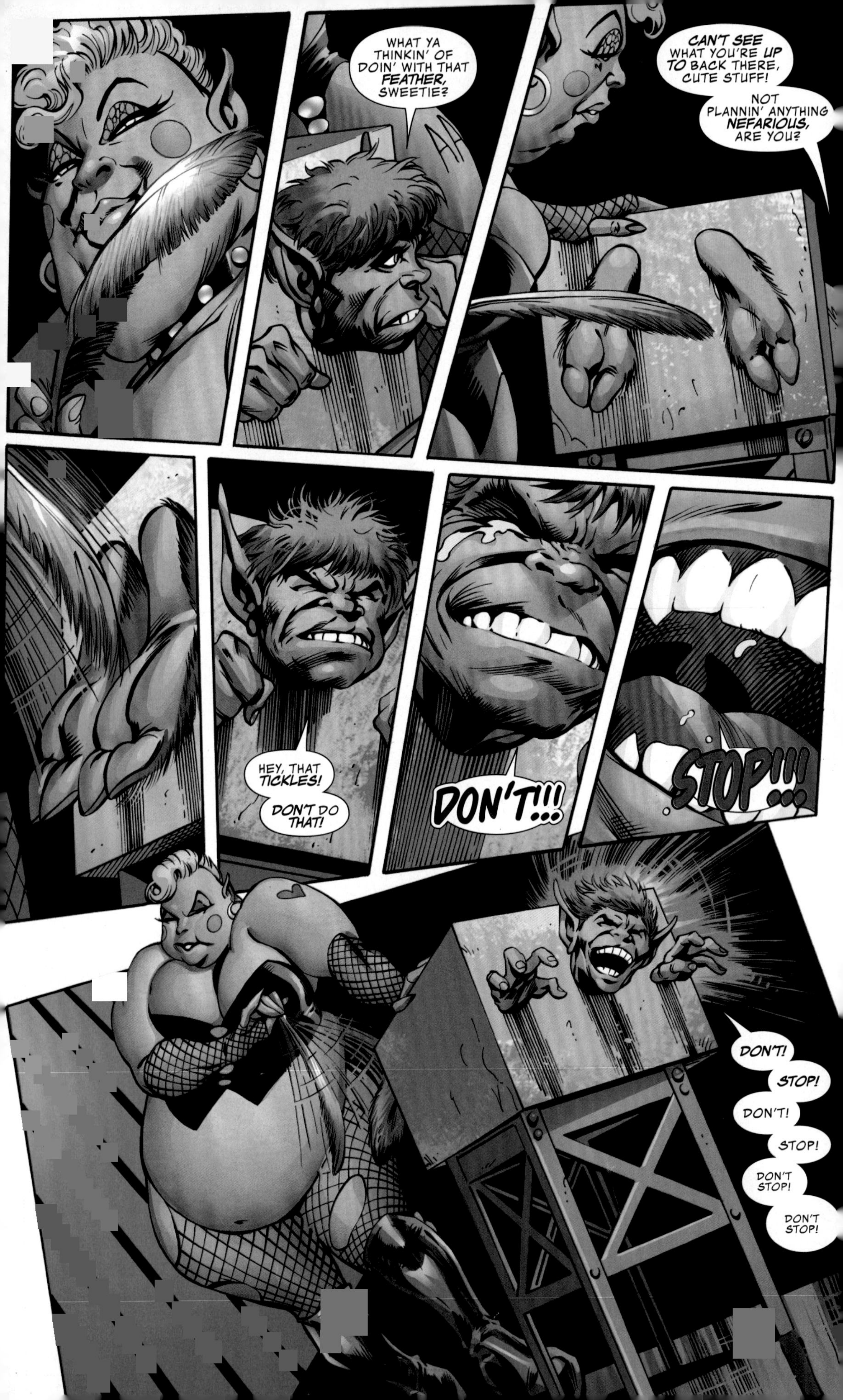

WHAT YA THINKIN' OF DOIN' WITH THAT FEATHER, SWEETIE?
CAN'T SEE WHAT YOU'RE UP TO BACK THERE, CUTE STUFF!
NOT PLANNIN' ANYTHING NEFARIOUS, ARE YOU?
HEY, THAT TICKLES!
DON'T DO THAT!
DON'T!!!
STOP!!!
DON'T!
STOP!
DON'T!
STOP!
DON'T STOP!
DON'T STOP!

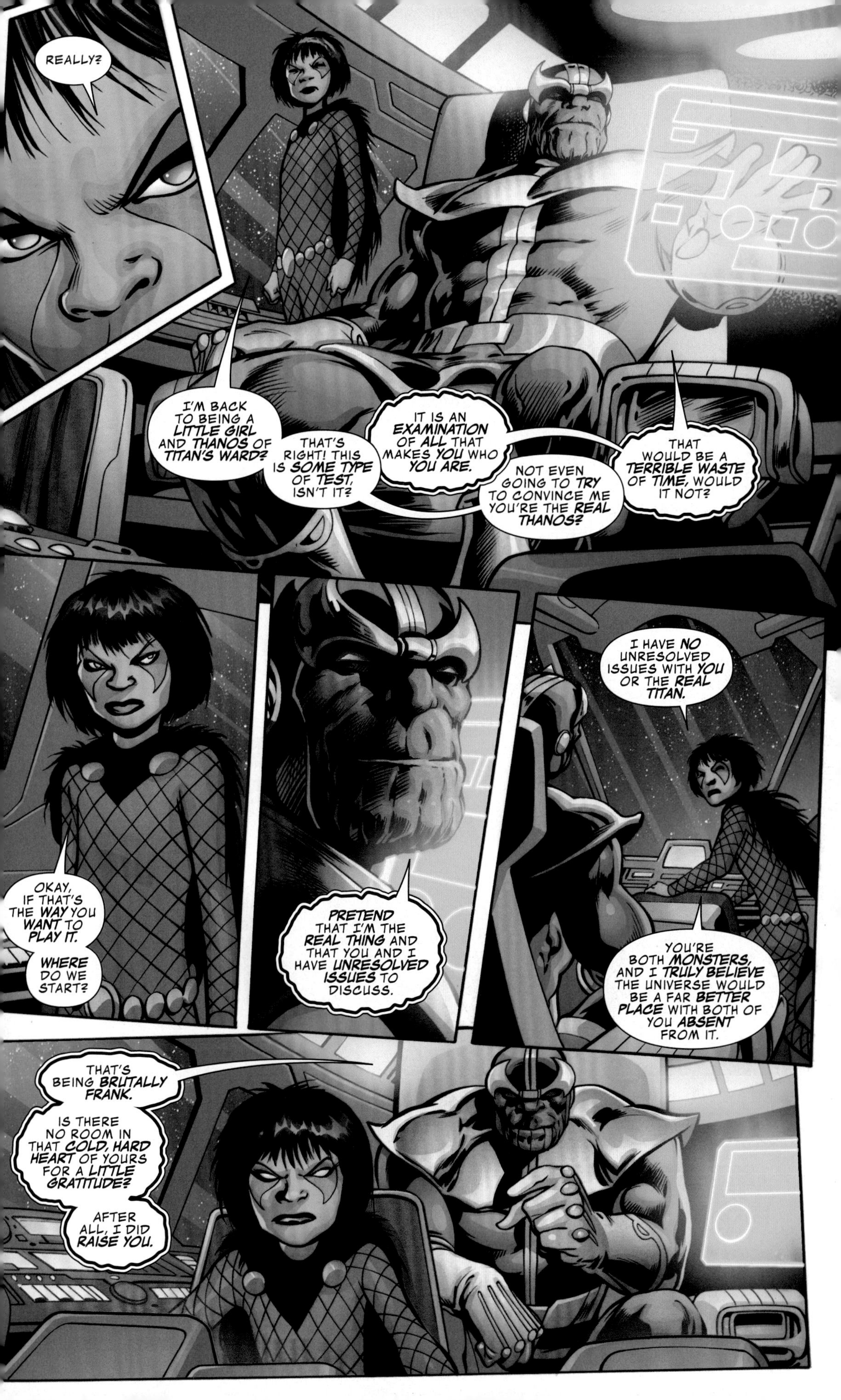
REALLY?
I'M BACK TO BEING A LITTLE GIRL AND THANOS OF TITAN'S WARD?
THAT'S RIGHT! THIS IS SOME TYPE OF TEST, ISN'T IT?
IT IS AN EXAMINATION OF ALL THAT MAKES YOU WHO YOU ARE.
NOT EVEN GOING TO TRY TO CONVINCE ME YOU'RE THE REAL THANOS?
THAT WOULD BE A TERRIBLE WASTE OF TIME, WOULD IT NOT?
OKAY, IF THAT'S THE WAY YOU WANT TO PLAY IT.
WHERE DO WE START?
PRETEND THAT I'M THE REAL THING AND THAT YOU AND I HAVE UNRESOLVED ISSUES TO DISCUSS.
I HAVE NO UNRESOLVED ISSUES WITH YOU OR THE REAL TITAN.
YOU'RE BOTH MONSTERS, AND I TRULY BELIEVE THE UNIVERSE WOULD BE A FAR BETTER PLACE WITH BOTH OF YOU ABSENT FROM IT.
THAT'S BEING BRUTALLY FRANK.
IS THERE NO ROOM IN THAT COLD, HARD HEART OF YOURS FOR A LITTLE GRATITUDE?
AFTER ALL, I DID RAISE YOU.

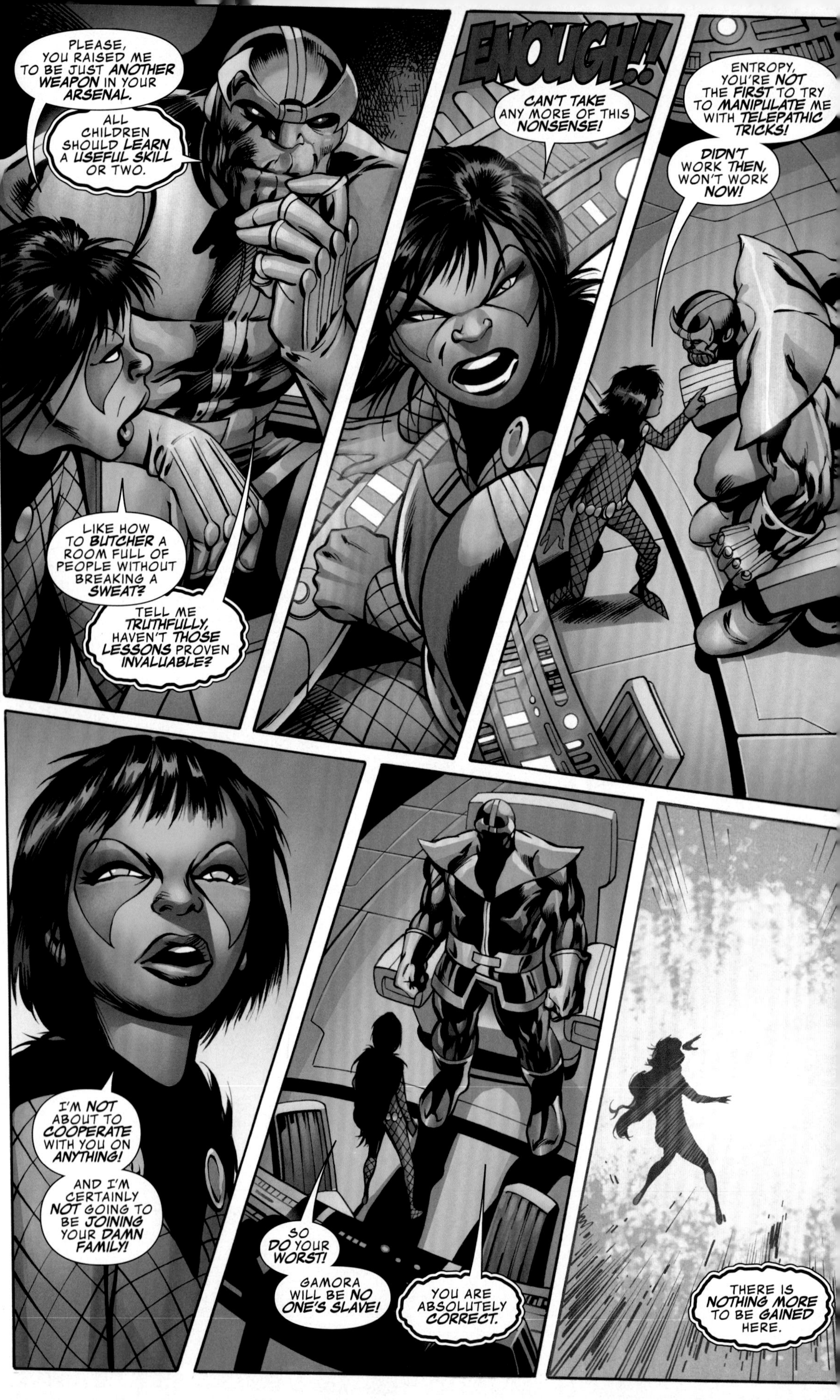
PLEASE, YOU RAISED ME TO BE JUST ANOTHER WEAPON IN YOUR ARSENAL.
ALL CHILDREN SHOULD LEARN A USEFUL SKILL OR TWO.
LIKE HOW TO BUTCHER A ROOM FULL OF PEOPLE WITHOUT BREAKING A SWEAT?
TELL ME TRUTHFULLY, HAVEN'T THOSE LESSONS PROVEN INVALUABLE?
ENOUGH!!
CAN'T TAKE ANY MORE OF THIS NONSENSE!
ENTROPY, YOU'RE NOT THE FIRST TO TRY TO MANIPULATE ME WITH TELEPATHIC TRICKS!
DIDN'T WORK THEN, WON'T WORK NOW!
I'M NOT ABOUT TO COOPERATE WITH YOU ON ANYTHING!
AND I'M CERTAINLY NOT GOING TO BE JOINING YOUR DAMN FAMILY!
SO DO YOUR WORST!
GAMORA WILL BE NO ONE'S SLAVE!
YOU ARE ABSOLUTELY CORRECT.
THERE IS NOTHING MORE TO BE GAINED HERE.

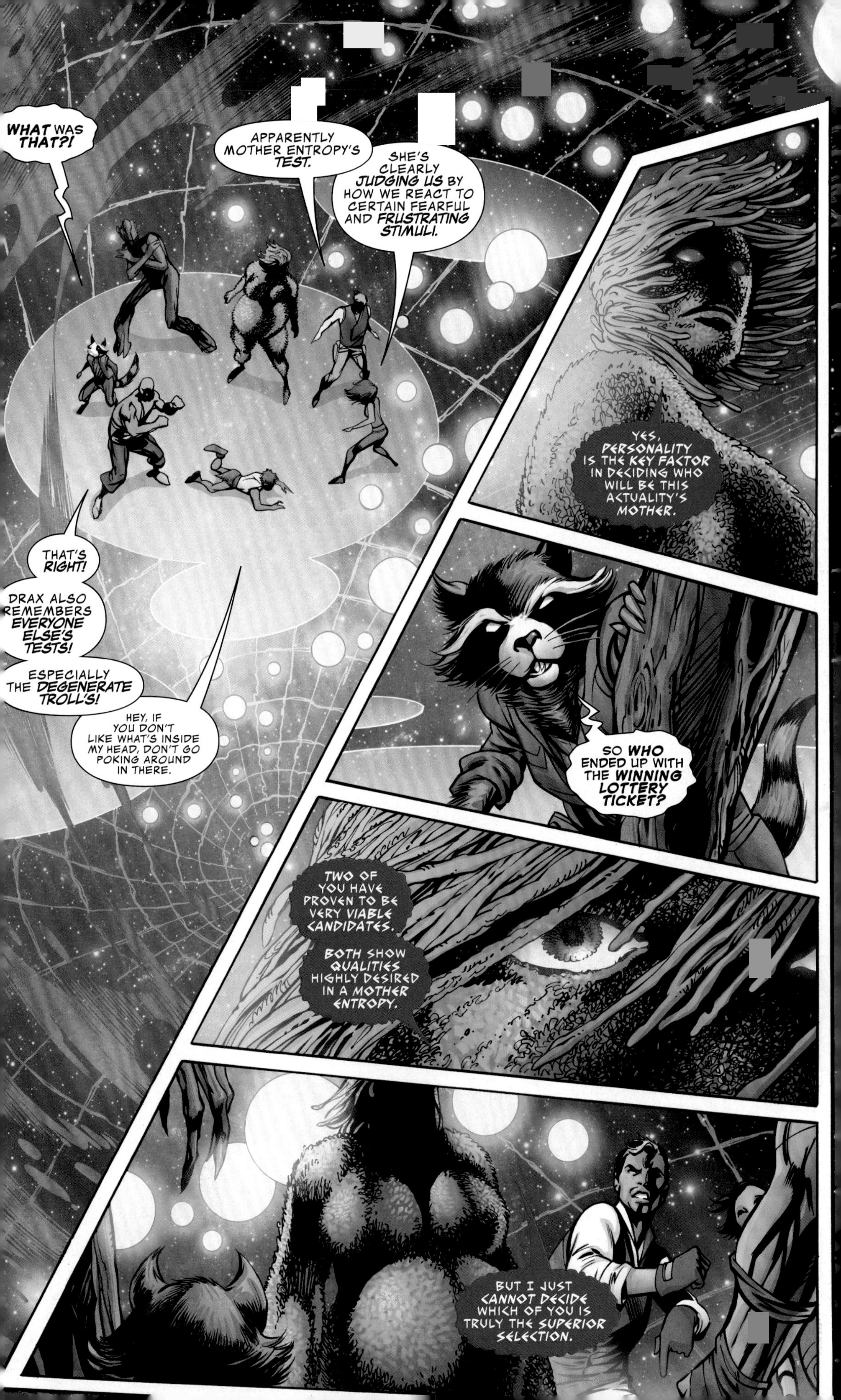
WHAT WAS THAT?!
APPARENTLY MOTHER ENTROPY'S TEST.
SHE'S CLEARLY JUDGING US BY HOW WE REACT TO CERTAIN FEARFUL AND FRUSTRATING STIMULI.
THAT'S RIGHT!
DRAX ALSO REMEMBERS EVERYONE ELSE'S TESTS!
ESPECIALLY THE DEGENERATE TROLL'S!
HEY, IF YOU DON'T LIKE WHAT'S INSIDE MY HEAD, DON'T GO POKING AROUND IN THERE.
YES, PERSONALITY IS THE KEY FACTOR IN DECIDING WHO WILL BE THIS ACTUALITY'S MOTHER.
SO WHO ENDED UP WITH THE WINNING LOTTERY TICKET?
TWO OF YOU HAVE PROVEN TO BE VERY VIABLE CANDIDATES.
BOTH SHOW QUALITIES HIGHLY DESIRED IN A MOTHER ENTROPY.
BUT I JUST CANNOT DECIDE WHICH OF YOU IS TRULY THE SUPERIOR SELECTION.

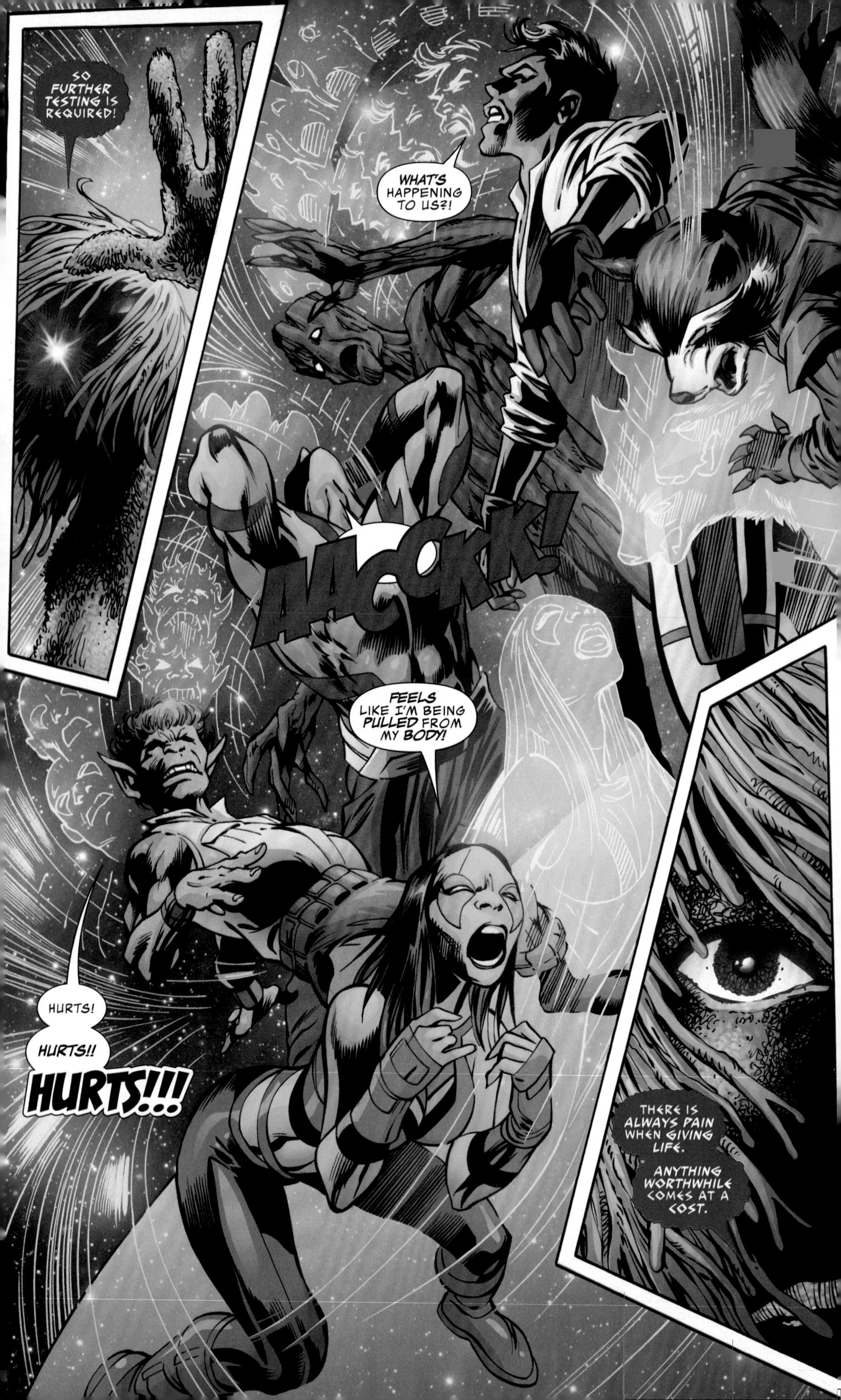
SO FURTHER TESTING IS REQUIRED!
WHAT'S HAPPENING TO US?!
AACCKK!
FEELS LIKE I'M BEING PULLED FROM MY BODY!
HURTS!
HURTS!!
HURTS!!!
THERE IS ALWAYS PAIN WHEN GIVING LIFE.
ANYTHING WORTHWHILE COMES AT A COST.

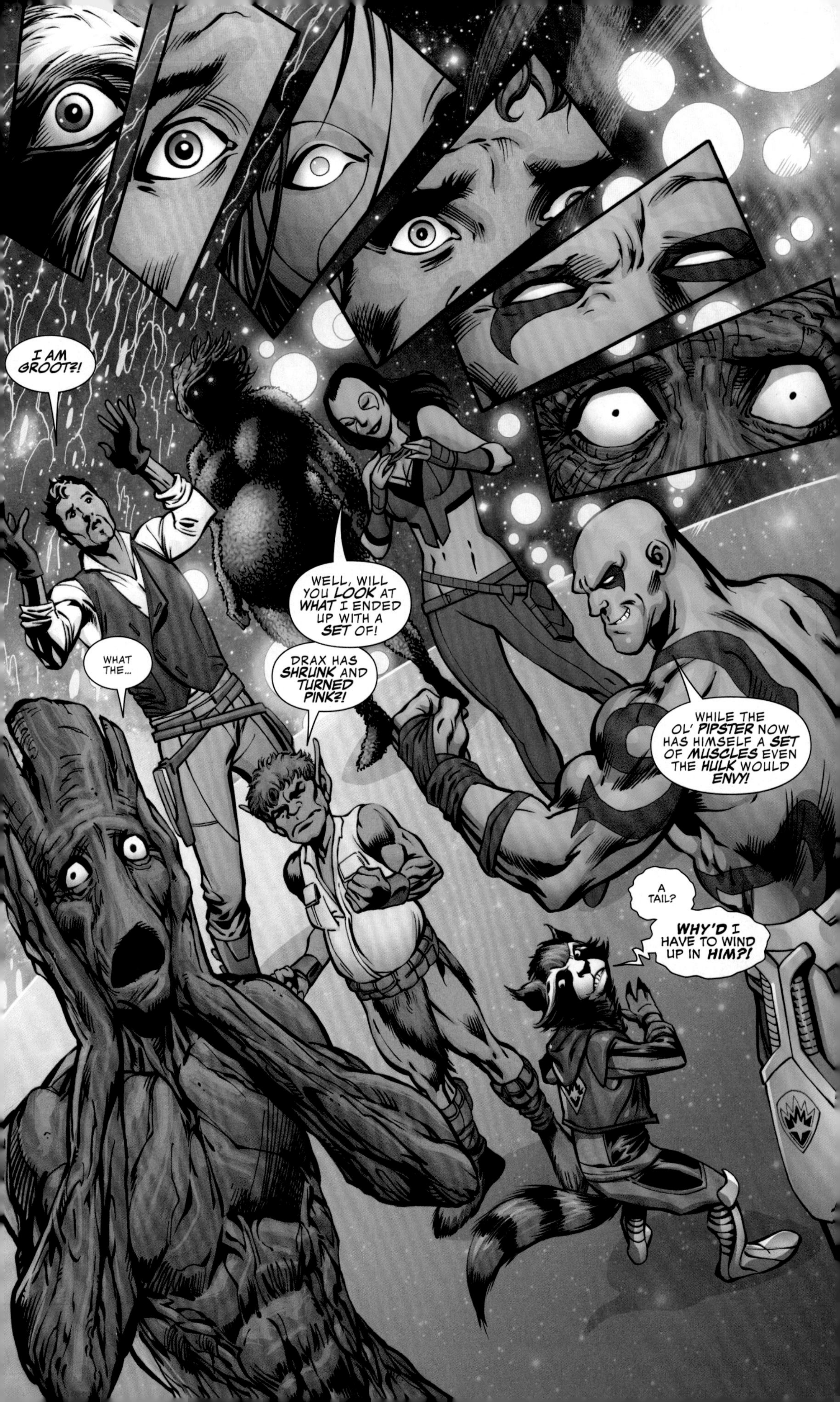
I AM GROOT?!
WELL, WILL YOU LOOK AT WHAT I ENDED UP WITH A SET OF!
WHAT THE...
DRAX HAS SHRUNK AND TURNED PINK?!
WHILE THE OL' PIPSTER NOW HAS HIMSELF A SET OF MUSCLES EVEN THE HULK WOULD ENVY!
A TAIL?
WHY'D I HAVE TO WIND UP IN HIM?!

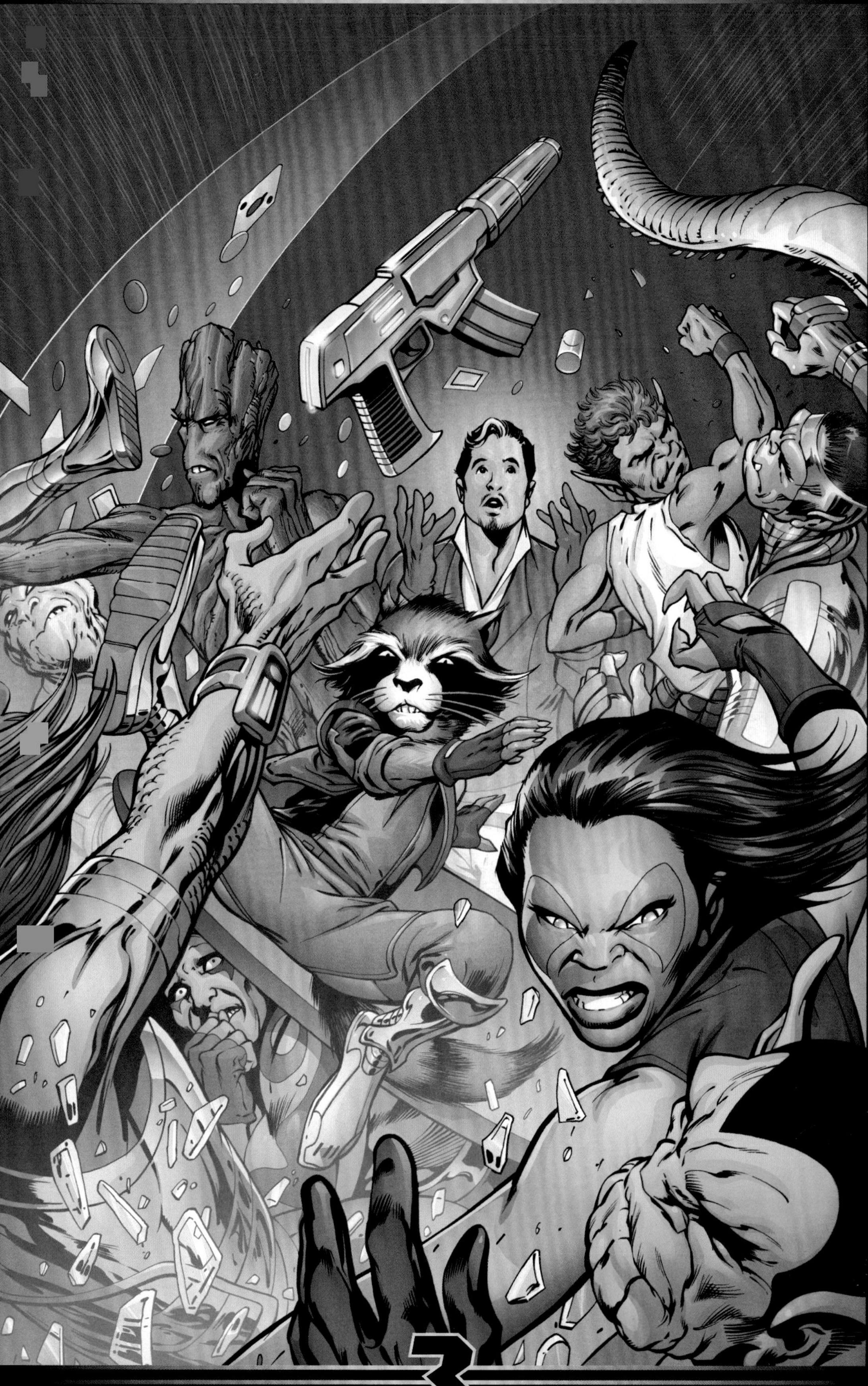

3

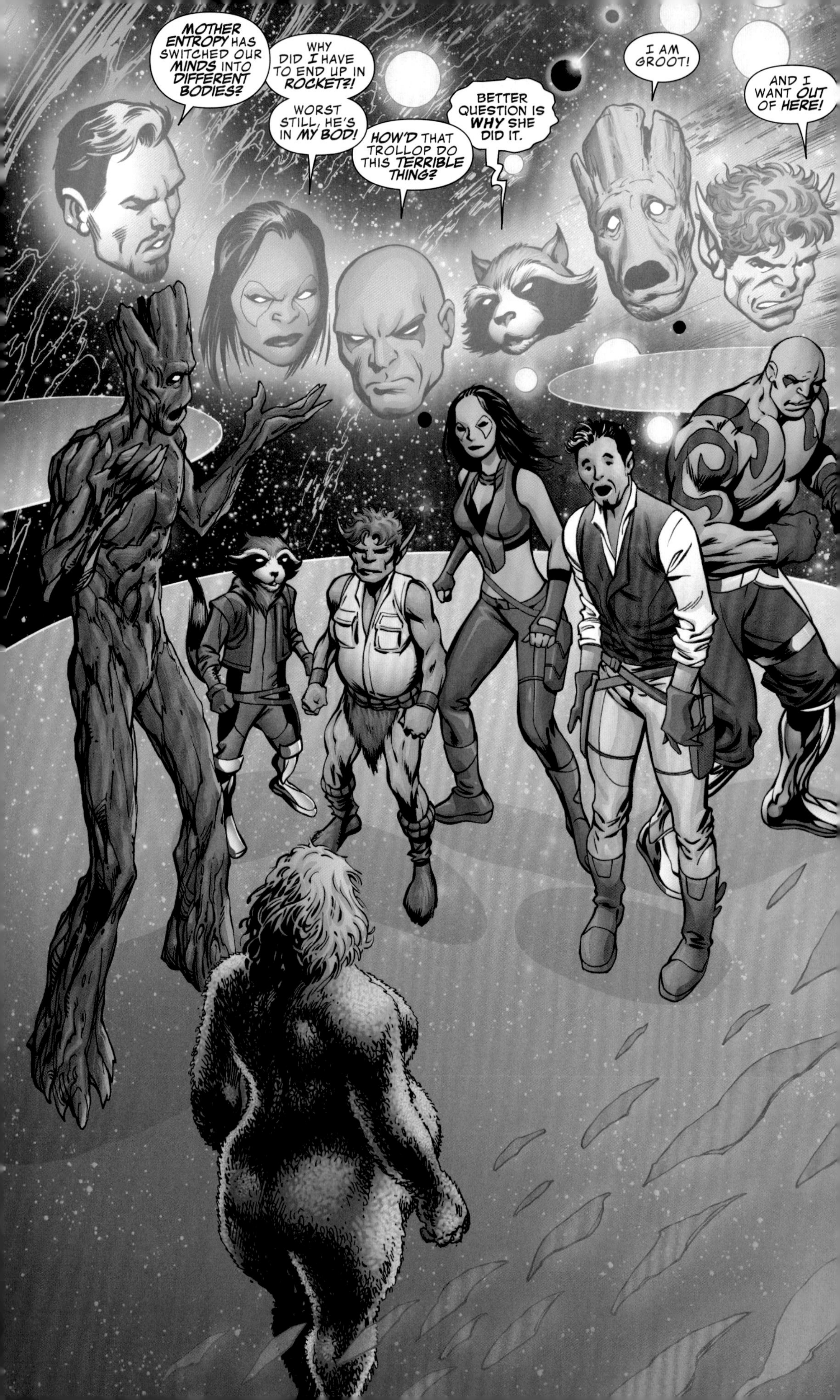
MOTHER ENTROPY HAS SWITCHED OUR MINDS INTO DIFFERENT BODIES?
WHY DID I HAVE TO END UP IN ROCKET?!
WORST STILL, HE'S IN MY BOD!
HOW'D THAT TROLLOP DO THIS TERRIBLE THING?
BETTER QUESTION IS WHY SHE DID IT.
I AM GROOT!
AND I WANT OUT OF HERE!

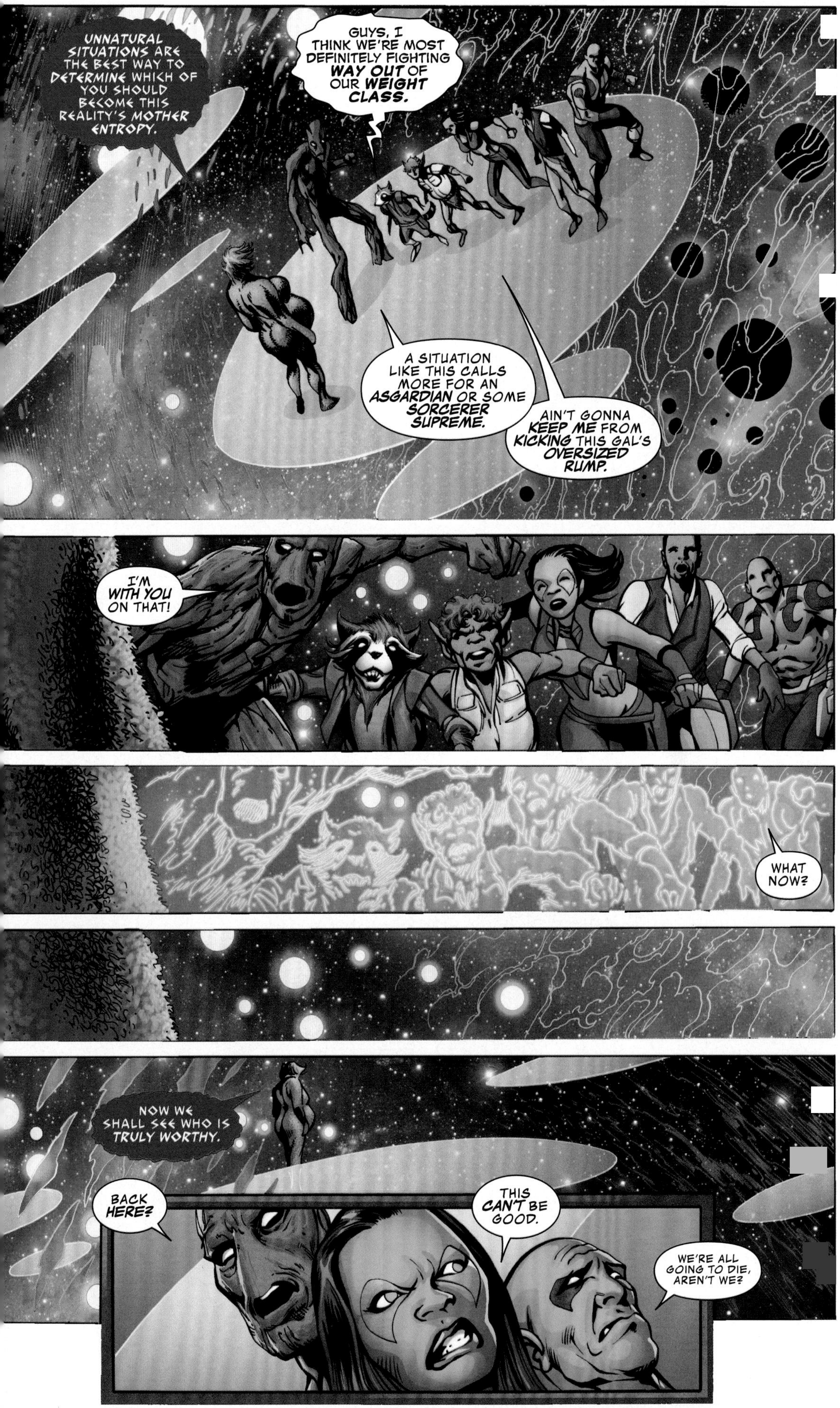
UNNATURAL SITUATIONS ARE THE BEST WAY TO DETERMINE WHICH OF YOU SHOULD BECOME THIS REALITY'S MOTHER ENTROPY.
GUYS, I THINK WE'RE MOST DEFINITELY FIGHTING WAY OUT OF OUR WEIGHT CLASS.
A SITUATION LIKE THIS CALLS MORE FOR AN ASGARDIAN OR SOME SORCERER SUPREME.
AIN'T GONNA KEEP ME FROM KICKING THIS GAL'S OVERSIZED RUMP.
I'M WITH YOU ON THAT!
WHAT NOW?
NOW WE SHALL SEE WHO IS TRULY WORTHY.
BACK HERE?
THIS CAN'T BE GOOD.
WE'RE ALL GOING TO DIE, AREN'T WE?

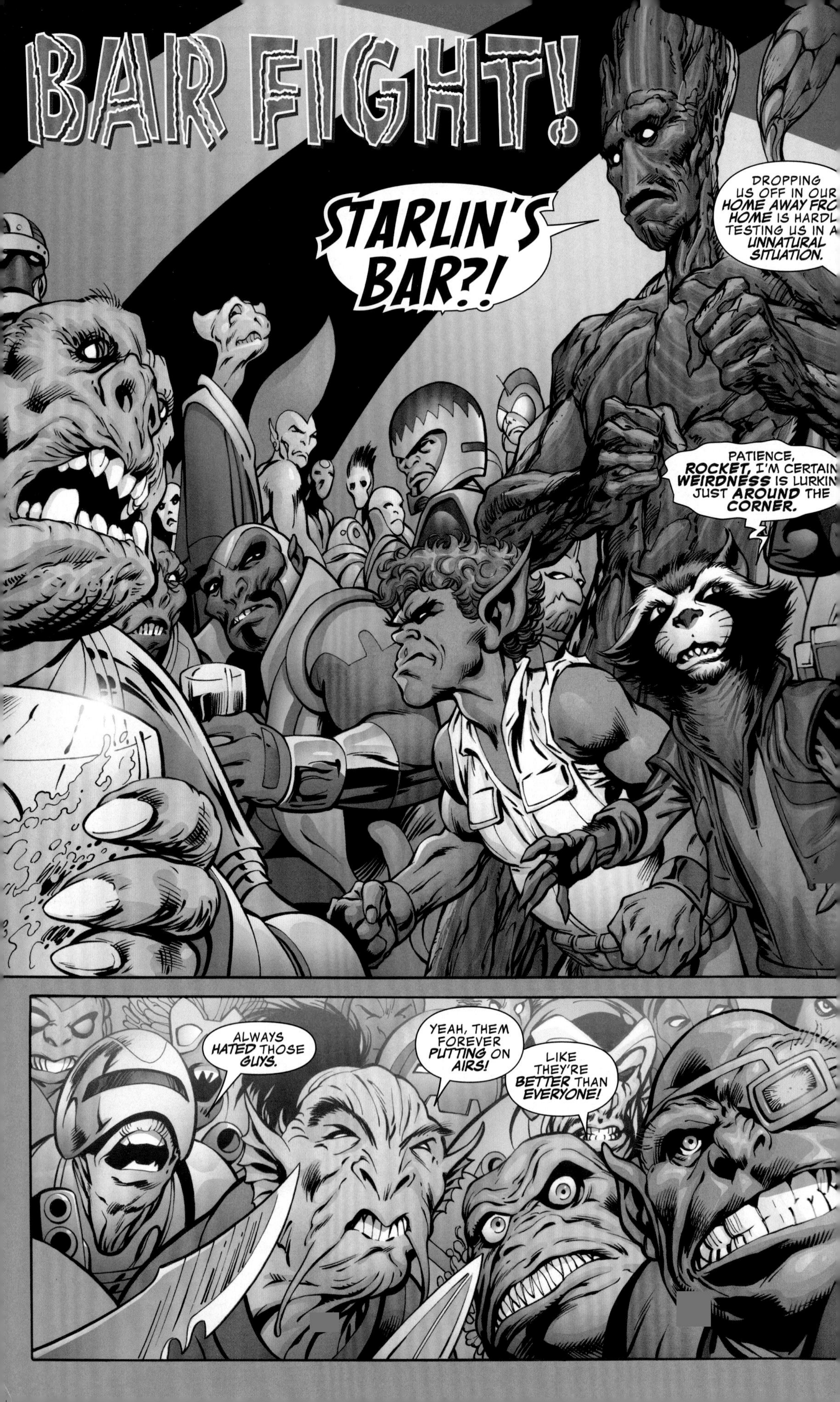

BAR FIGHT!
STARLIN'S BAR?!
DROPPING US OFF IN OUR HOME AWAY FRO HOME IS HARDL TESTING US IN A UNNATURAL SITUATION.
PATIENCE, ROCKET, I'M CERTAIN WEIRDNESS IS LURKIN JUST AROUND THE CORNER.
ALWAYS HATED THOSE GUYS.
YEAH, THEM FOREVER PUTTING ON AIRS!
LIKE THEY'RE BETTER THAN EVERYONE!

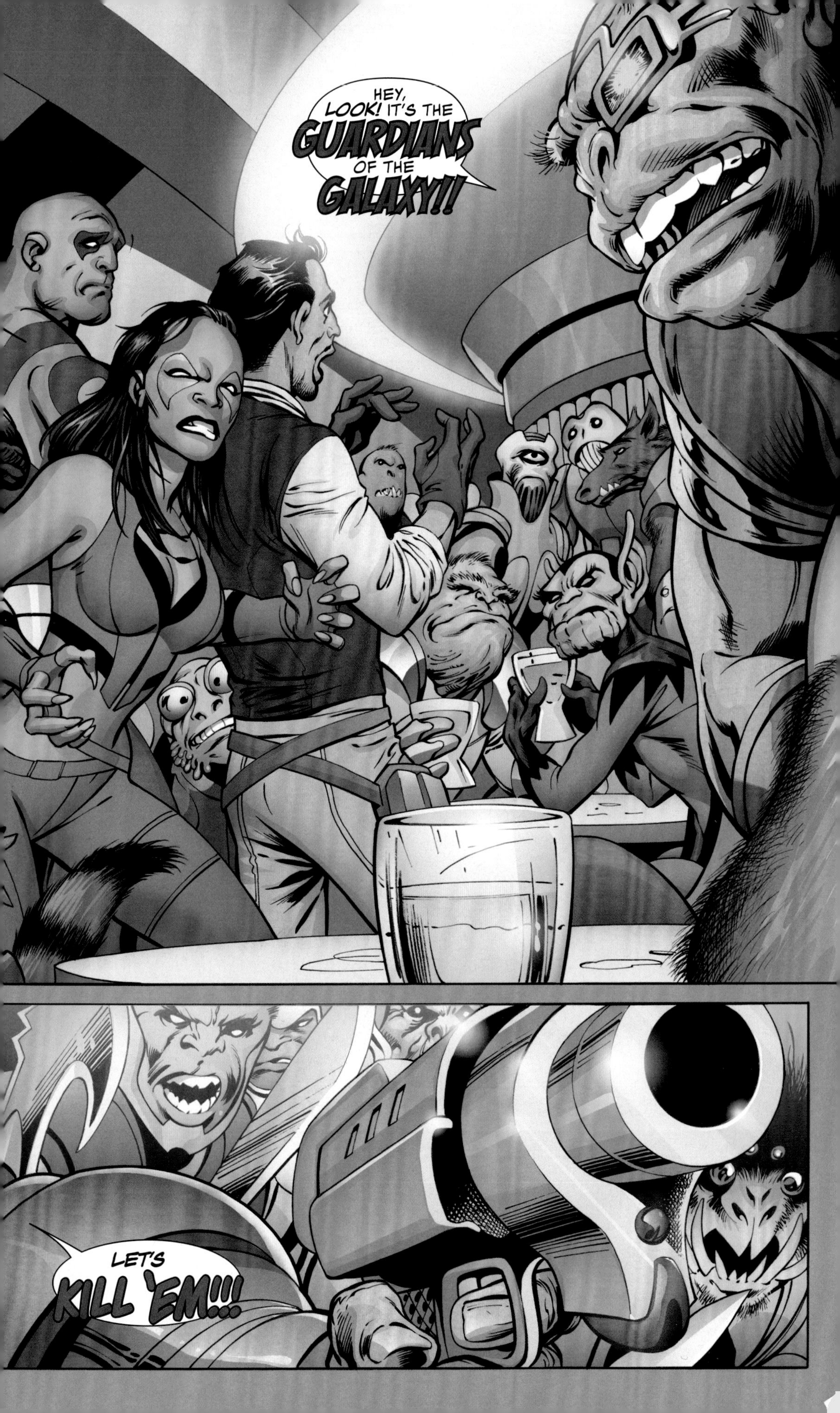
HEY, LOOK! IT'S THE GUARDIANS OF THE GALAXY!!
LET'S KILL 'EM!!!

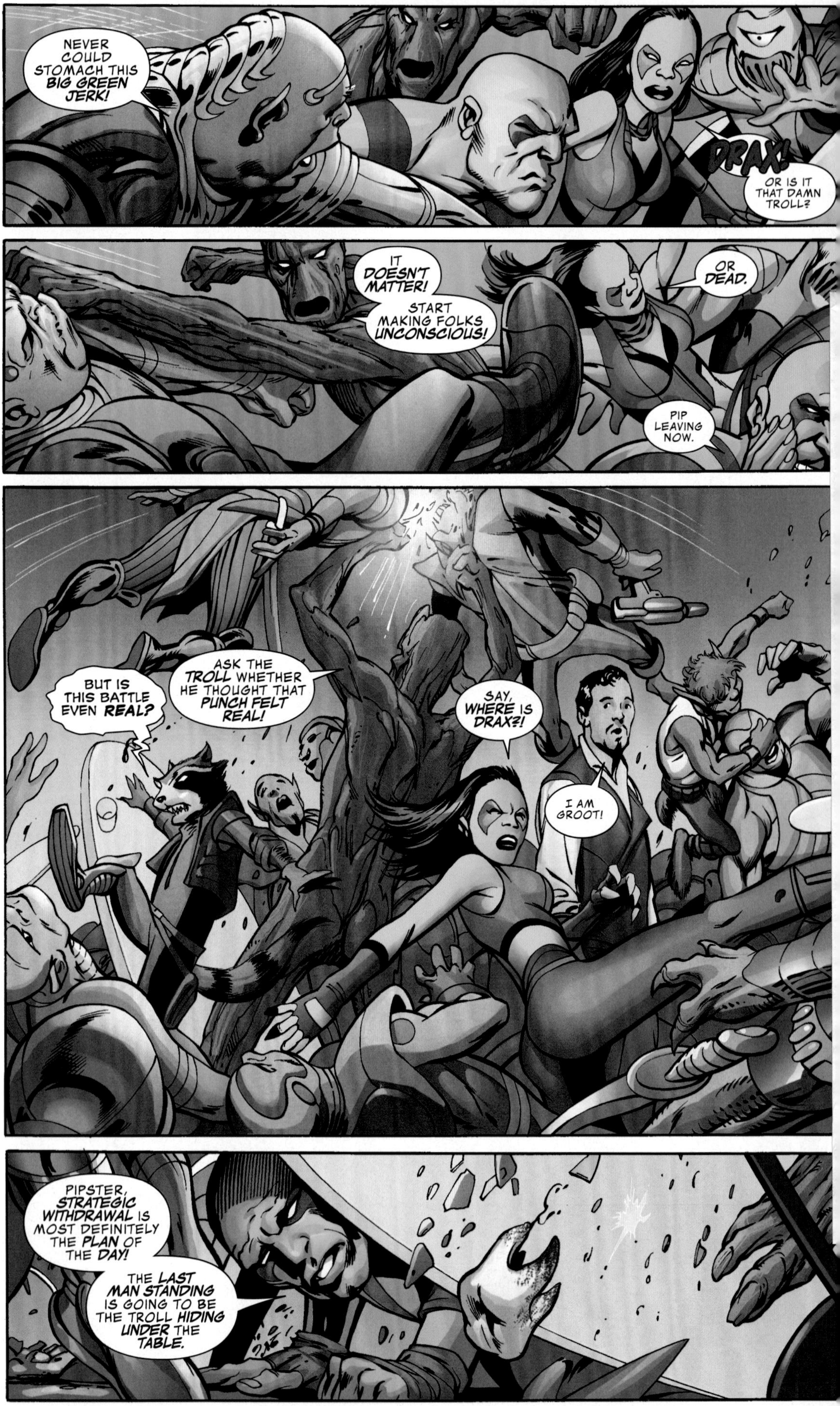
NEVER COULD STOMACH THIS BIG GREEN JERK!
DRAX!
OR IS IT THAT DAMN TROLL?
IT DOESN'T MATTER!
START MAKING FOLKS UNCONSCIOUS!
OR DEAD.
PIP LEAVING NOW.
BUT IS THIS BATTLE EVEN REAL?
ASK THE TROLL WHETHER HE THOUGHT THAT PUNCH FELT REAL!
SAY, WHERE IS DRAX?!
I AM GROOT!
PIPSTER, STRATEGIC WITHDRAWAL IS MOST DEFINITELY THE PLAN OF THE DAY!
THE LAST MAN STANDING IS GOING TO BE THE TROLL HIDING UNDER THE TABLE.

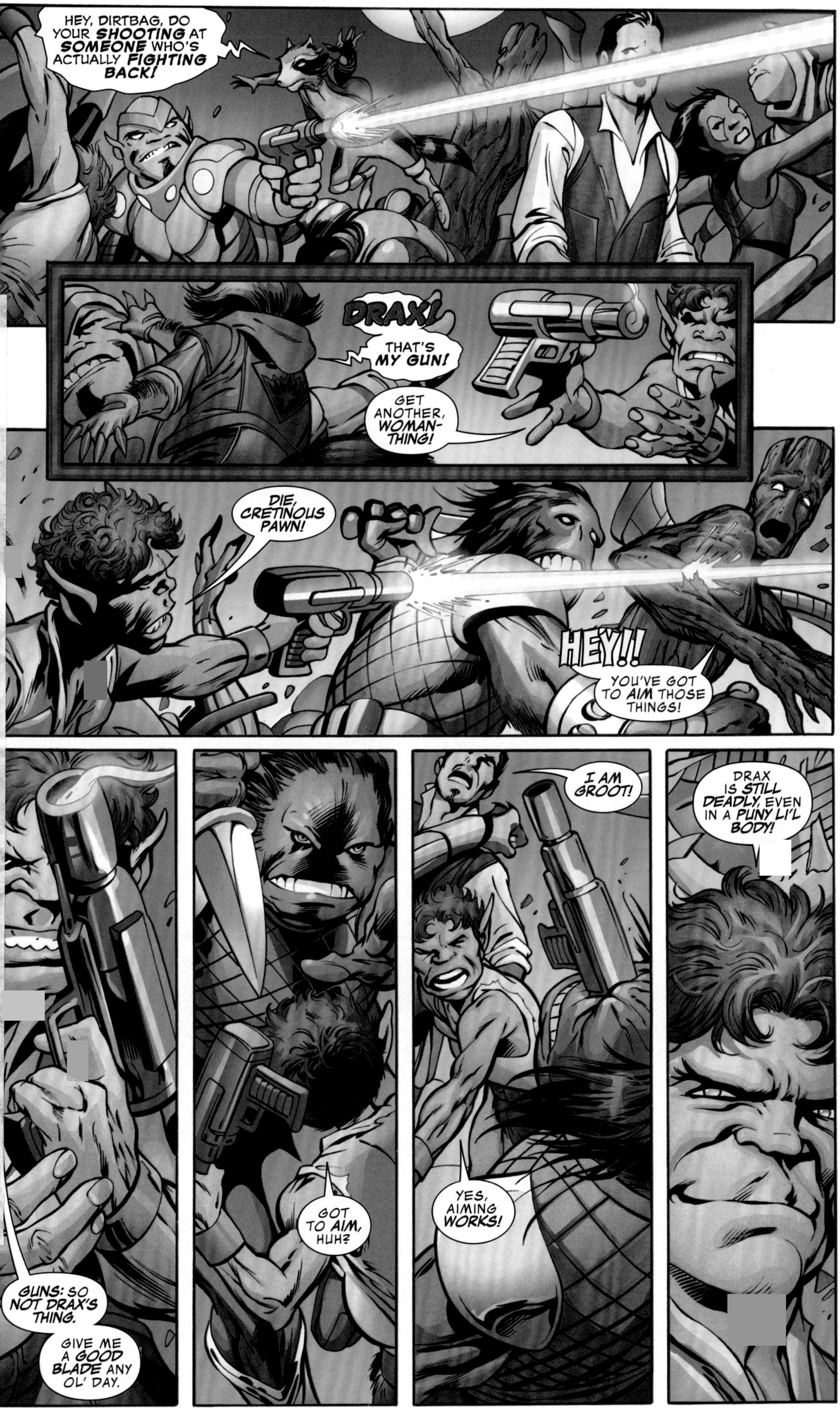
HEY, DIRTBAG, DO YOUR SHOOTING AT SOMEONE WHO'S ACTUALLY FIGHTING BACK!
DRAX!
THAT'S MY GUN!
GET ANOTHER, WOMAN-THING!
DIE, CRETINOUS PAWN!
HEY!!
YOU'VE GOT TO AIM THOSE THINGS!
GUNS: SO NOT DRAX'S THING.
GIVE ME A GOOD BLADE ANY OL' DAY.
GOT TO AIM, HUH?
I AM GROOT!
YES, AIMING WORKS!
DRAX IS STILL DEADLY, EVEN IN A PUNY LI'L BODY!

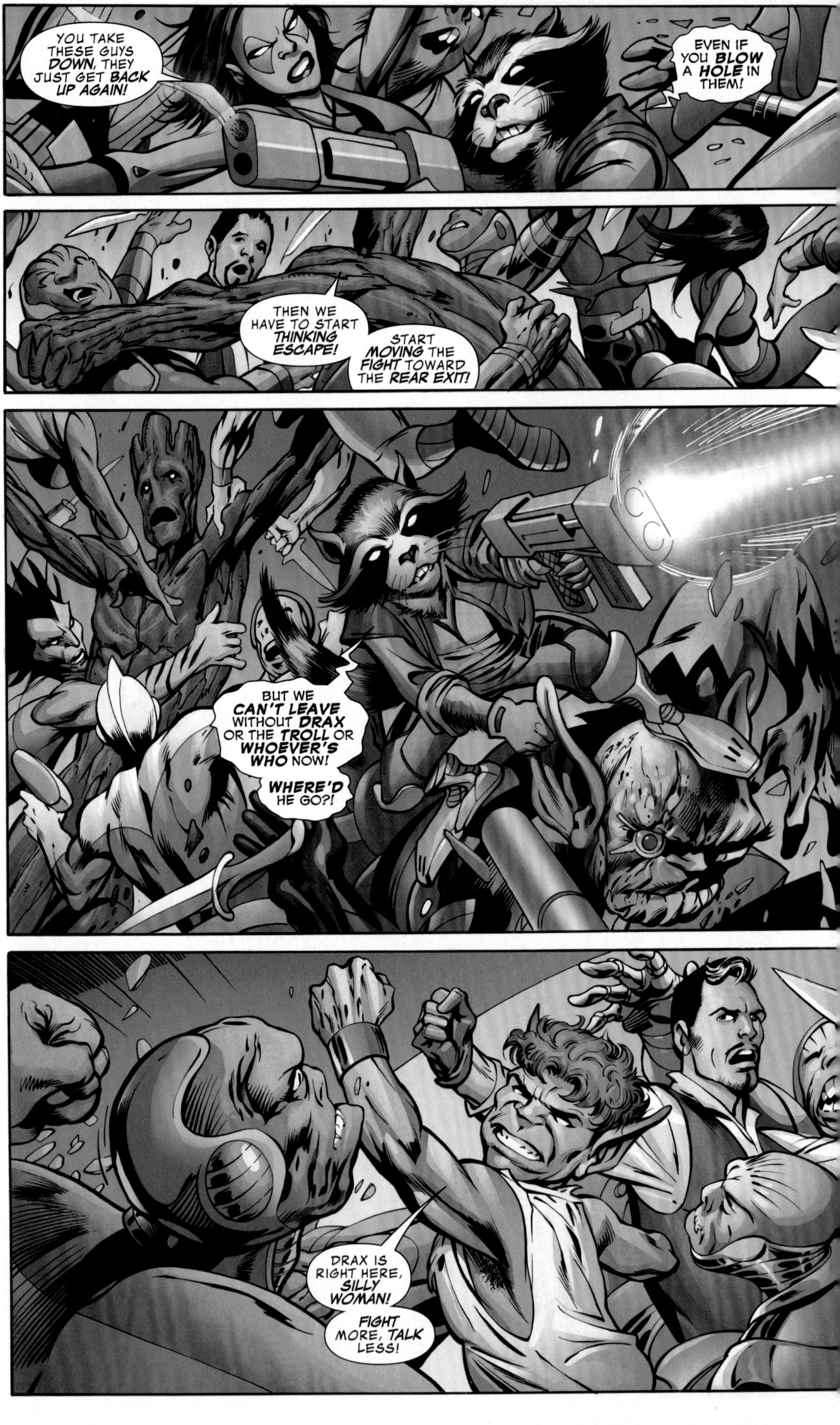
YOU TAKE THESE GUYS DOWN, THEY JUST GET BACK UP AGAIN!
EVEN IF YOU BLOW A HOLE IN THEM!
THEN WE HAVE TO START THINKING ESCAPE!
START MOVING THE FIGHT TOWARD THE REAR EXIT!
BUT WE CAN'T LEAVE WITHOUT DRAX OR THE TROLL OR WHOEVER'S WHO NOW!
WHERE'D HE GO?!
DRAX IS RIGHT HERE, SILLY WOMAN!
FIGHT MORE, TALK LESS!

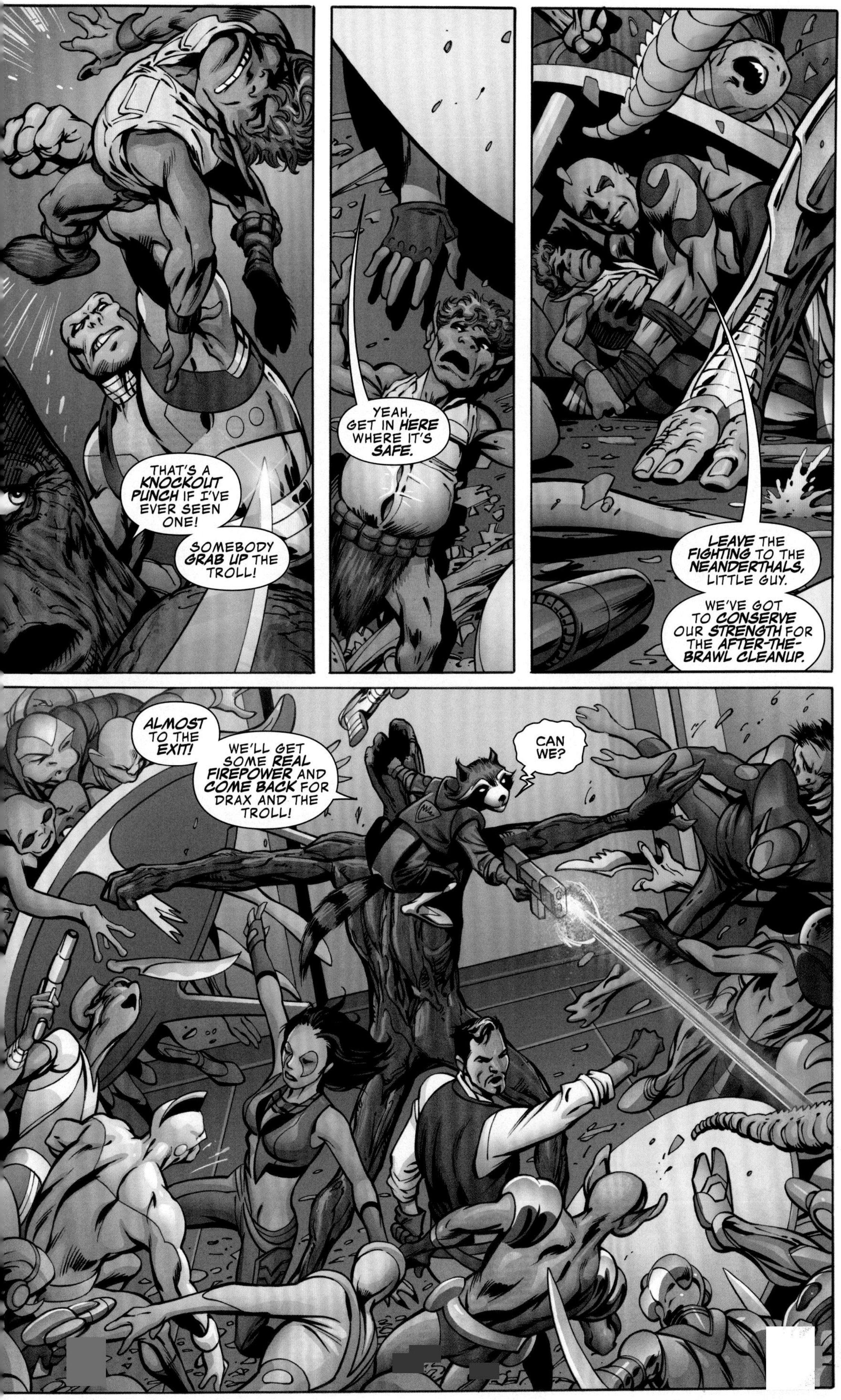

THAT'S A KNOCKOUT PUNCH IF I'VE EVER SEEN ONE!
SOMEBODY GRAB UP THE TROLL!
YEAH, GET IN HERE WHERE IT'S SAFE.
LEAVE THE FIGHTING TO THE NEANDERTHALS, LITTLE GUY.
WE'VE GOT TO CONSERVE OUR STRENGTH FOR THE AFTER-THE-BRAWL CLEANUP.
ALMOST TO THE EXIT!
WE'LL GET SOME REAL FIREPOWER AND COME BACK FOR DRAX AND THE TROLL!
CAN WE?

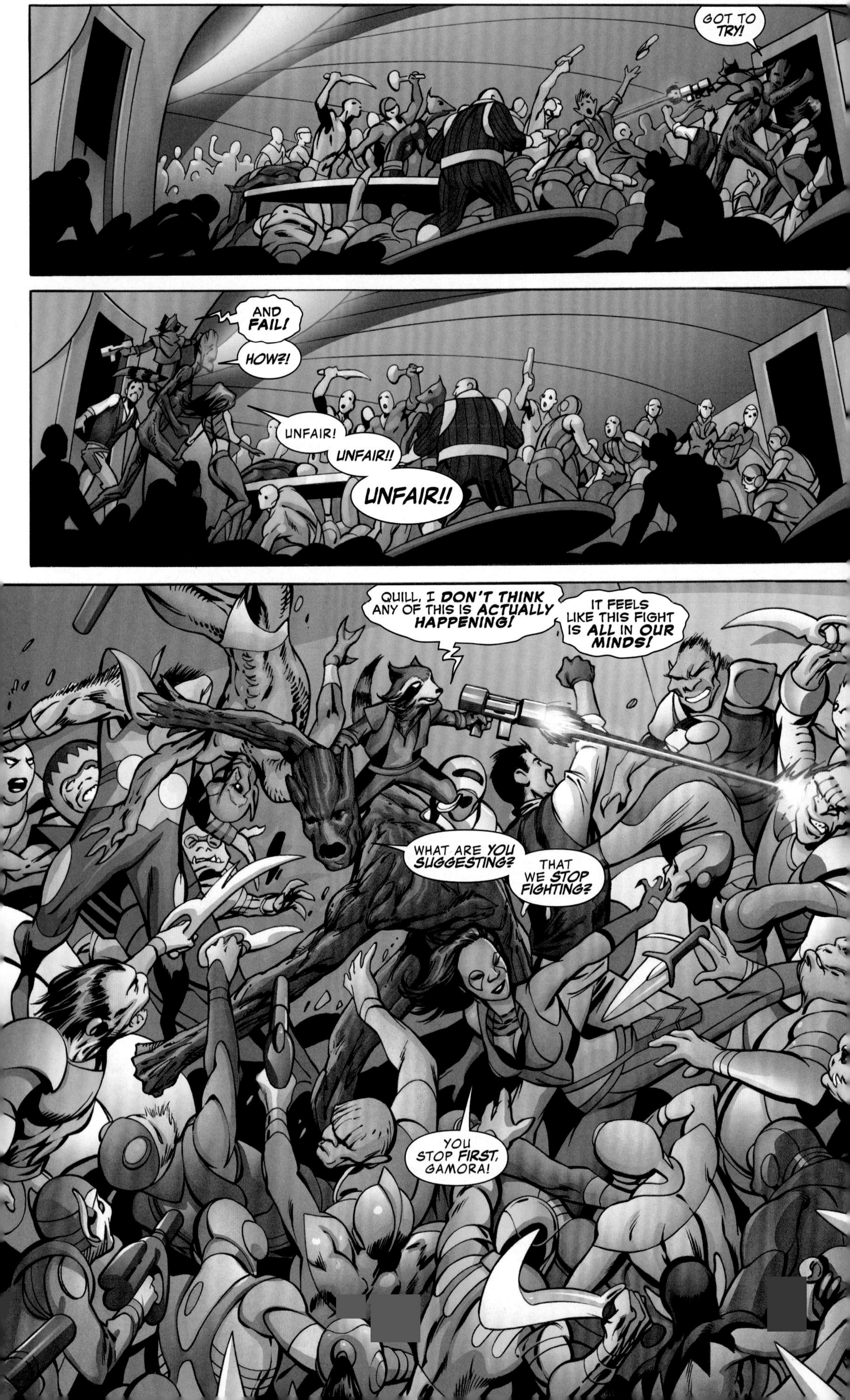
GOT TO TRY!
AND FAIL!
HOW?!
UNFAIR!
UNFAIR!!
UNFAIR!!
QUILL, I DON'T THINK ANY OF THIS IS ACTUALLY HAPPENING!
IT FEELS LIKE THIS FIGHT IS ALL IN OUR MINDS!
WHAT ARE YOU SUGGESTING?
THAT WE STOP FIGHTING?
YOU STOP FIRST, GAMORA!

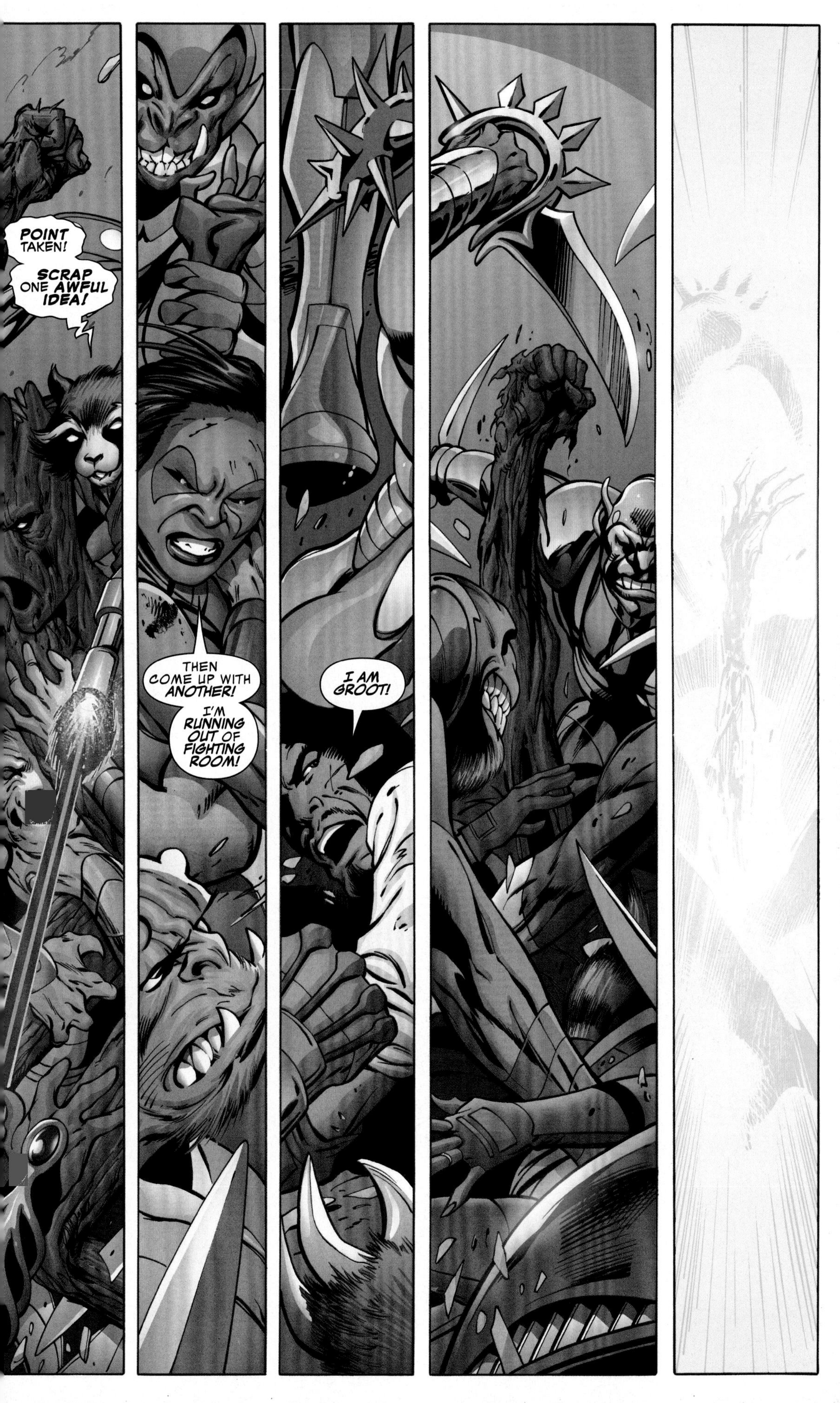

POINT TAKEN!
SCRAP ONE AWFUL IDEA!
THEN COME UP WITH ANOTHER!
I'M RUNNING OUT OF FIGHTING ROOM!
I AM GROOT!

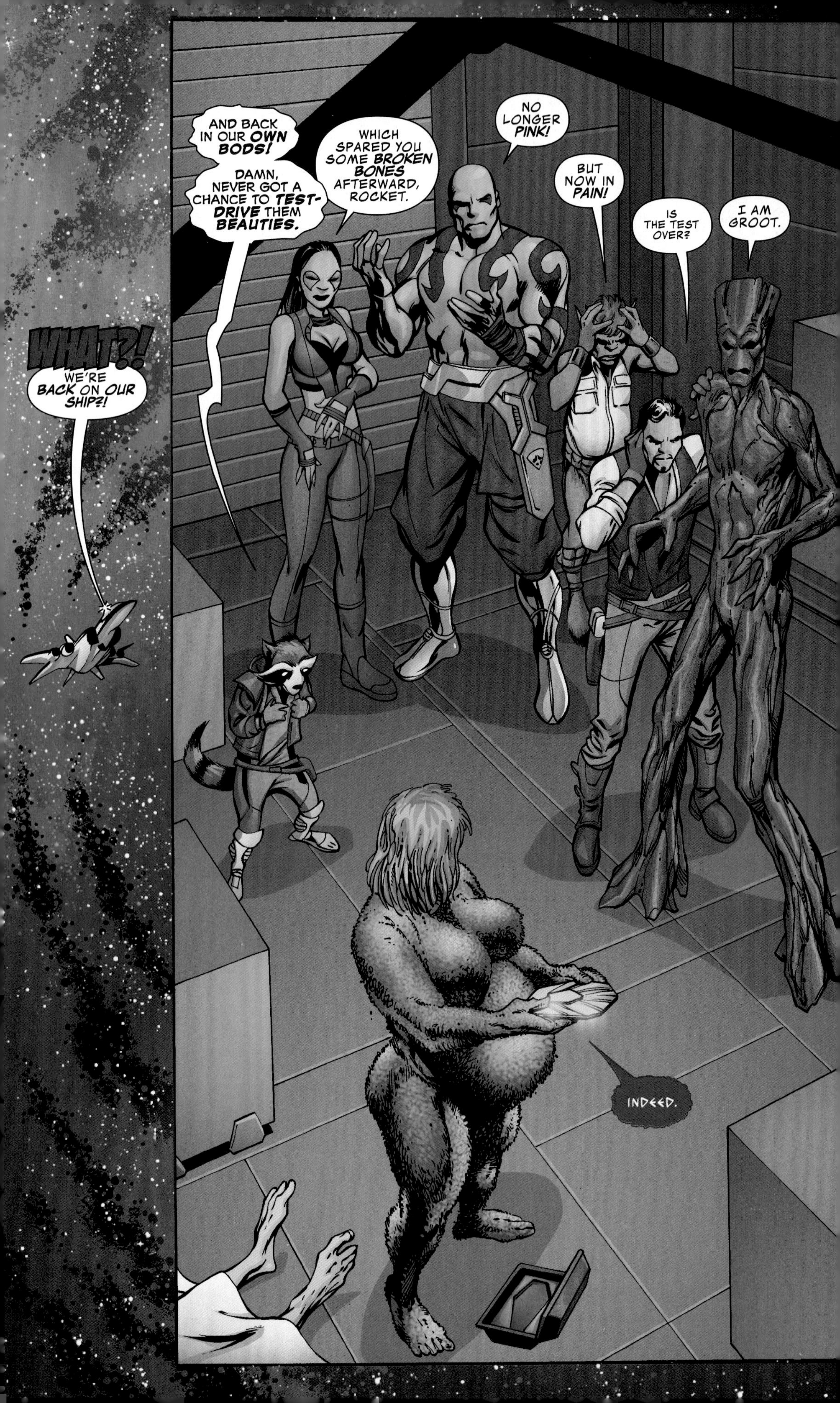

WHAT?!
WE'RE BACK ON OUR SHIP?!
AND BACK IN OUR OWN BODS!
DAMN, NEVER GOT A CHANCE TO TEST-DRIVE THEM BEAUTIES.
WHICH SPARED YOU SOME BROKEN BONES AFTERWARD, ROCKET.
NO LONGER PINK!
BUT NOW IN PAIN!
IS THE TEST OVER?
I AM GROOT.
INDEED.

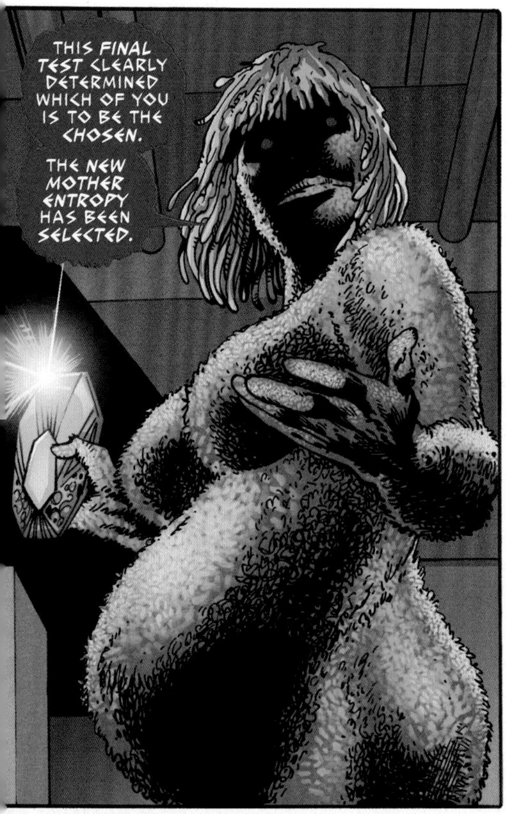

THIS FINAL TEST CLEARLY DETERMINED WHICH OF YOU IS TO BE THE CHOSEN.
THE NEW MOTHER ENTROPY HAS BEEN SELECTED.

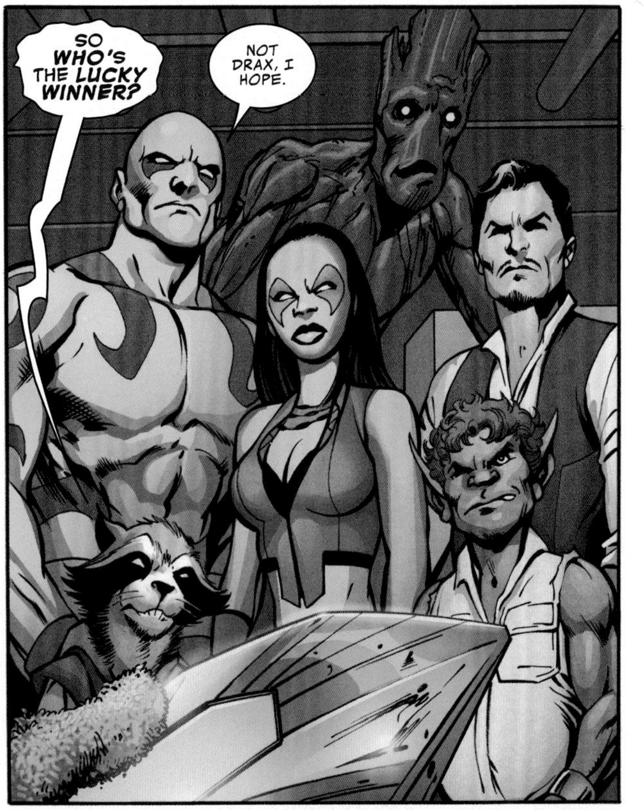

SO WHO'S THE LUCKY WINNER?
NOT DRAX, I HOPE.

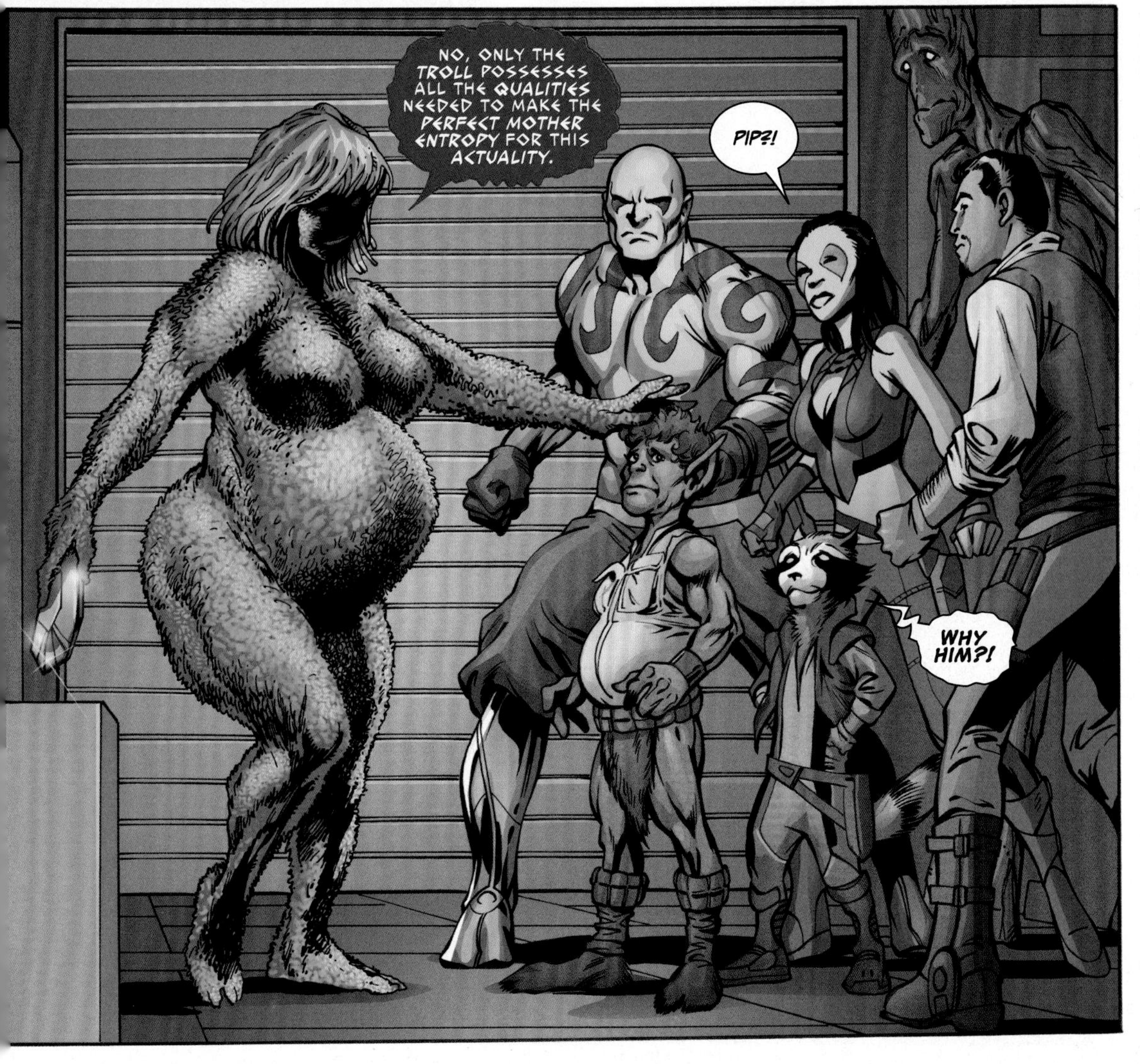

NO, ONLY THE TROLL POSSESSES ALL THE QUALITIES NEEDED TO MAKE THE PERFECT MOTHER ENTROPY FOR THIS ACTUALITY.
PIP?!
WHY HIM?!

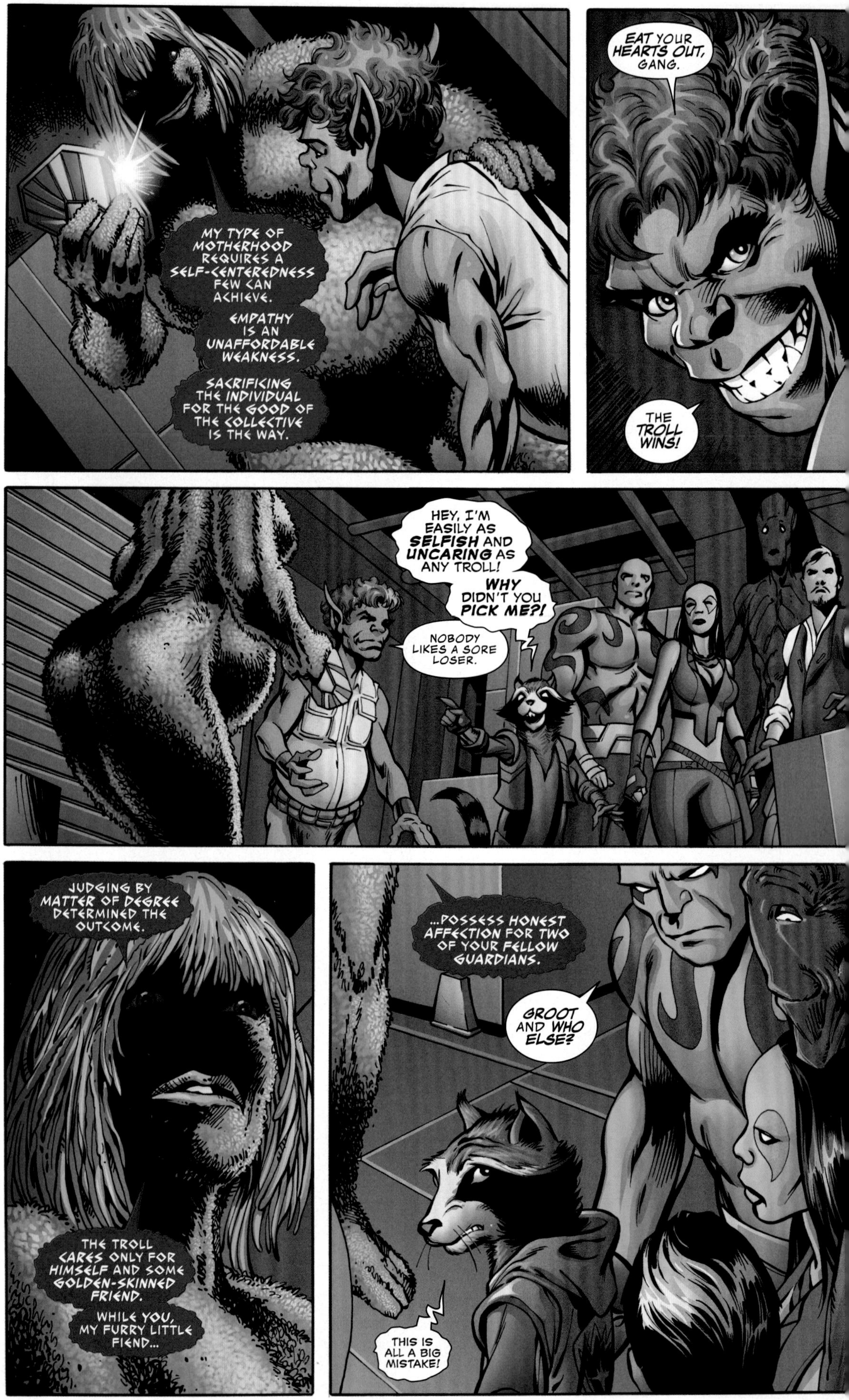

MY TYPE OF MOTHERHOOD REQUIRES A SELF-CENTEREDNESS FEW CAN ACHIEVE.
EMPATHY IS AN UNAFFORDABLE WEAKNESS.
SACRIFICING THE INDIVIDUAL FOR THE GOOD OF THE COLLECTIVE IS THE WAY.
EAT YOUR HEARTS OUT, GANG.
THE TROLL WINS!
HEY, I'M EASILY AS SELFISH AND UNCARING AS ANY TROLL!
WHY DIDN'T YOU PICK ME?!
NOBODY LIKES A SORE LOSER.
JUDGING BY MATTER OF DEGREE DETERMINED THE OUTCOME.
THE TROLL CARES ONLY FOR HIMSELF AND SOME GOLDEN-SKINNED FRIEND.
WHILE YOU, MY FURRY LITTLE FIEND...
...POSSESS HONEST AFFECTION FOR TWO OF YOUR FELLOW GUARDIANS.
GROOT AND WHO ELSE?
THIS IS ALL A BIG MISTAKE!

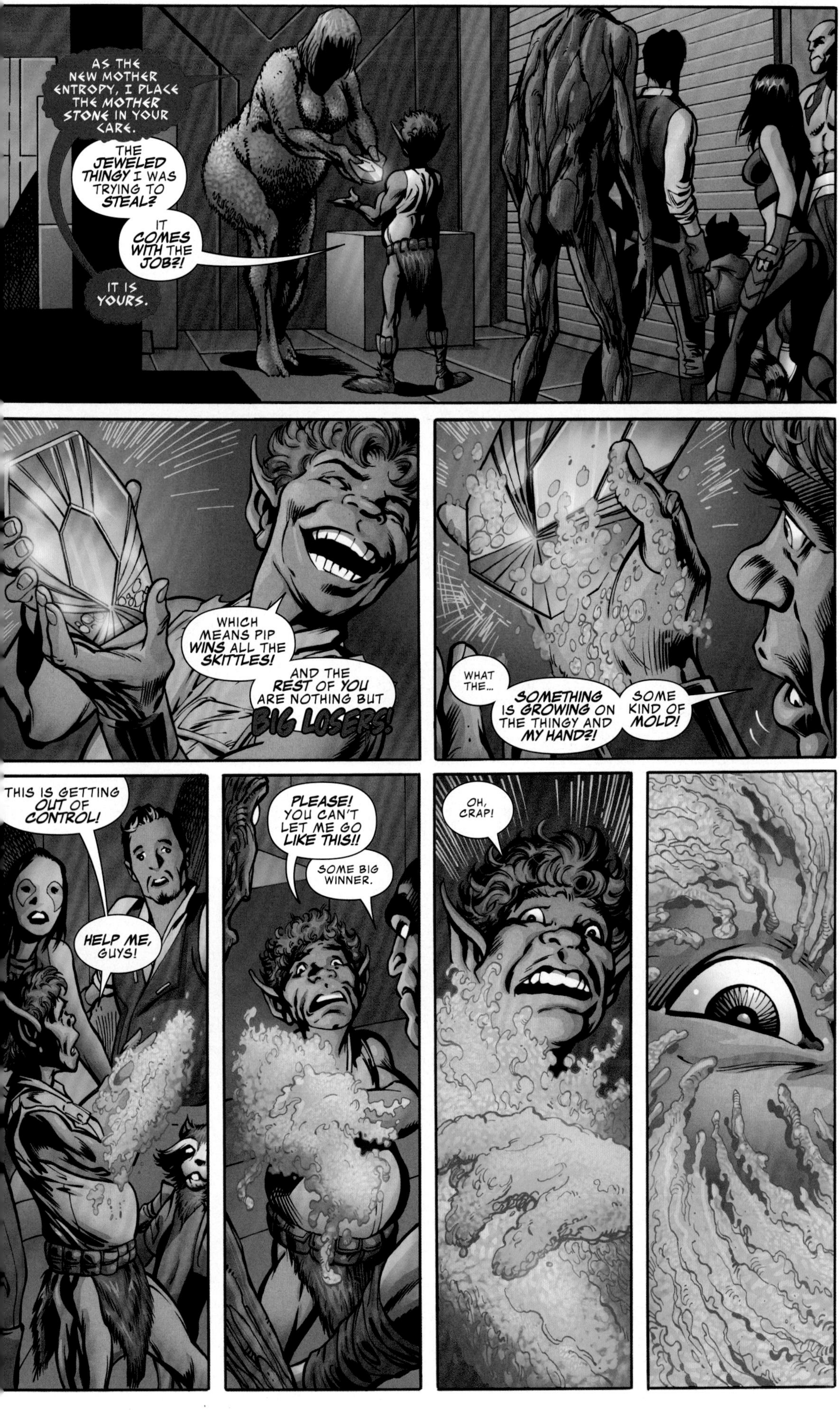

AS THE NEW MOTHER ENTROPY, I PLACE THE MOTHER STONE IN YOUR CARE.
THE JEWELED THINGY I WAS TRYING TO STEAL?
IT COMES WITH THE JOB?!
IT IS YOURS.
WHICH MEANS PIP WINS ALL THE SKITTLES!
AND THE REST OF YOU ARE NOTHING BUT BIG LOSERS!
WHAT THE...
SOMETHING IS GROWING ON THE THINGY AND MY HAND?!
SOME KIND OF MOLD!
THIS IS GETTING OUT OF CONTROL!
HELP ME, GUYS!
PLEASE! YOU CAN'T LET ME GO LIKE THIS!!
SOME BIG WINNER.
OH, CRAP!

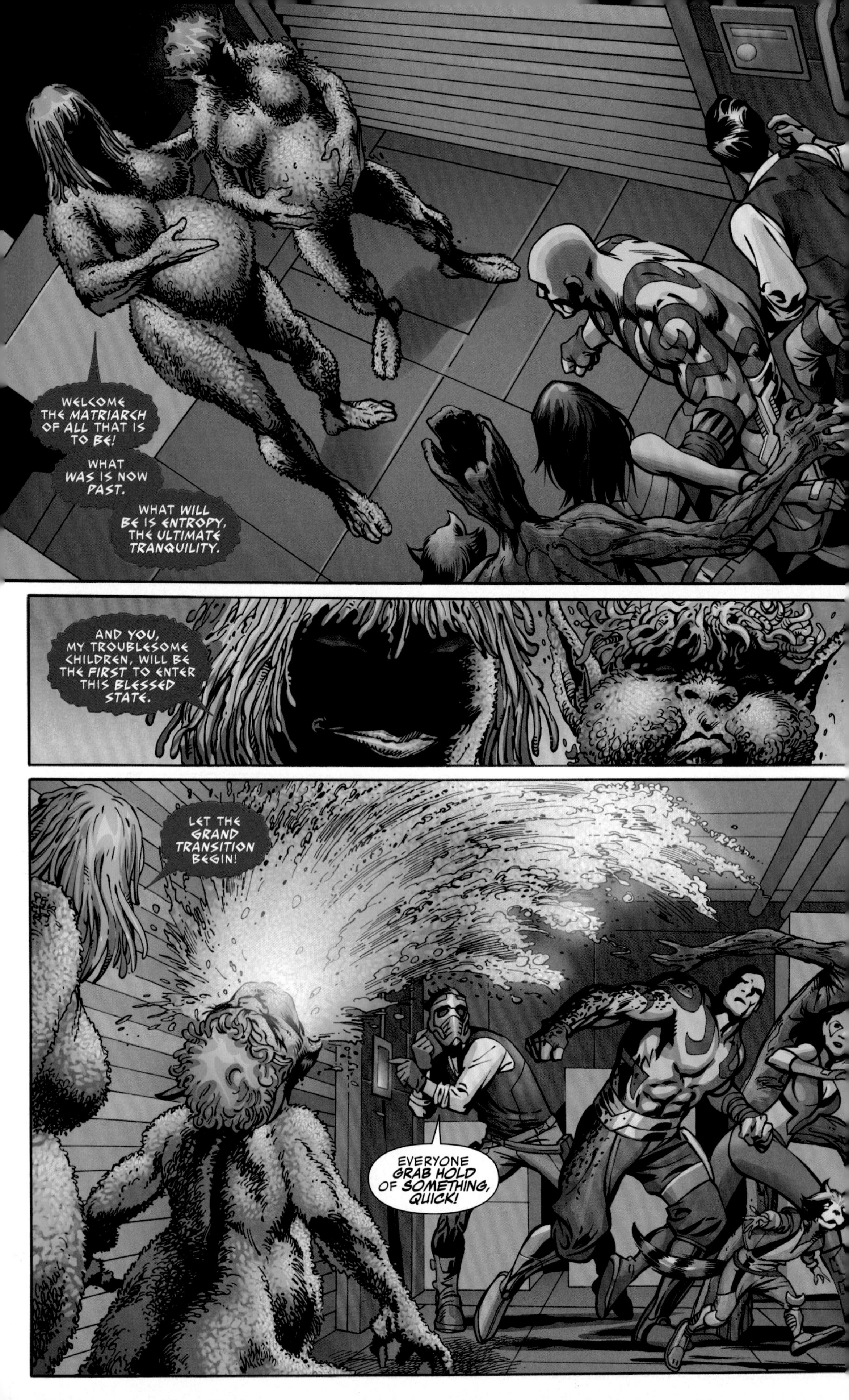
WELCOME THE MATRIARCH OF ALL THAT IS TO BE!
WHAT WAS IS NOW PAST.
WHAT WILL BE IS ENTROPY, THE ULTIMATE TRANQUILITY.
AND YOU, MY TROUBLESOME CHILDREN, WILL BE THE FIRST TO ENTER THIS BLESSED STATE.
LET THE GRAND TRANSITION BEGIN!
EVERYONE GRAB HOLD OF SOMETHING, QUICK!

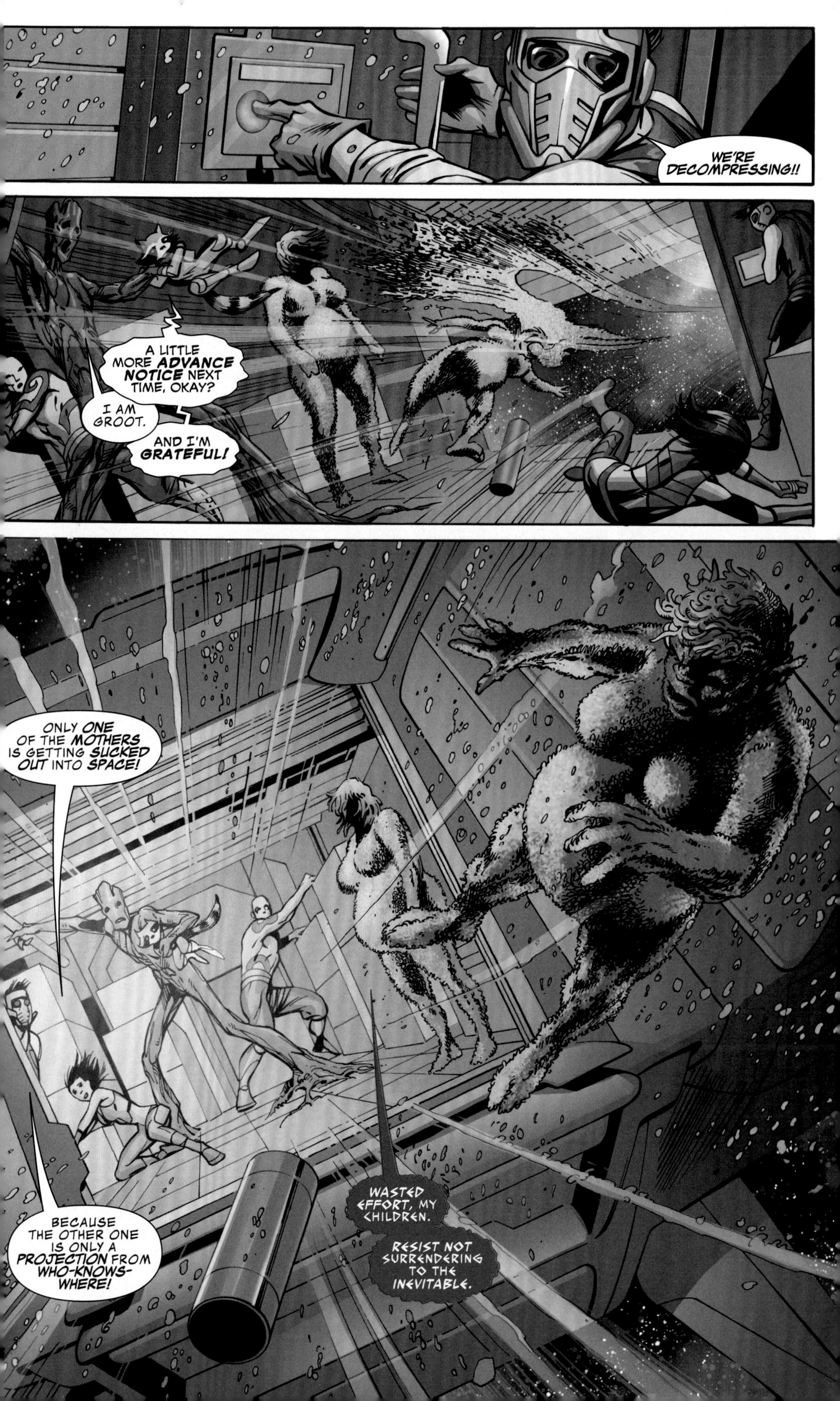
WE'RE DECOMPRESSING!!
A LITTLE MORE ADVANCE NOTICE NEXT TIME, OKAY?
I AM GROOT.
AND I'M GRATEFUL!
ONLY ONE OF THE MOTHERS IS GETTING SUCKED OUT INTO SPACE!
BECAUSE THE OTHER ONE IS ONLY A PROJECTION FROM WHO-KNOWS-WHERE!
WASTED EFFORT, MY CHILDREN.
RESIST NOT SURRENDERING TO THE INEVITABLE.

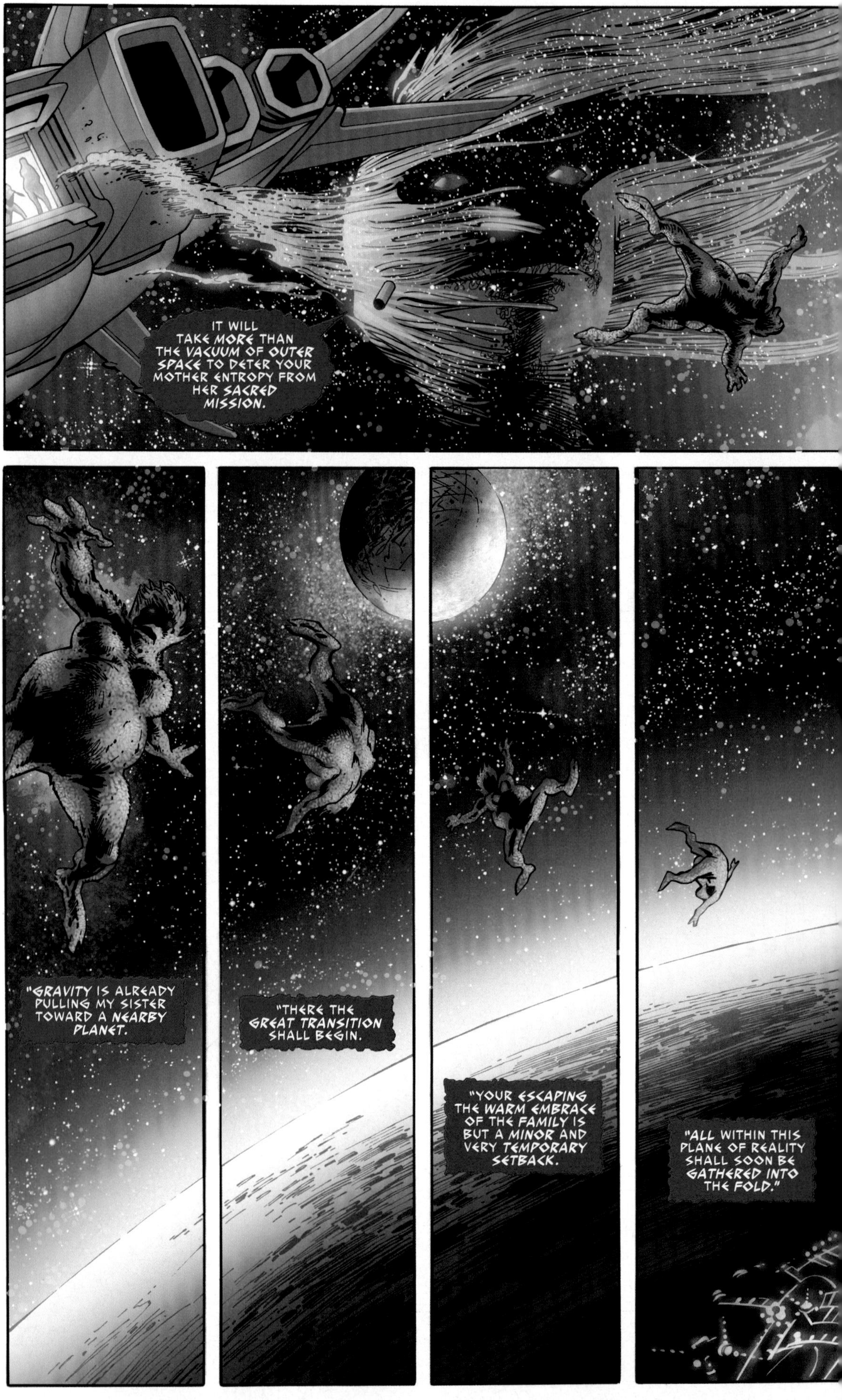
IT WILL TAKE MORE THAN THE VACUUM OF OUTER SPACE TO DETER YOUR MOTHER ENTROPY FROM HER SACRED MISSION.
"GRAVITY IS ALREADY PULLING MY SISTER TOWARD A NEARBY PLANET.
"THERE THE GREAT TRANSITION SHALL BEGIN.
"YOUR ESCAPING THE WARM EMBRACE OF THE FAMILY IS BUT A MINOR AND VERY TEMPORARY SETBACK.
"ALL WITHIN THIS PLANE OF REALITY SHALL SOON BE GATHERED INTO THE FOLD."

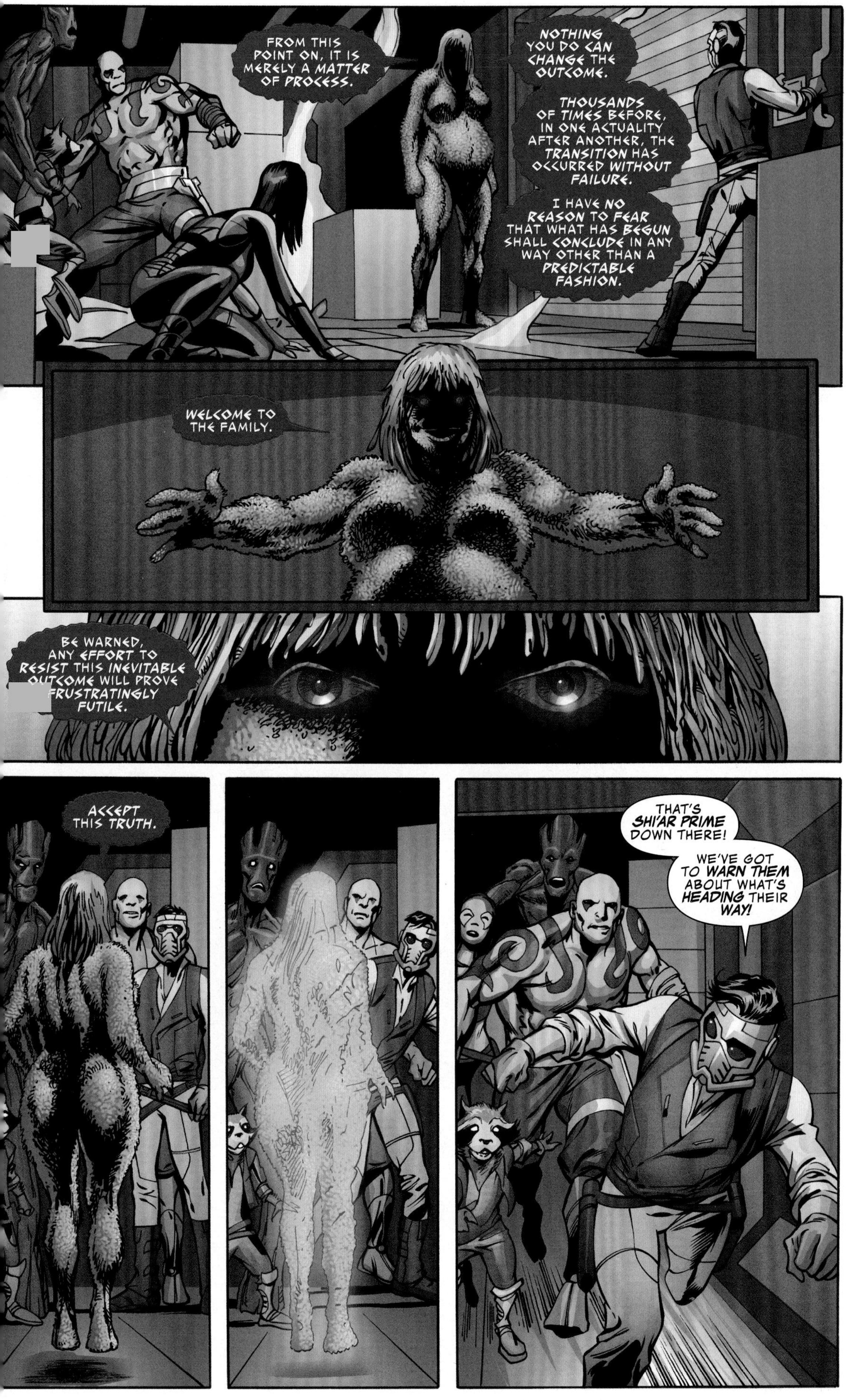

FROM THIS POINT ON, IT IS MERELY A MATTER OF PROCESS.
NOTHING YOU DO CAN CHANGE THE OUTCOME.
THOUSANDS OF TIMES BEFORE, IN ONE ACTUALITY AFTER ANOTHER, THE TRANSITION HAS OCCURRED WITHOUT FAILURE.
I HAVE NO REASON TO FEAR THAT WHAT HAS BEGUN SHALL CONCLUDE IN ANY WAY OTHER THAN A PREDICTABLE FASHION.
WELCOME TO THE FAMILY.
BE WARNED, ANY EFFORT TO RESIST THIS INEVITABLE OUTCOME WILL PROVE FRUSTRATINGLY FUTILE.
ACCEPT THIS TRUTH.
THAT'S SHI'AR PRIME DOWN THERE!
WE'VE GOT TO WARN THEM ABOUT WHAT'S HEADING THEIR WAY!

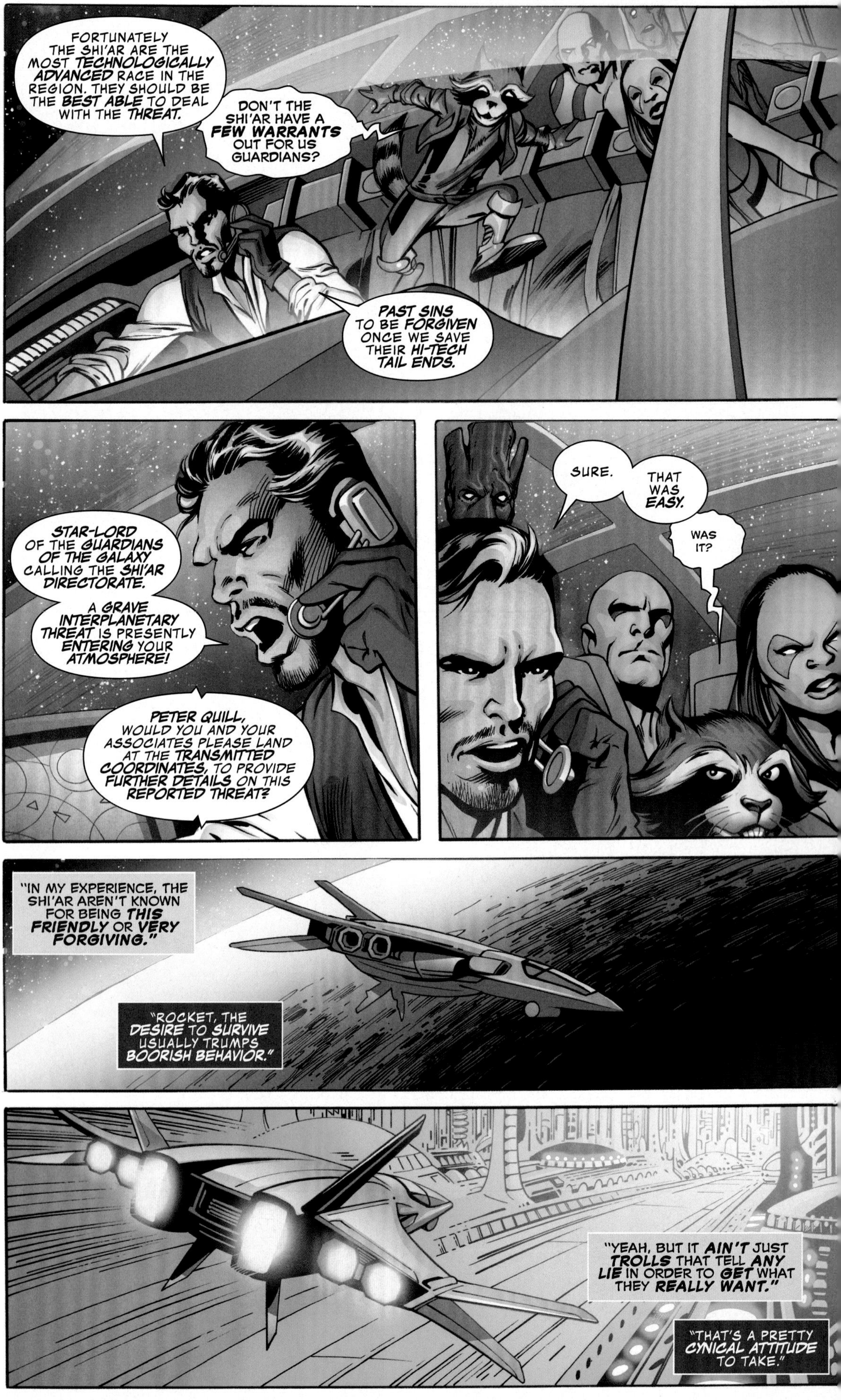
FORTUNATELY THE SHI'AR ARE THE MOST TECHNOLOGICALLY ADVANCED RACE IN THE REGION. THEY SHOULD BE THE BEST ABLE TO DEAL WITH THE THREAT.
DON'T THE SHI'AR HAVE A FEW WARRANTS OUT FOR US GUARDIANS?
PAST SINS TO BE FORGIVEN ONCE WE SAVE THEIR HI-TECH TAIL ENDS.
STAR-LORD OF THE GUARDIANS OF THE GALAXY CALLING THE SHI'AR DIRECTORATE.
A GRAVE INTERPLANETARY THREAT IS PRESENTLY ENTERING YOUR ATMOSPHERE!
PETER QUILL, WOULD YOU AND YOUR ASSOCIATES PLEASE LAND AT THE TRANSMITTED COORDINATES, TO PROVIDE FURTHER DETAILS ON THIS REPORTED THREAT?
SURE.
THAT WAS EASY.
WAS IT?
"IN MY EXPERIENCE, THE SHI'AR AREN'T KNOWN FOR BEING THIS FRIENDLY OR VERY FORGIVING."
"ROCKET, THE DESIRE TO SURVIVE USUALLY TRUMPS BOORISH BEHAVIOR."
"YEAH, BUT IT AIN'T JUST TROLLS THAT TELL ANY LIE IN ORDER TO GET WHAT THEY REALLY WANT."
"THAT'S A PRETTY CYNICAL ATTITUDE TO TAKE."

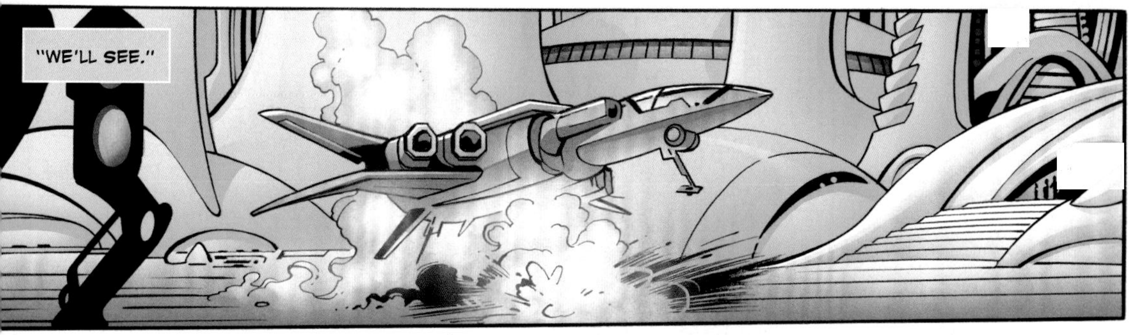
"WE'LL SEE."

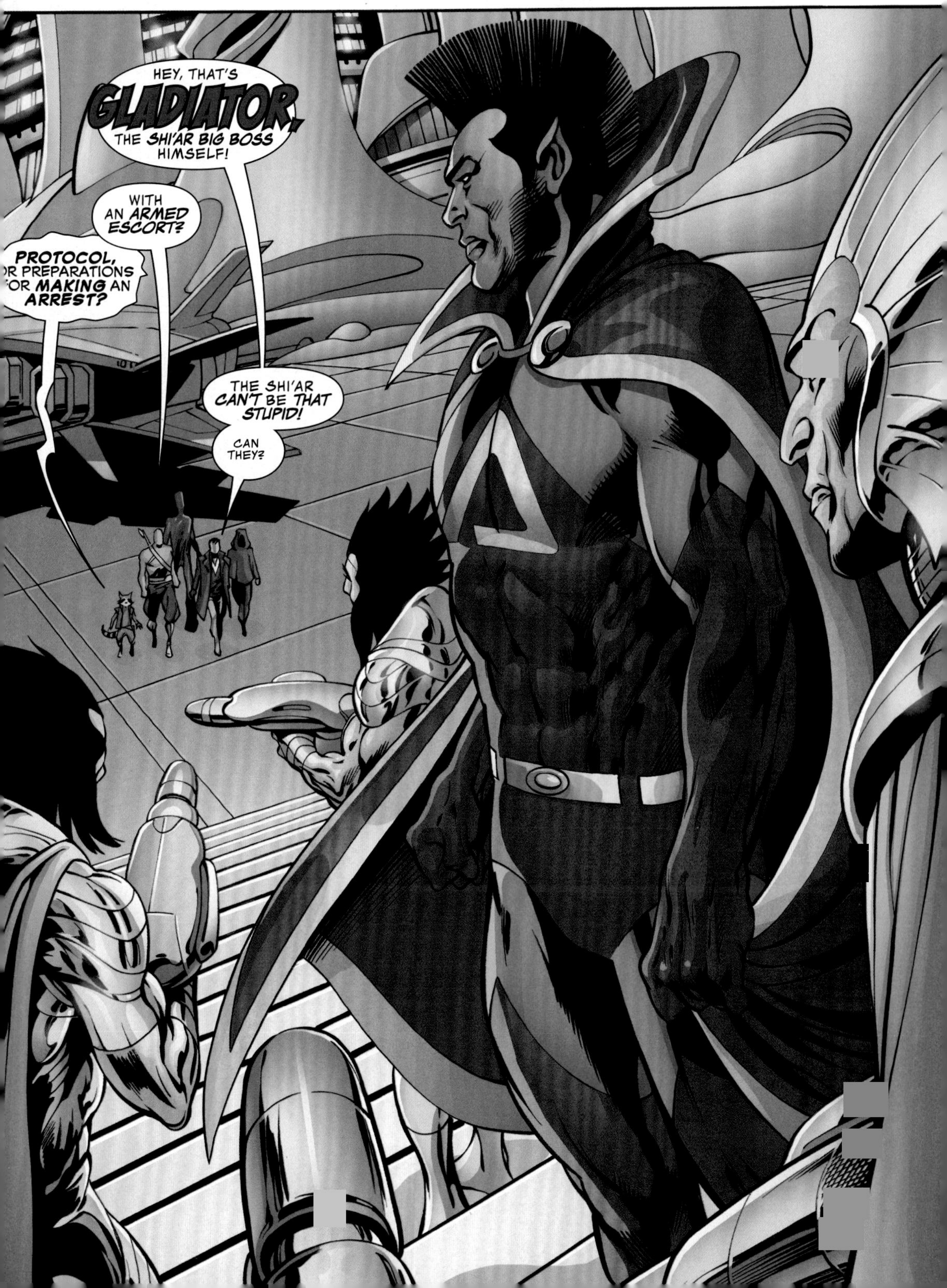
HEY, THAT'S GLADIATOR, THE SHI'AR BIG BOSS HIMSELF!
WITH AN ARMED ESCORT?
PROTOCOL, R PREPARATIONS OR MAKING AN ARREST?
THE SHI'AR CAN'T BE THAT STUPID!
CAN THEY?

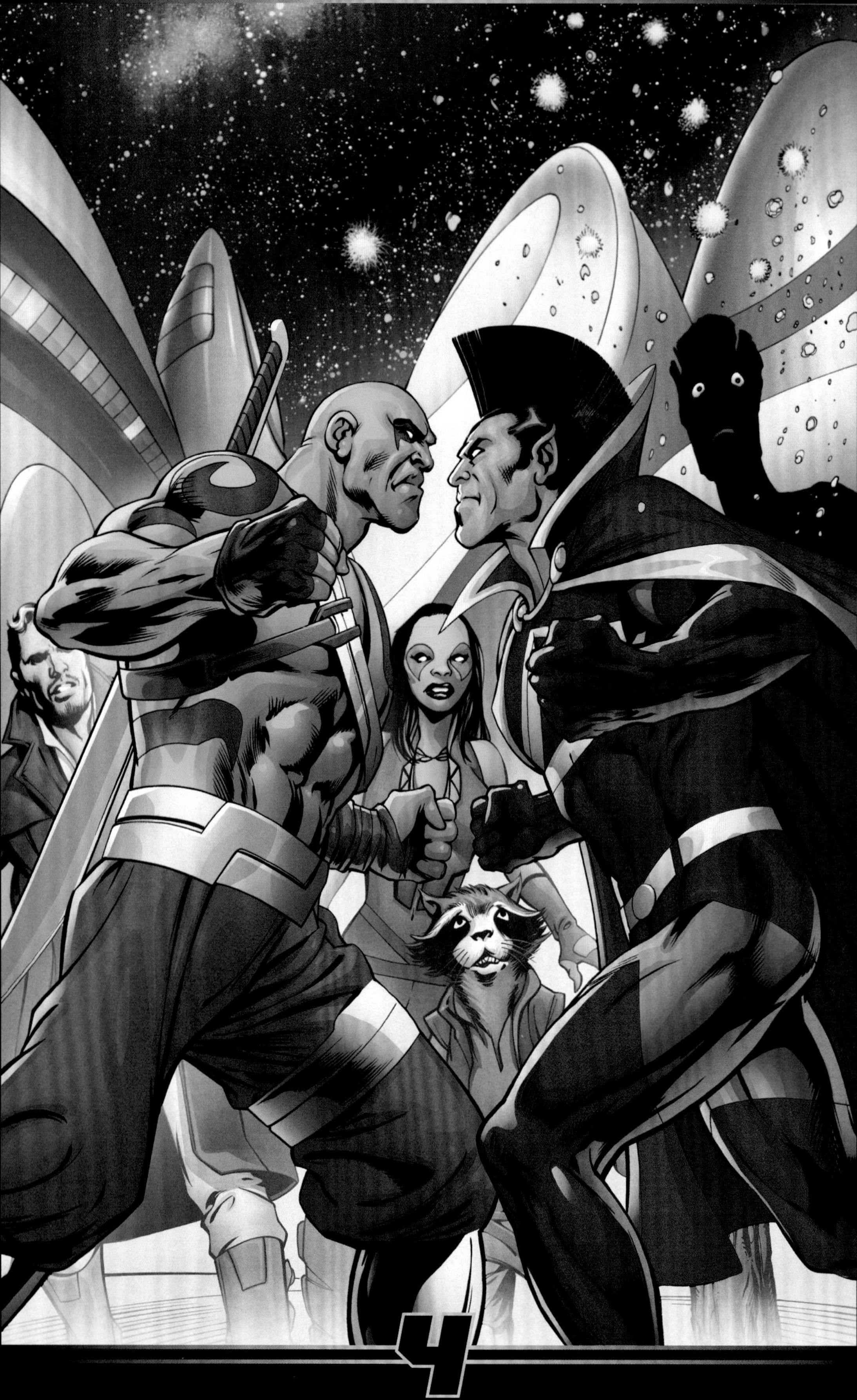
4

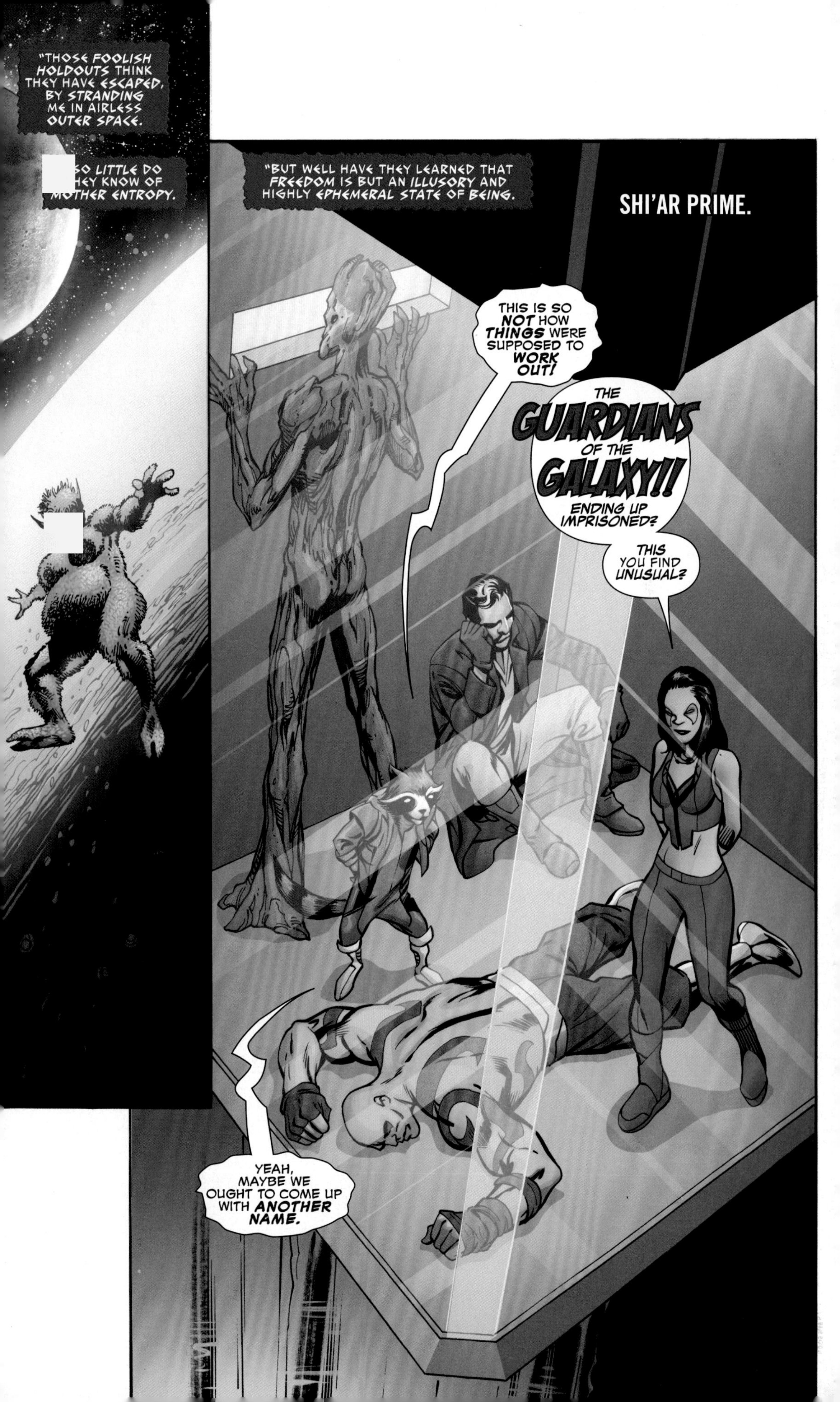
"THOSE FOOLISH HOLDOUTS THINK THEY HAVE ESCAPED, BY STRANDING ME IN AIRLESS OUTER SPACE.
SO LITTLE DO HEY KNOW OF MOTHER ENTROPY.
"BUT WELL HAVE THEY LEARNED THAT FREEDOM IS BUT AN ILLUSORY AND HIGHLY EPHEMERAL STATE OF BEING.
SHI'AR PRIME.
THIS IS SO NOT HOW THINGS WERE SUPPOSED TO WORK OUT!
THE GUARDIANS OF THE GALAXY!! ENDING UP IMPRISONED?
THIS YOU FIND UNUSUAL?
YEAH, MAYBE WE OUGHT TO COME UP WITH ANOTHER NAME.

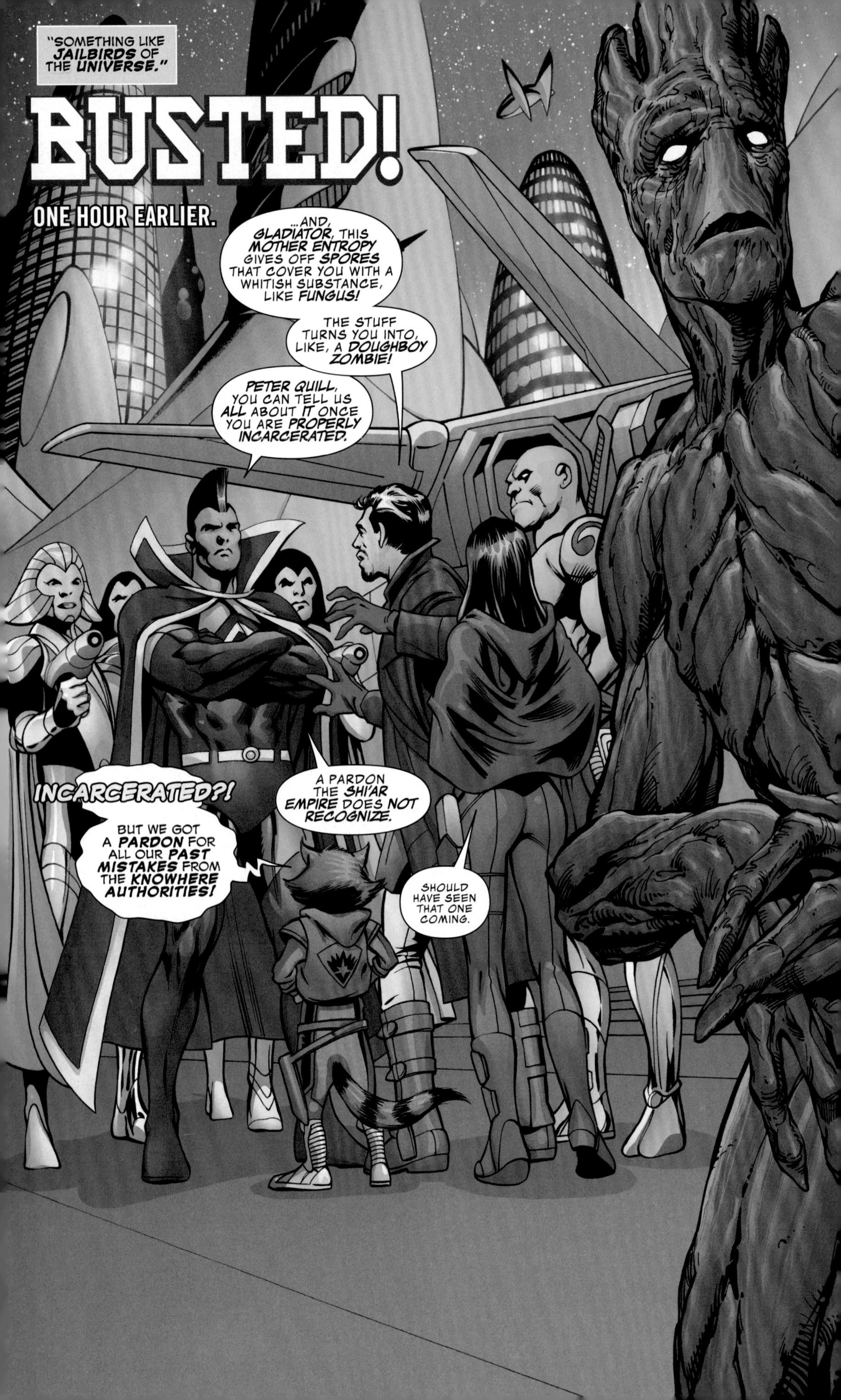

"SOMETHING LIKE JAILBIRDS OF THE UNIVERSE."
BUSTED!
ONE HOUR EARLIER.
...AND, GLADIATOR, THIS MOTHER ENTROPY GIVES OFF SPORES THAT COVER YOU WITH A WHITISH SUBSTANCE, LIKE FUNGUS!
THE STUFF TURNS YOU INTO, LIKE, A DOUGHBOY ZOMBIE!
PETER QUILL, YOU CAN TELL US ALL ABOUT IT ONCE YOU ARE PROPERLY INCARCERATED.
INCARCERATED?!
BUT WE GOT A PARDON FOR ALL OUR PAST MISTAKES FROM THE KNOWHERE AUTHORITIES!
A PARDON THE SHI'AR EMPIRE DOES NOT RECOGNIZE.
SHOULD HAVE SEEN THAT ONE COMING.

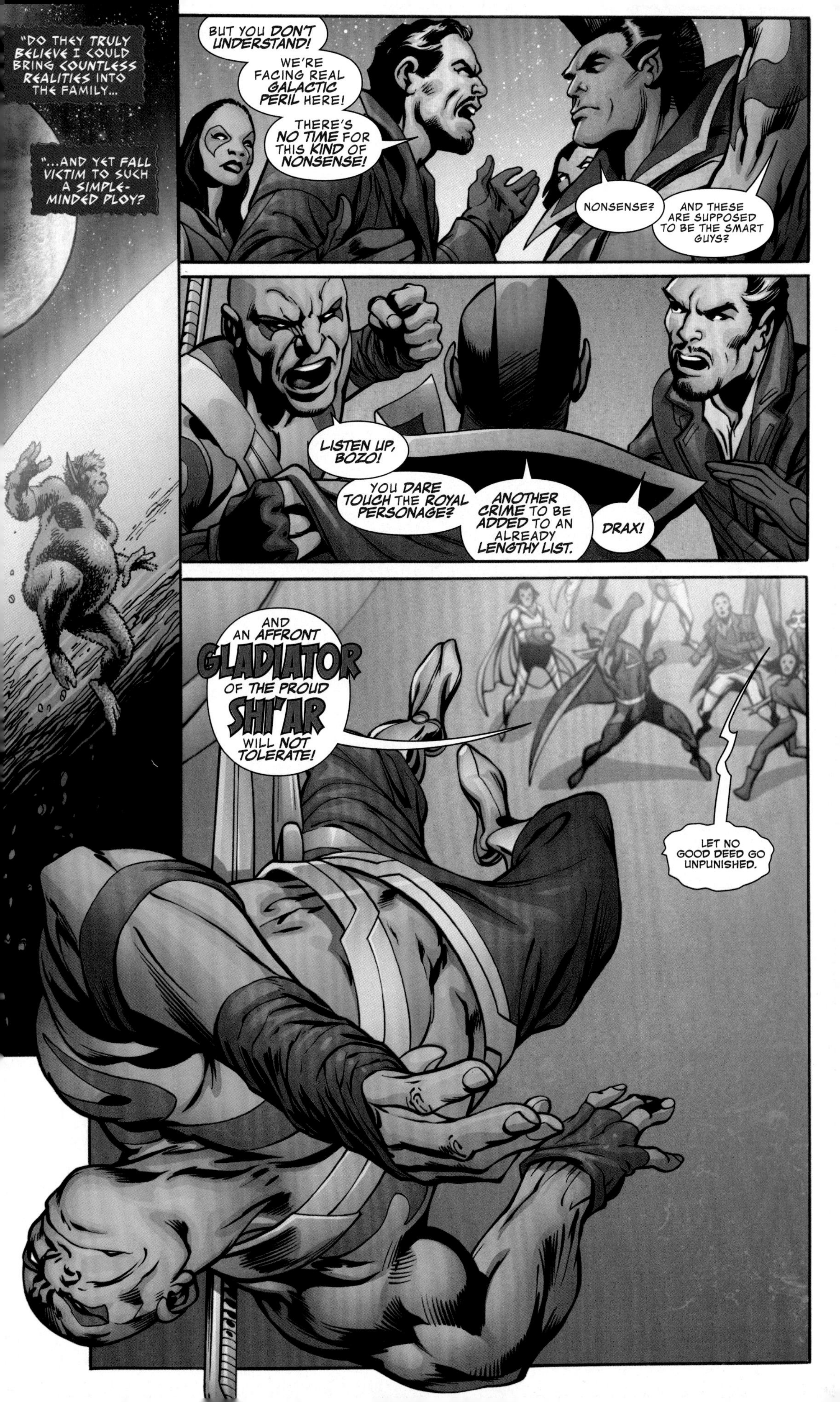
"DO THEY TRULY BELIEVE I COULD BRING COUNTLESS REALITIES INTO THE FAMILY...
"...AND YET FALL VICTIM TO SUCH A SIMPLE-MINDED PLOY?
BUT YOU DON'T UNDERSTAND!
WE'RE FACING REAL GALACTIC PERIL HERE!
THERE'S NO TIME FOR THIS KIND OF NONSENSE!
NONSENSE?
AND THESE ARE SUPPOSED TO BE THE SMART GUYS?
LISTEN UP, BOZO!
YOU DARE TOUCH THE ROYAL PERSONAGE?
ANOTHER CRIME TO BE ADDED TO AN ALREADY LENGTHY LIST.
DRAX!
AND AN AFFRONT GLADIATOR OF THE PROUD SHI'AR WILL NOT TOLERATE!
LET NO GOOD DEED GO UNPUNISHED.

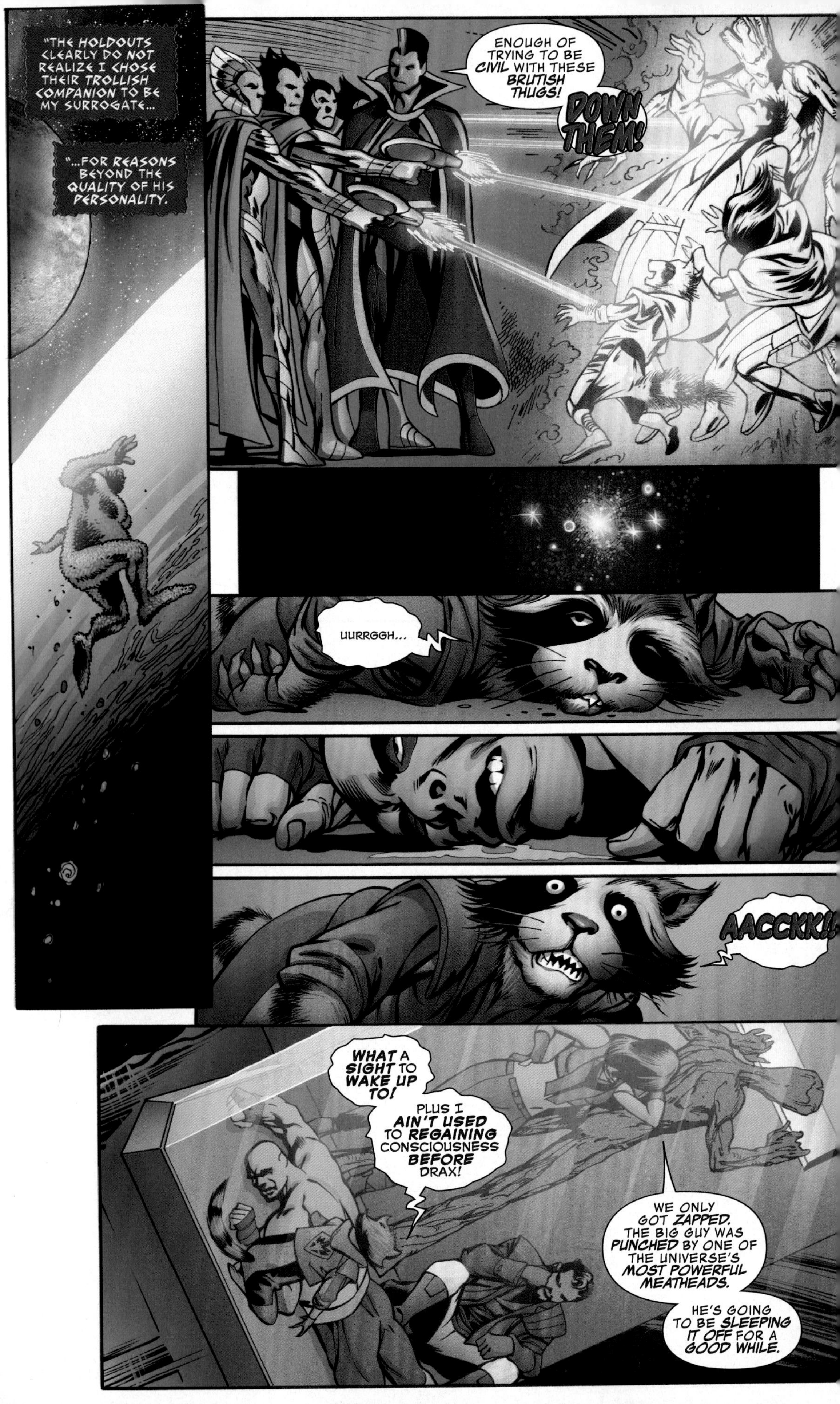
"THE HOLDOUTS CLEARLY DO NOT REALIZE I CHOSE THEIR TROLLISH COMPANION TO BE MY SURROGATE...
"...FOR REASONS BEYOND THE QUALITY OF HIS PERSONALITY.
ENOUGH OF TRYING TO BE CIVIL WITH THESE BRUTISH THUGS!
DOWN THEM!
UURRGGH...
AACCKK!!
WHAT A SIGHT TO WAKE UP TO!
PLUS I AIN'T USED TO REGAINING CONSCIOUSNESS BEFORE DRAX!
WE ONLY GOT ZAPPED. THE BIG GUY WAS PUNCHED BY ONE OF THE UNIVERSE'S MOST POWERFUL MEATHEADS.
HE'S GOING TO BE SLEEPING IT OFF FOR A GOOD WHILE.

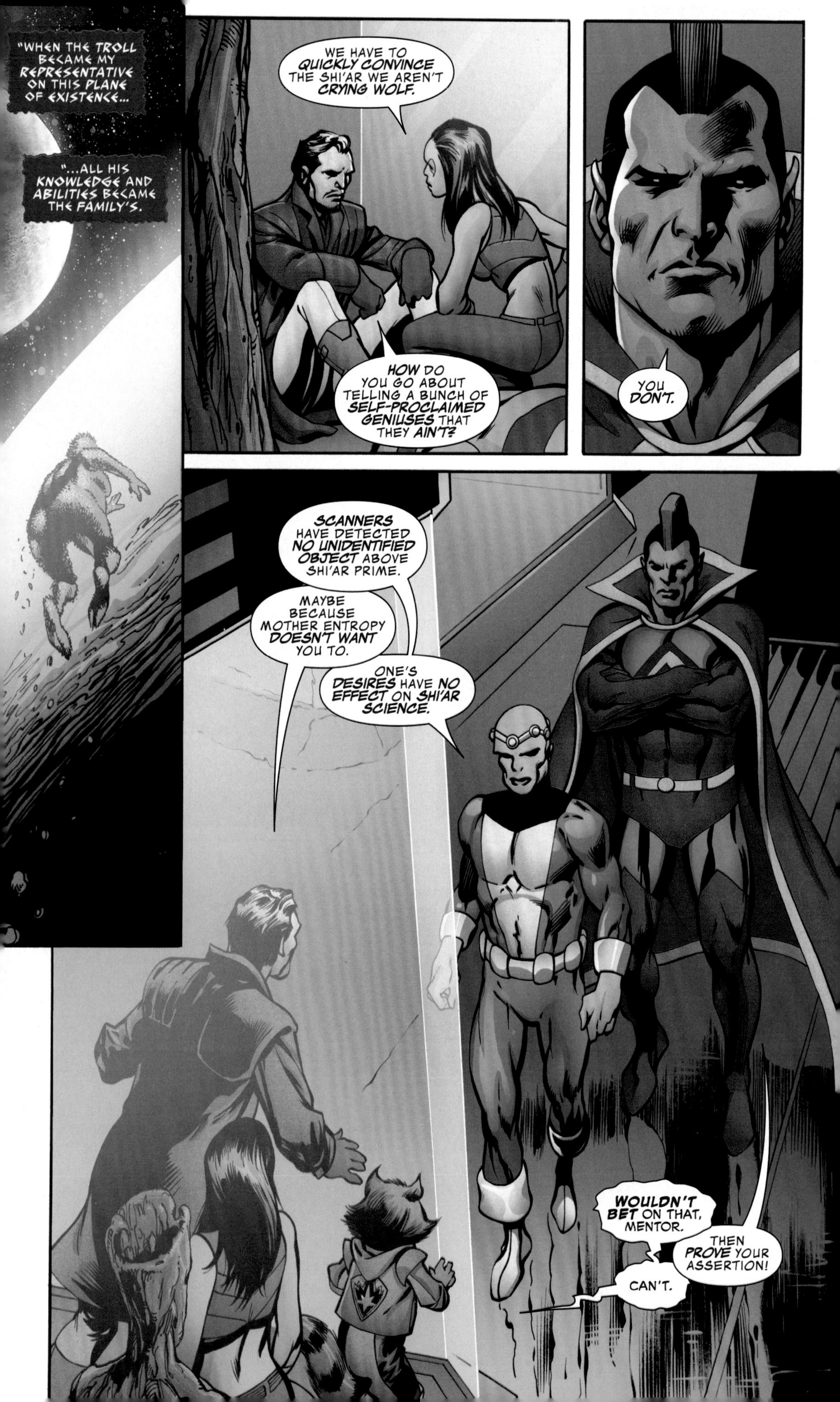
"WHEN THE TROLL BECAME MY REPRESENTATIVE ON THIS PLANE OF EXISTENCE...
"...ALL HIS KNOWLEDGE AND ABILITIES BECAME THE FAMILY'S.
WE HAVE TO QUICKLY CONVINCE THE SHI'AR WE AREN'T CRYING WOLF.
HOW DO YOU GO ABOUT TELLING A BUNCH OF SELF-PROCLAIMED GENIUSES THAT THEY AIN'T?
YOU DON'T.
SCANNERS HAVE DETECTED NO UNIDENTIFIED OBJECT ABOVE SHI'AR PRIME.
MAYBE BECAUSE MOTHER ENTROPY DOESN'T WANT YOU TO.
ONE'S DESIRES HAVE NO EFFECT ON SHI'AR SCIENCE.
WOULDN'T BET ON THAT, MENTOR.
THEN PROVE YOUR ASSERTION!
CAN'T.

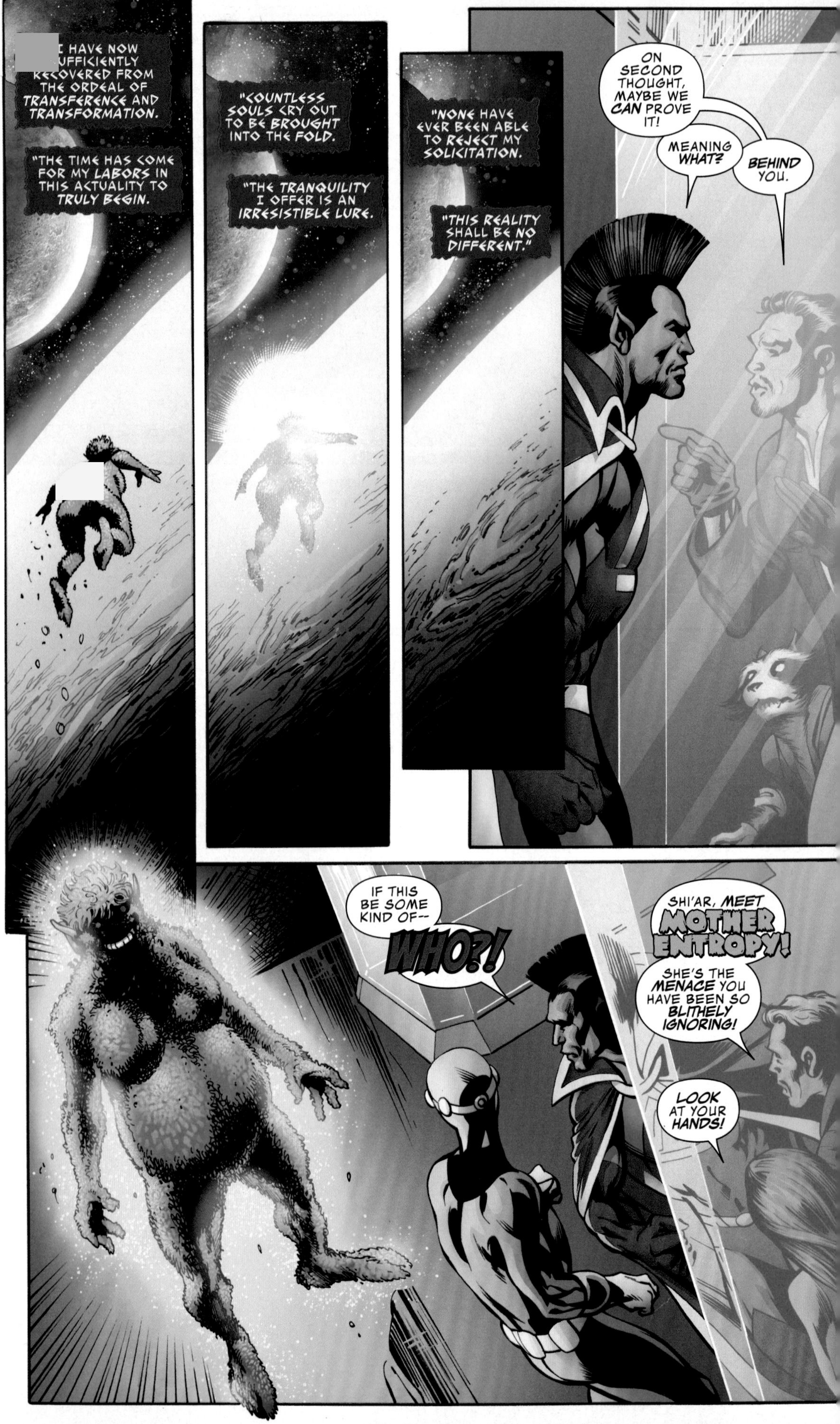
I HAVE NOW UFFICIENTLY RECOVERED FROM THE ORDEAL OF TRANSFERENCE AND TRANSFORMATION.
"THE TIME HAS COME FOR MY LABORS IN THIS ACTUALITY TO TRULY BEGIN.
"COUNTLESS SOULS CRY OUT TO BE BROUGHT INTO THE FOLD.
"THE TRANQUILITY I OFFER IS AN IRRESISTIBLE LURE.
"NONE HAVE EVER BEEN ABLE TO REJECT MY SOLICITATION.
"THIS REALITY SHALL BE NO DIFFERENT."
ON SECOND THOUGHT, MAYBE WE CAN PROVE IT!
MEANING WHAT?
BEHIND YOU.
IF THIS BE SOME KIND OF--
WHO?!
SHI'AR, MEET MOTHER ENTROPY!
SHE'S THE MENACE YOU HAVE BEEN SO BLITHELY IGNORING!
LOOK AT YOUR HANDS!

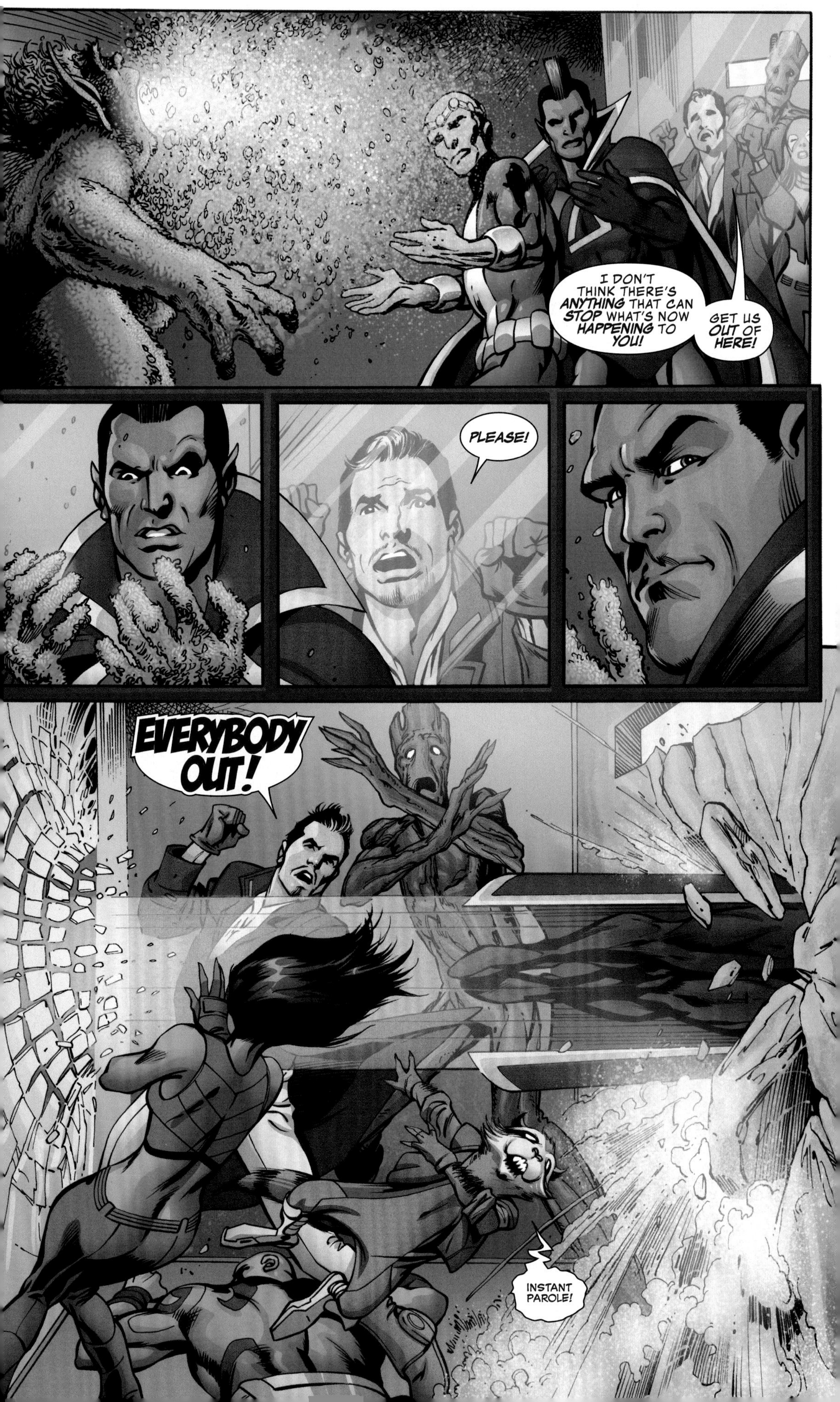
I DON'T THINK THERE'S ANYTHING THAT CAN STOP WHAT'S NOW HAPPENING TO YOU!
GET US OUT OF HERE!
PLEASE!
EVERYBODY OUT!
INSTANT PAROLE!

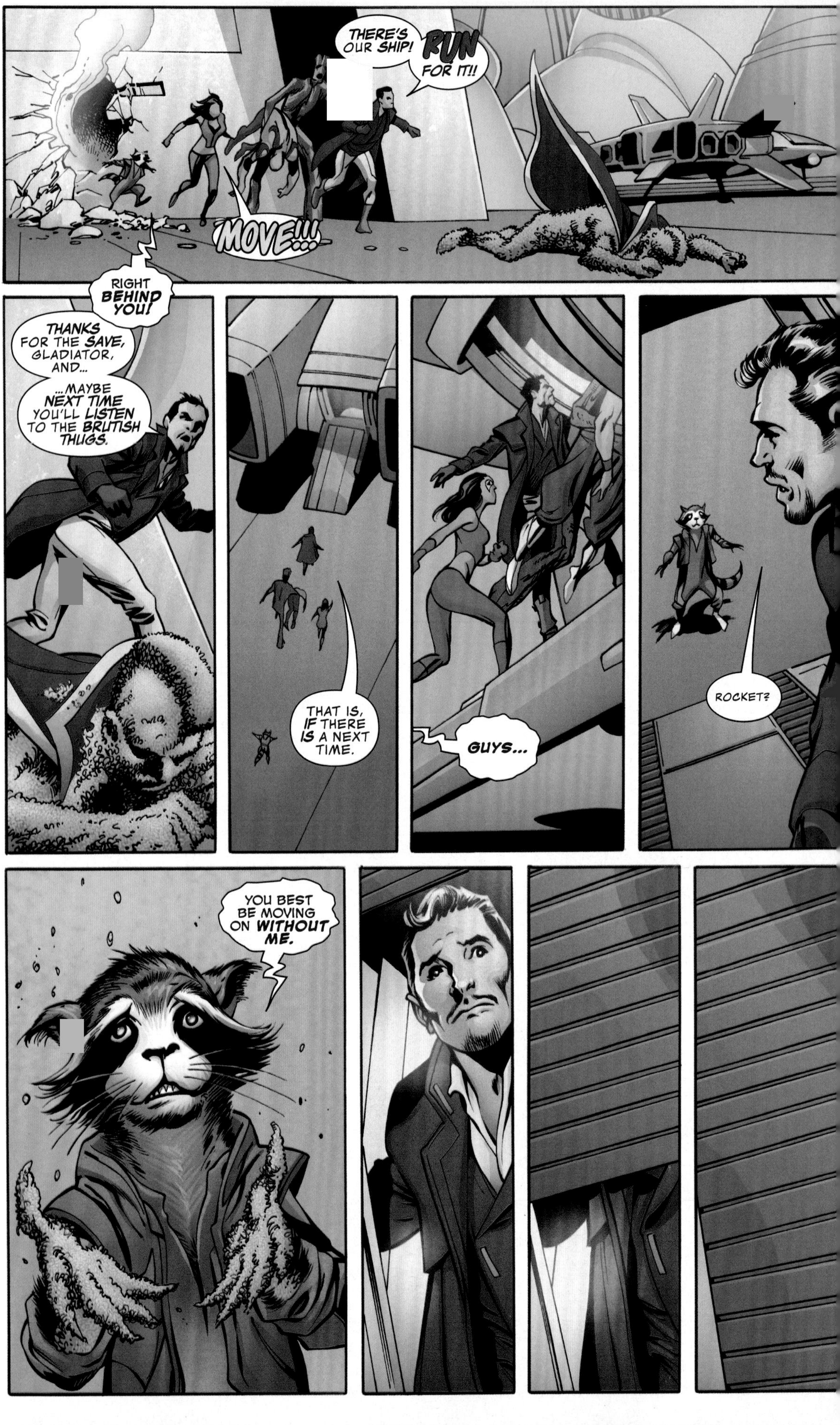
THERE'S OUR SHIP!
RUN FOR IT!!
MOVE!!!
RIGHT BEHIND YOU!
THANKS FOR THE SAVE, GLADIATOR, AND...
...MAYBE NEXT TIME YOU'LL LISTEN TO THE BRUTISH THUGS.
THAT IS, IF THERE IS A NEXT TIME.
GUYS...
ROCKET?
YOU BEST BE MOVING ON WITHOUT ME.

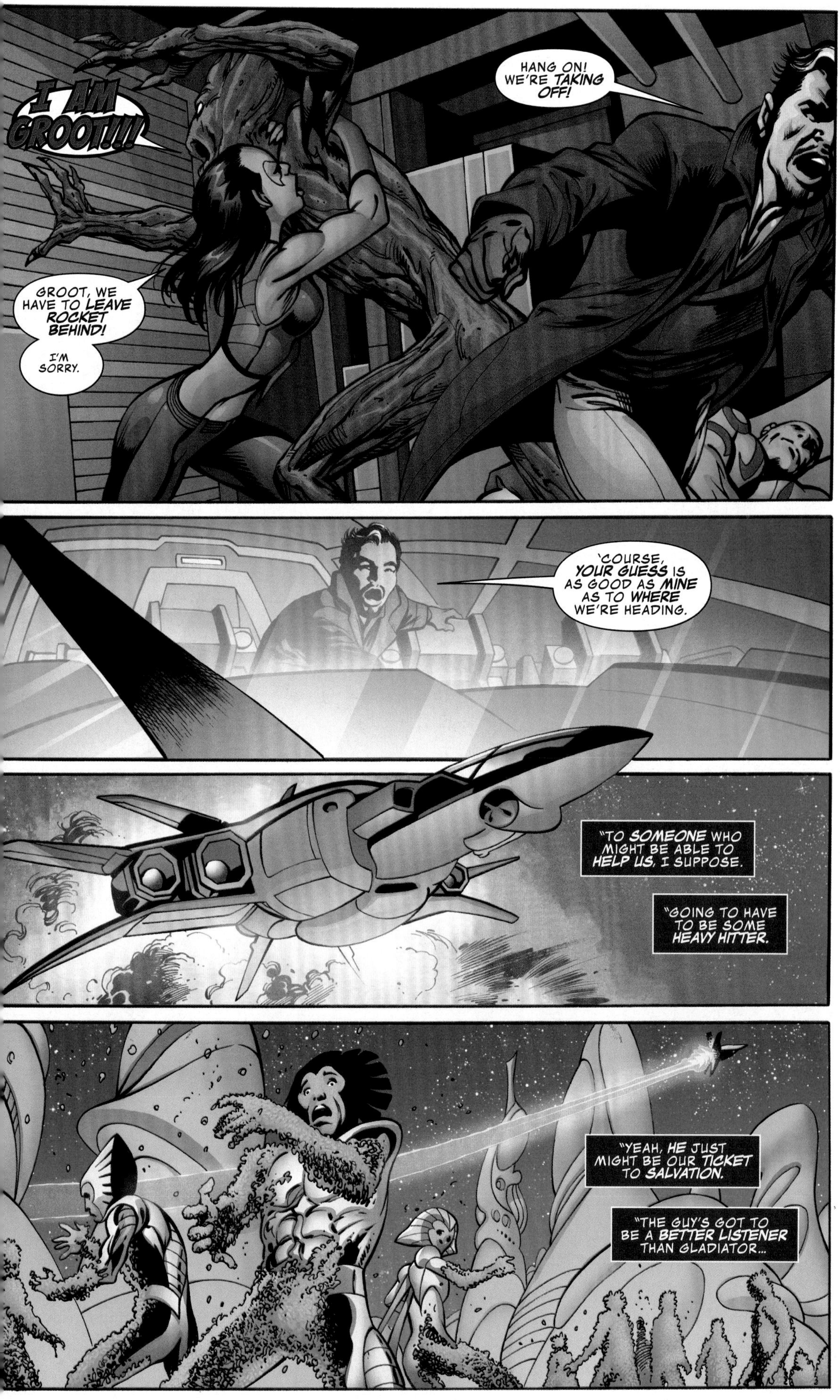
I AM GROOT!!!
HANG ON! WE'RE TAKING OFF!
GROOT, WE HAVE TO LEAVE ROCKET BEHIND!
I'M SORRY.
'COURSE, YOUR GUESS IS AS GOOD AS MINE AS TO WHERE WE'RE HEADING.
"TO SOMEONE WHO MIGHT BE ABLE TO HELP US, I SUPPOSE.
"GOING TO HAVE TO BE SOME HEAVY HITTER.
"YEAH, HE JUST MIGHT BE OUR TICKET TO SALVATION.
"THE GUY'S GOT TO BE A BETTER LISTENER THAN GLADIATOR...

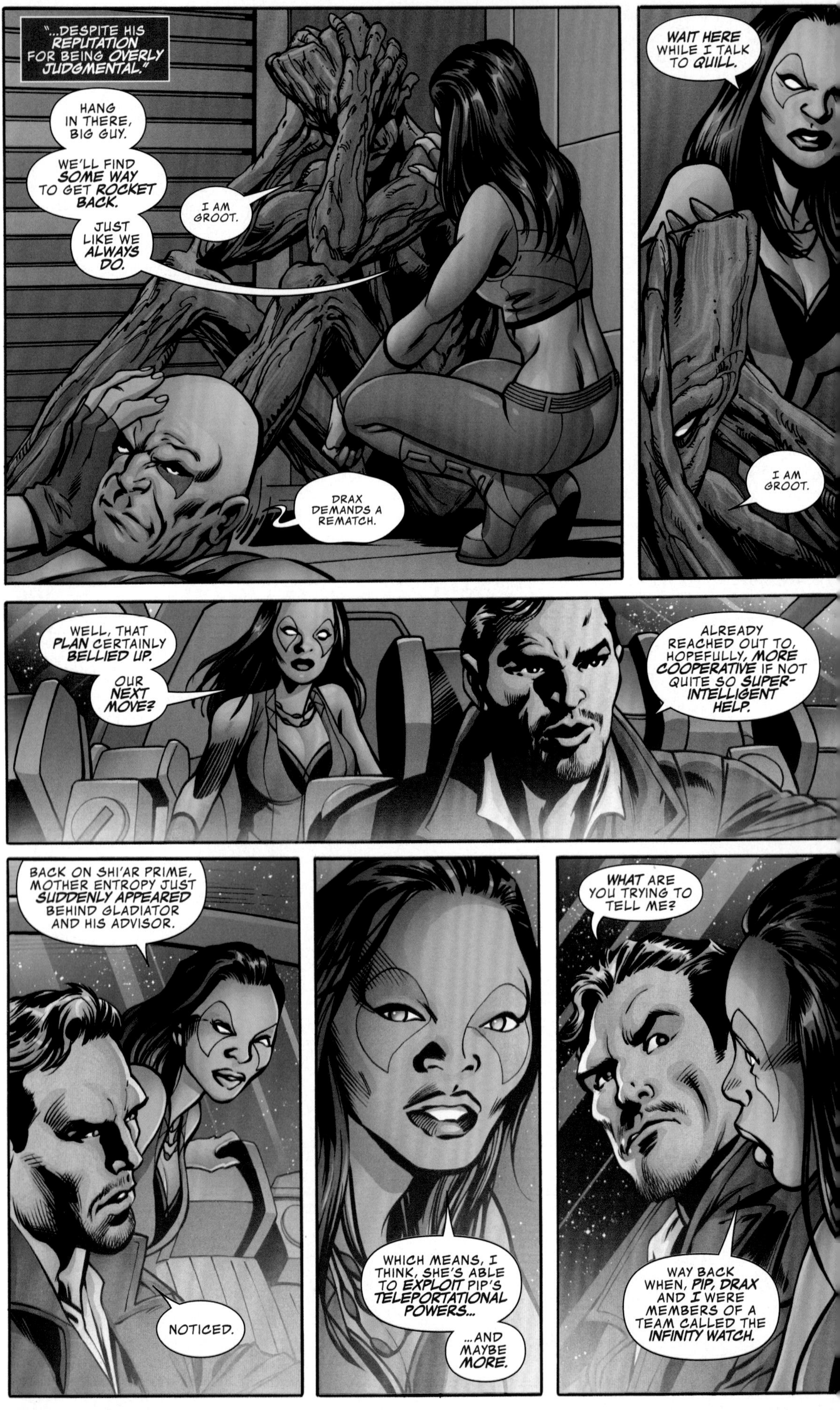
"...DESPITE HIS REPUTATION FOR BEING OVERLY JUDGMENTAL."
HANG IN THERE, BIG GUY.
WE'LL FIND SOME WAY TO GET ROCKET BACK.
JUST LIKE WE ALWAYS DO.
I AM GROOT.
DRAX DEMANDS A REMATCH.
WAIT HERE WHILE I TALK TO QUILL.
I AM GROOT.
WELL, THAT PLAN CERTAINLY BELLIED UP.
OUR NEXT MOVE?
ALREADY REACHED OUT TO, HOPEFULLY, MORE COOPERATIVE IF NOT QUITE SO SUPER-INTELLIGENT HELP.
BACK ON SHI'AR PRIME, MOTHER ENTROPY JUST SUDDENLY APPEARED BEHIND GLADIATOR AND HIS ADVISOR.
NOTICED.
WHICH MEANS, I THINK, SHE'S ABLE TO EXPLOIT PIP'S TELEPORTATIONAL POWERS...
...AND MAYBE MORE.
WHAT ARE YOU TRYING TO TELL ME?
WAY BACK WHEN, PIP, DRAX AND I WERE MEMBERS OF A TEAM CALLED THE INFINITY WATCH.

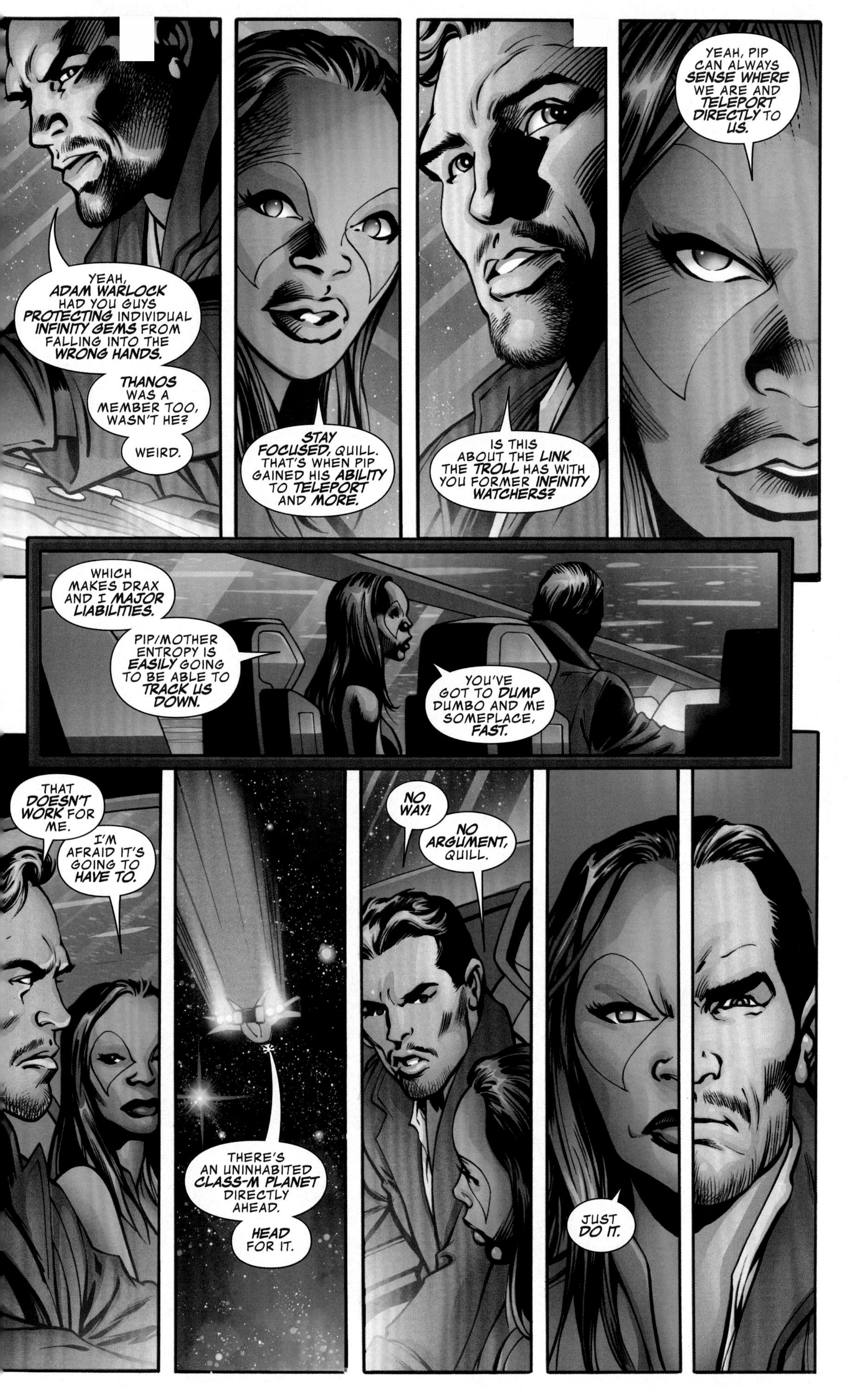

YEAH, ADAM WARLOCK HAD YOU GUYS PROTECTING INDIVIDUAL INFINITY GEMS FROM FALLING INTO THE WRONG HANDS.
THANOS WAS A MEMBER TOO, WASN'T HE?
WEIRD.
STAY FOCUSED, QUILL. THAT'S WHEN PIP GAINED HIS ABILITY TO TELEPORT AND MORE.
IS THIS ABOUT THE LINK THE TROLL HAS WITH YOU FORMER INFINITY WATCHERS?
YEAH, PIP CAN ALWAYS SENSE WHERE WE ARE AND TELEPORT DIRECTLY TO US.
WHICH MAKES DRAX AND I MAJOR LIABILITIES.
PIP/MOTHER ENTROPY IS EASILY GOING TO BE ABLE TO TRACK US DOWN.
YOU'VE GOT TO DUMP DUMBO AND ME SOMEPLACE, FAST.
THAT DOESN'T WORK FOR ME.
I'M AFRAID IT'S GOING TO HAVE TO.
THERE'S AN UNINHABITED CLASS-M PLANET DIRECTLY AHEAD.
HEAD FOR IT.
NO WAY!
NO ARGUMENT, QUILL.
JUST DO IT.

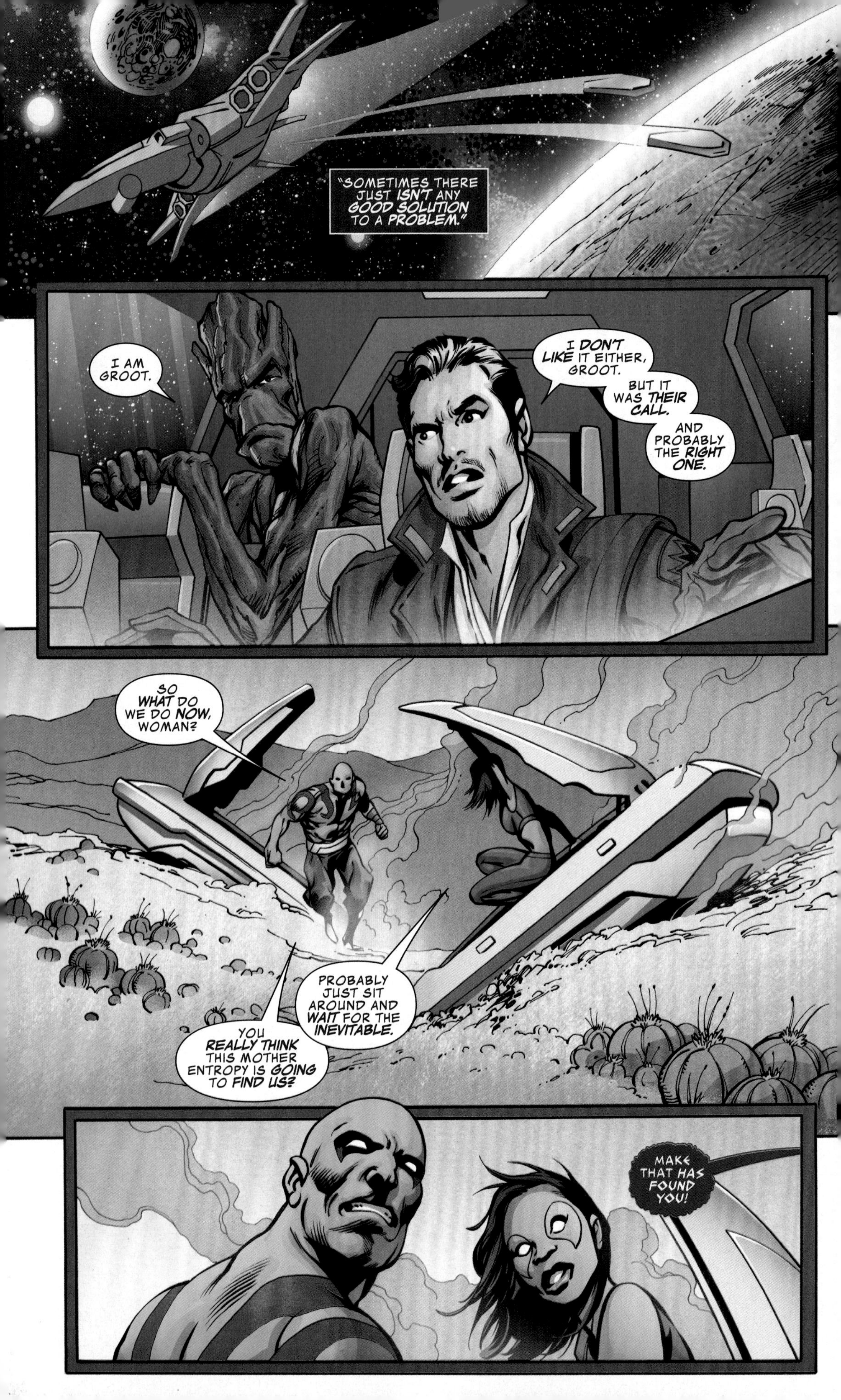
"SOMETIMES THERE JUST ISN'T ANY GOOD SOLUTION TO A PROBLEM."
I AM GROOT.
I DON'T LIKE IT EITHER, GROOT.
BUT IT WAS THEIR CALL.
AND PROBABLY THE RIGHT ONE.
SO WHAT DO WE DO NOW, WOMAN?
PROBABLY JUST SIT AROUND AND WAIT FOR THE INEVITABLE.
YOU REALLY THINK THIS MOTHER ENTROPY IS GOING TO FIND US?
MAKE THAT HAS FOUND YOU!

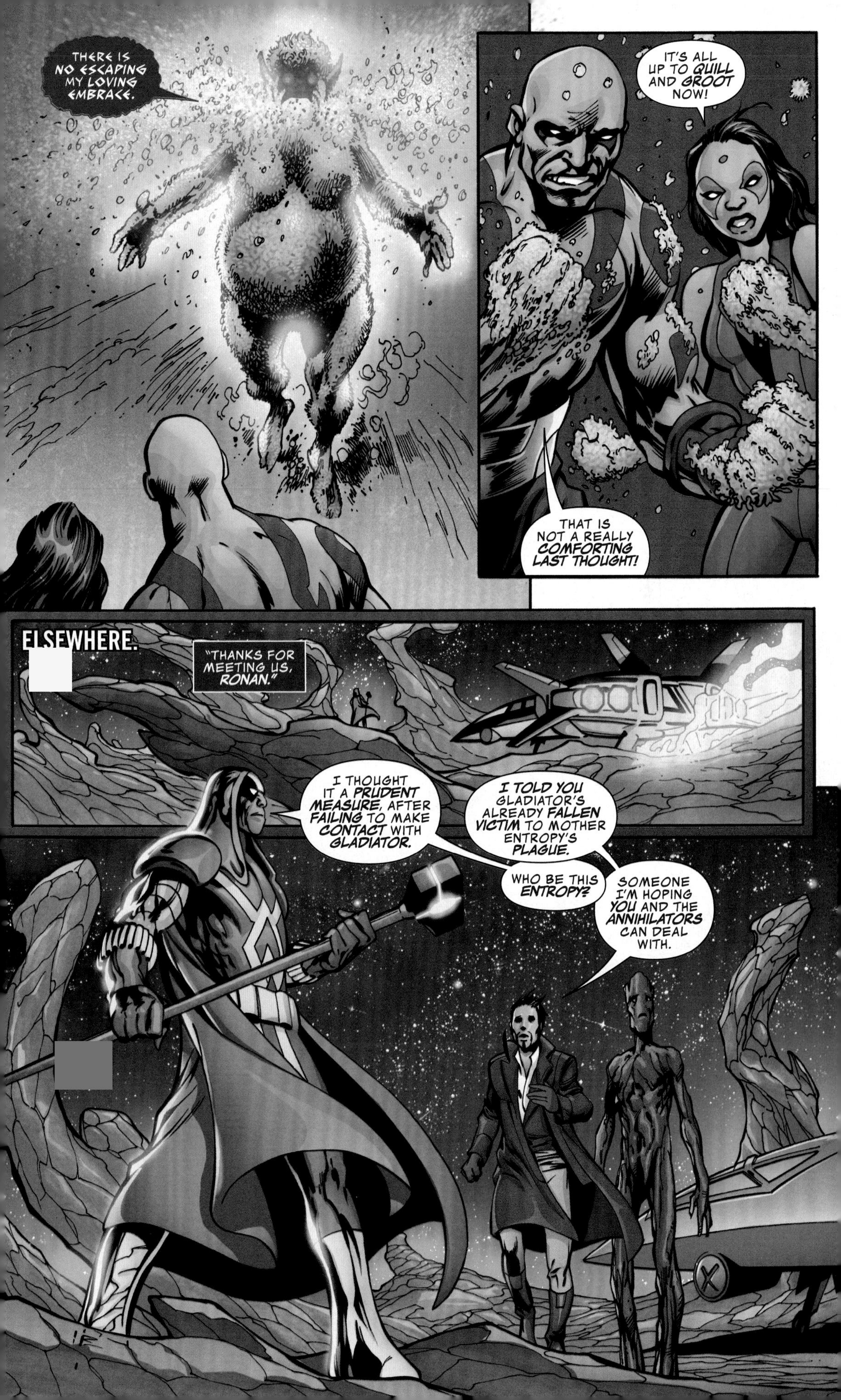
THERE IS NO ESCAPING MY LOVING EMBRACE.
IT'S ALL UP TO QUILL AND GROOT NOW!
THAT IS NOT A REALLY COMFORTING LAST THOUGHT!
ELSEWHERE.
"THANKS FOR MEETING US, RONAN."
I THOUGHT IT A PRUDENT MEASURE, AFTER FAILING TO MAKE CONTACT WITH GLADIATOR.
I TOLD YOU GLADIATOR'S ALREADY FALLEN VICTIM TO MOTHER ENTROPY'S PLAGUE.
WHO BE THIS ENTROPY?
SOMEONE I'M HOPING YOU AND THE ANNIHILATORS CAN DEAL WITH.

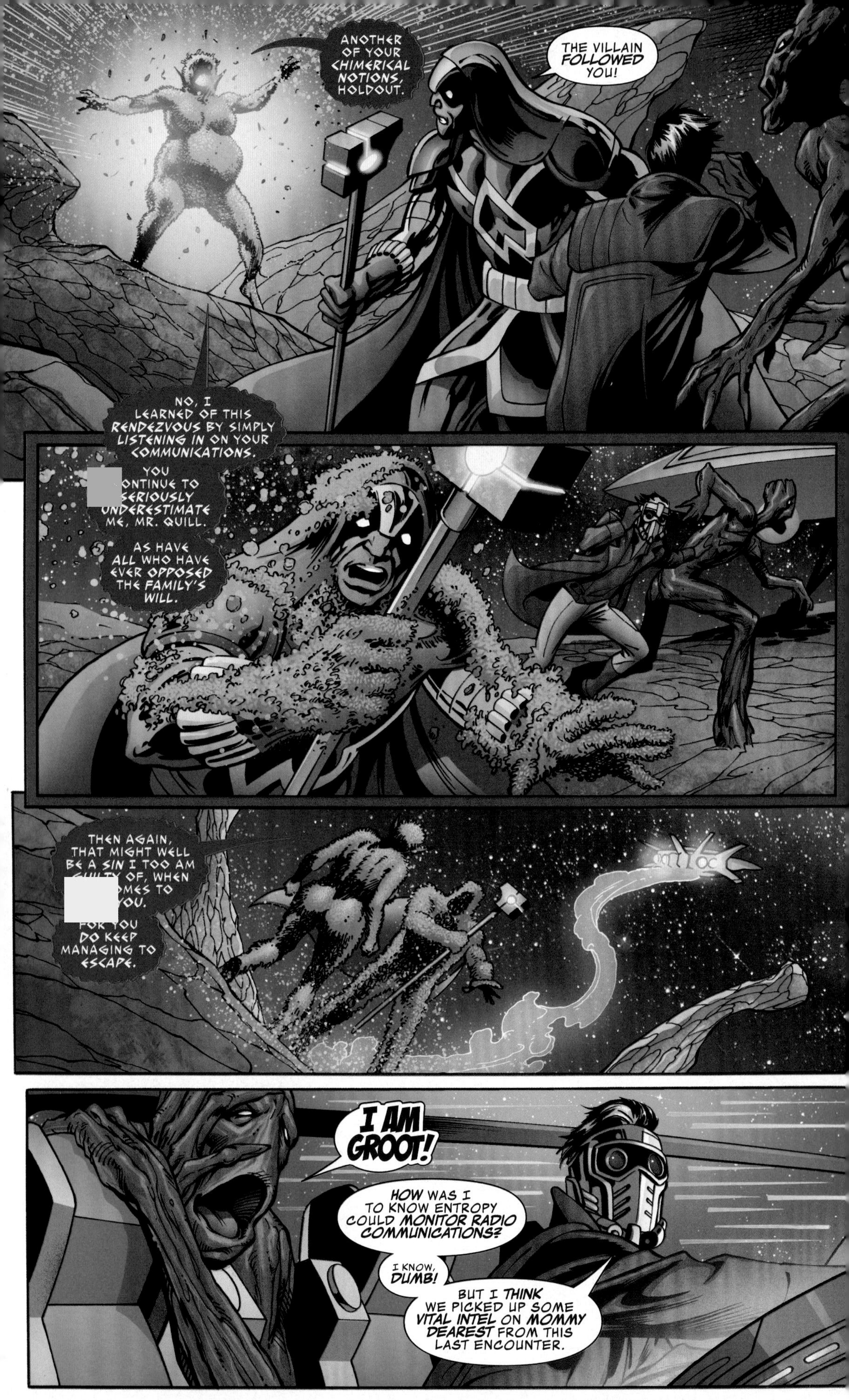

ANOTHER OF YOUR CHIMERICAL NOTIONS, HOLDOUT.
THE VILLAIN FOLLOWED YOU!
NO, I LEARNED OF THIS RENDEZVOUS BY SIMPLY LISTENING IN ON YOUR COMMUNICATIONS.
YOU ONTINUE TO ERIOUSLY UNDERESTIMATE ME, MR. QUILL.
AS HAVE ALL WHO HAVE EVER OPPOSED THE FAMILY'S WILL.
THEN AGAIN, THAT MIGHT WELL BE A SIN I TOO AM ...
FOR YOU DO KEEP MANAGING TO ESCAPE.
I AM GROOT!
HOW WAS I TO KNOW ENTROPY COULD MONITOR RADIO COMMUNICATIONS?
I KNOW, DUMB!
BUT I THINK WE PICKED UP SOME VITAL INTEL ON MOMMY DEAREST FROM THIS LAST ENCOUNTER.

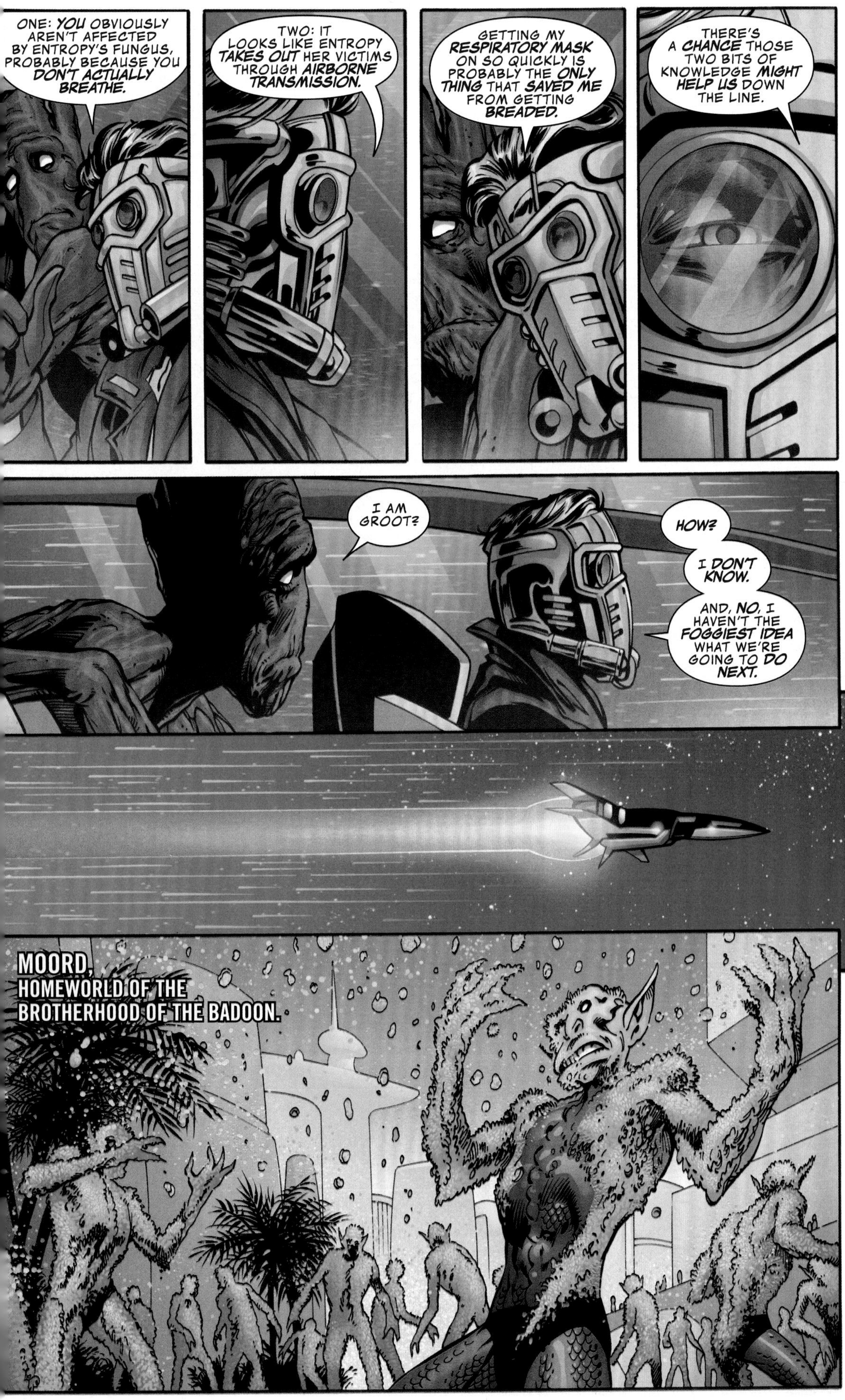

ONE: YOU OBVIOUSLY AREN'T AFFECTED BY ENTROPY'S FUNGUS, PROBABLY BECAUSE YOU DON'T ACTUALLY BREATHE.
TWO: IT LOOKS LIKE ENTROPY TAKES OUT HER VICTIMS THROUGH AIRBORNE TRANSMISSION.
GETTING MY RESPIRATORY MASK ON SO QUICKLY IS PROBABLY THE ONLY THING THAT SAVED ME FROM GETTING BREADED.
THERE'S A CHANCE THOSE TWO BITS OF KNOWLEDGE MIGHT HELP US DOWN THE LINE.
I AM GROOT?
HOW?
I DON'T KNOW.
AND, NO, I HAVEN'T THE FOGGIEST IDEA WHAT WE'RE GOING TO DO NEXT.
MOORD, HOMEWORLD OF THE BROTHERHOOD OF THE BADOON.

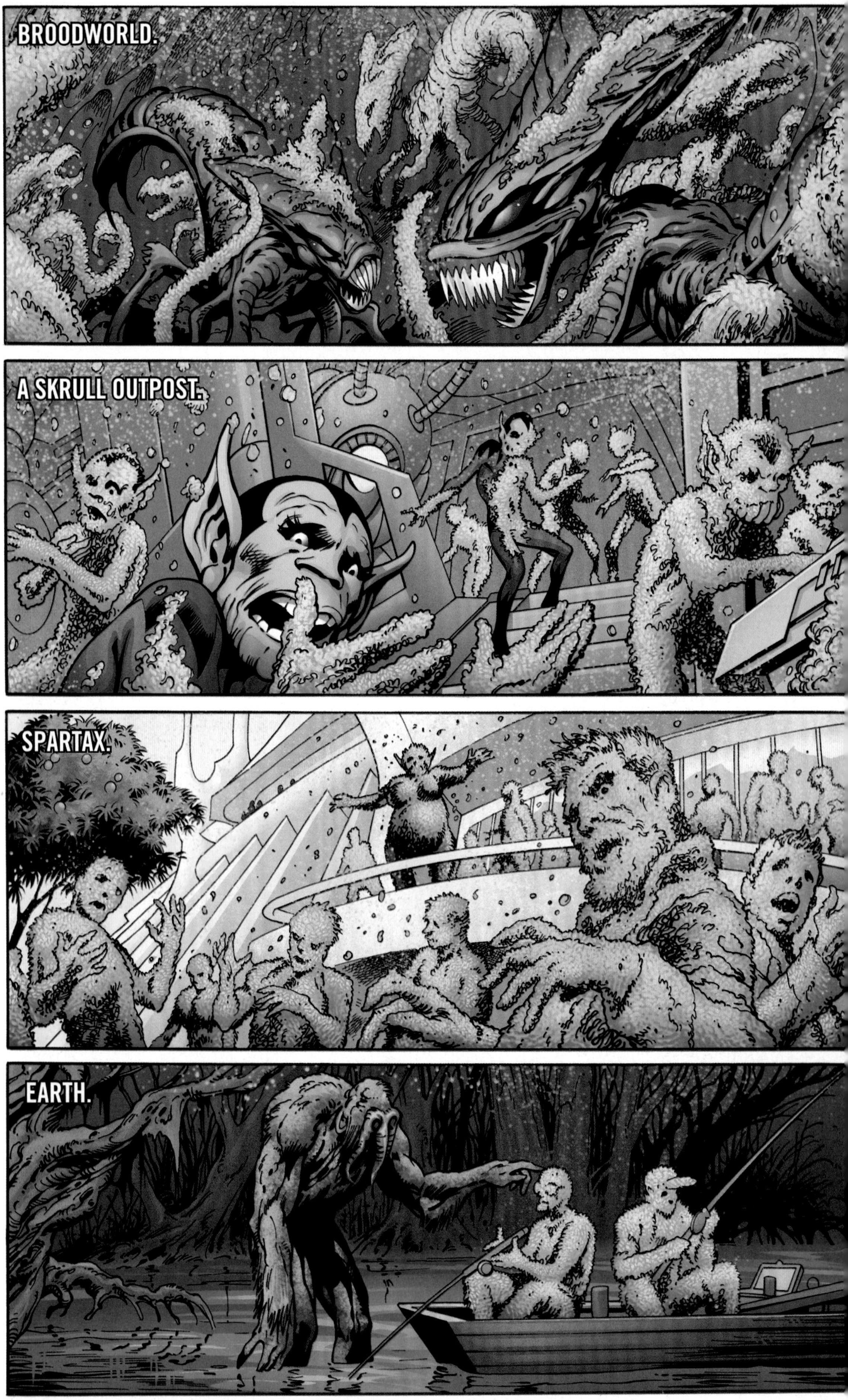
BROODWORLD.
A SKRULL OUTPOST.
SPARTAX.
EARTH.

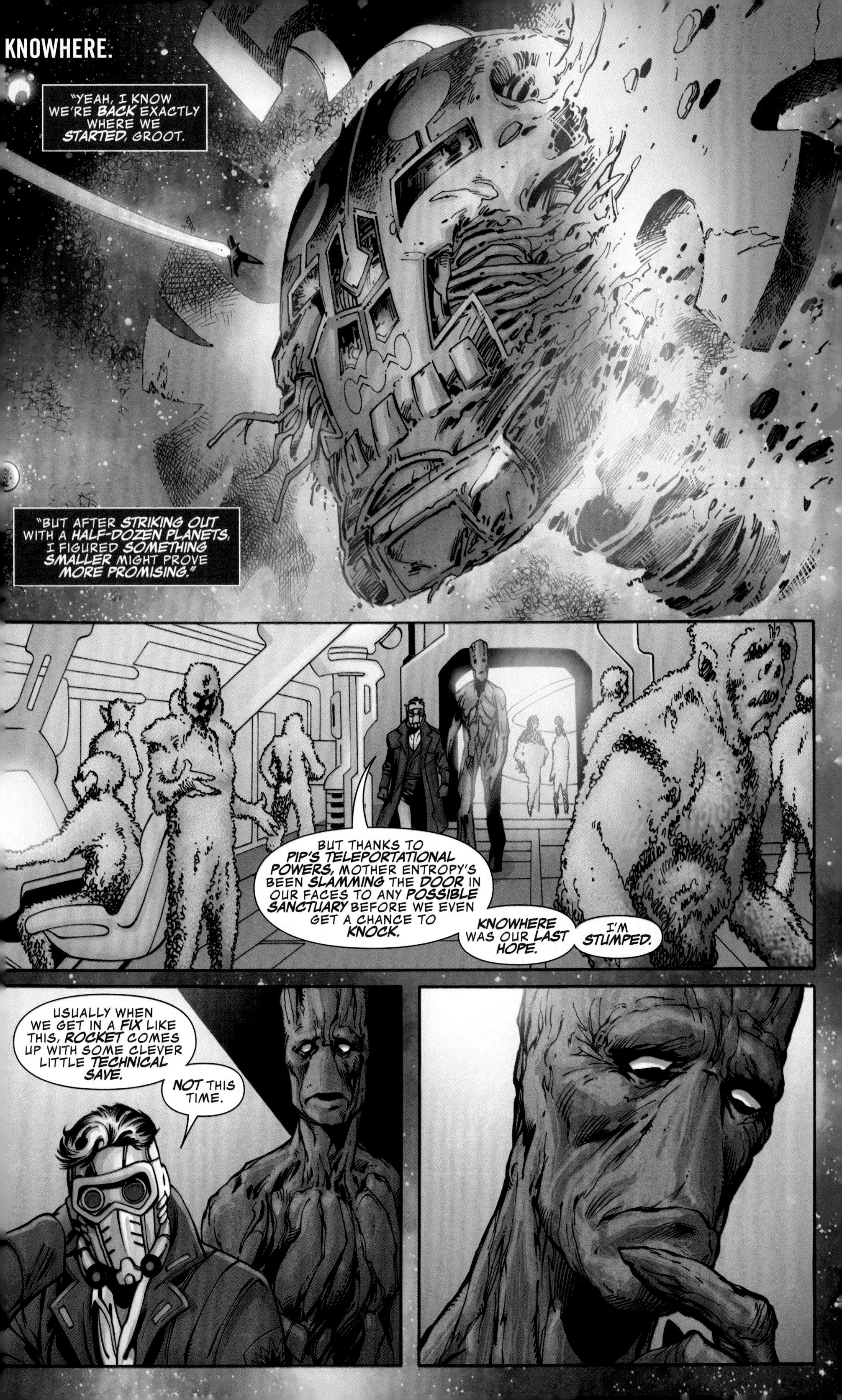
KNOWHERE.
"YEAH, I KNOW WE'RE BACK EXACTLY WHERE WE STARTED, GROOT.
"BUT AFTER STRIKING OUT WITH A HALF-DOZEN PLANETS, I FIGURED SOMETHING SMALLER MIGHT PROVE MORE PROMISING."
BUT THANKS TO PIP'S TELEPORTATIONAL POWERS, MOTHER ENTROPY'S BEEN SLAMMING THE DOOR IN OUR FACES TO ANY POSSIBLE SANCTUARY BEFORE WE EVEN GET A CHANCE TO KNOCK.
KNOWHERE WAS OUR LAST HOPE.
I'M STUMPED.
USUALLY WHEN WE GET IN A FIX LIKE THIS, ROCKET COMES UP WITH SOME CLEVER LITTLE TECHNICAL SAVE.
NOT THIS TIME.

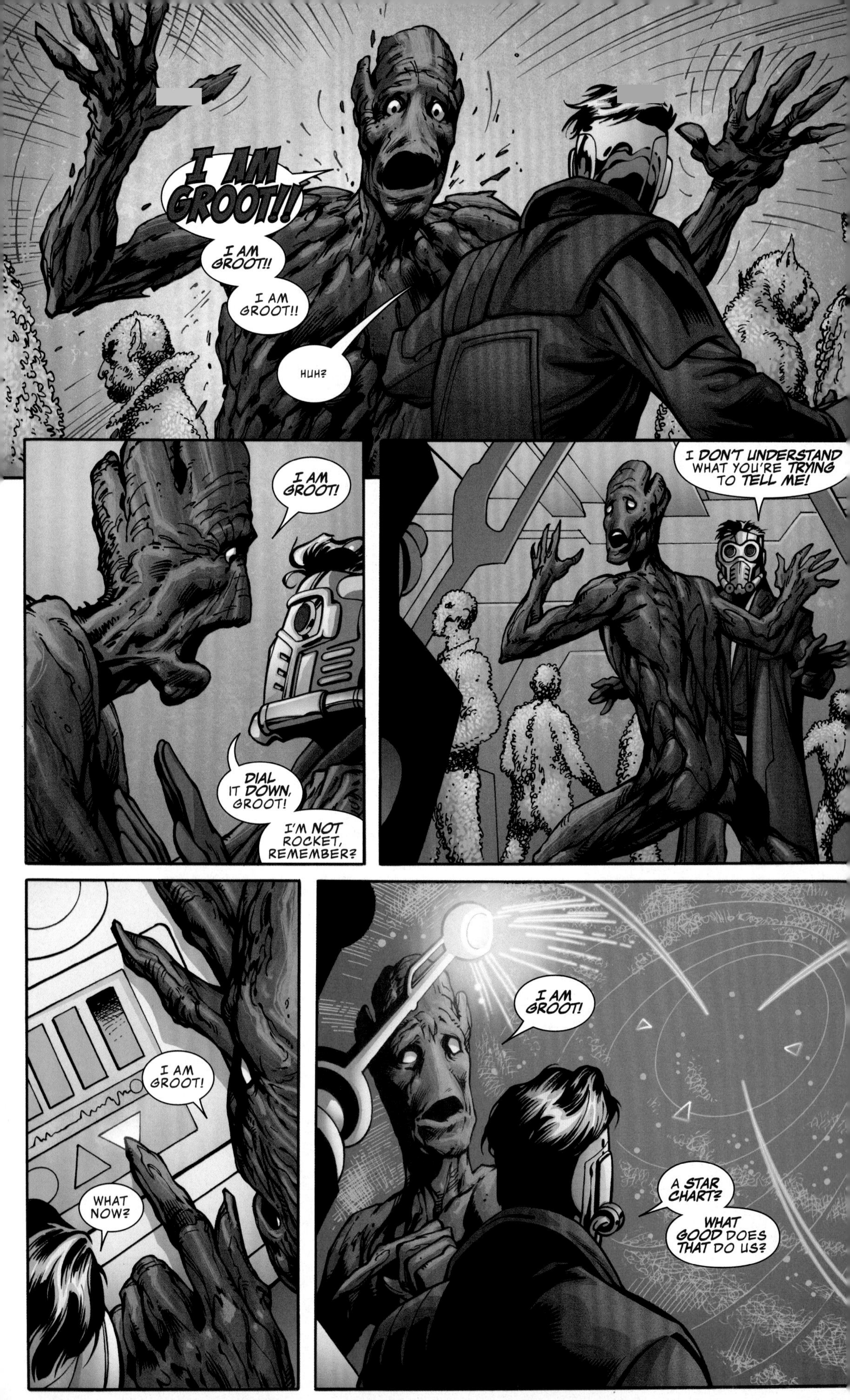
I AM GROOT!!
I AM GROOT!!
I AM GROOT!!
HUH?
I AM GROOT!
DIAL IT DOWN, GROOT!
I'M NOT ROCKET, REMEMBER?
I DON'T UNDERSTAND WHAT YOU'RE TRYING TO TELL ME!
I AM GROOT!
WHAT NOW?
I AM GROOT!
A STAR CHART?
WHAT GOOD DOES THAT DO US?

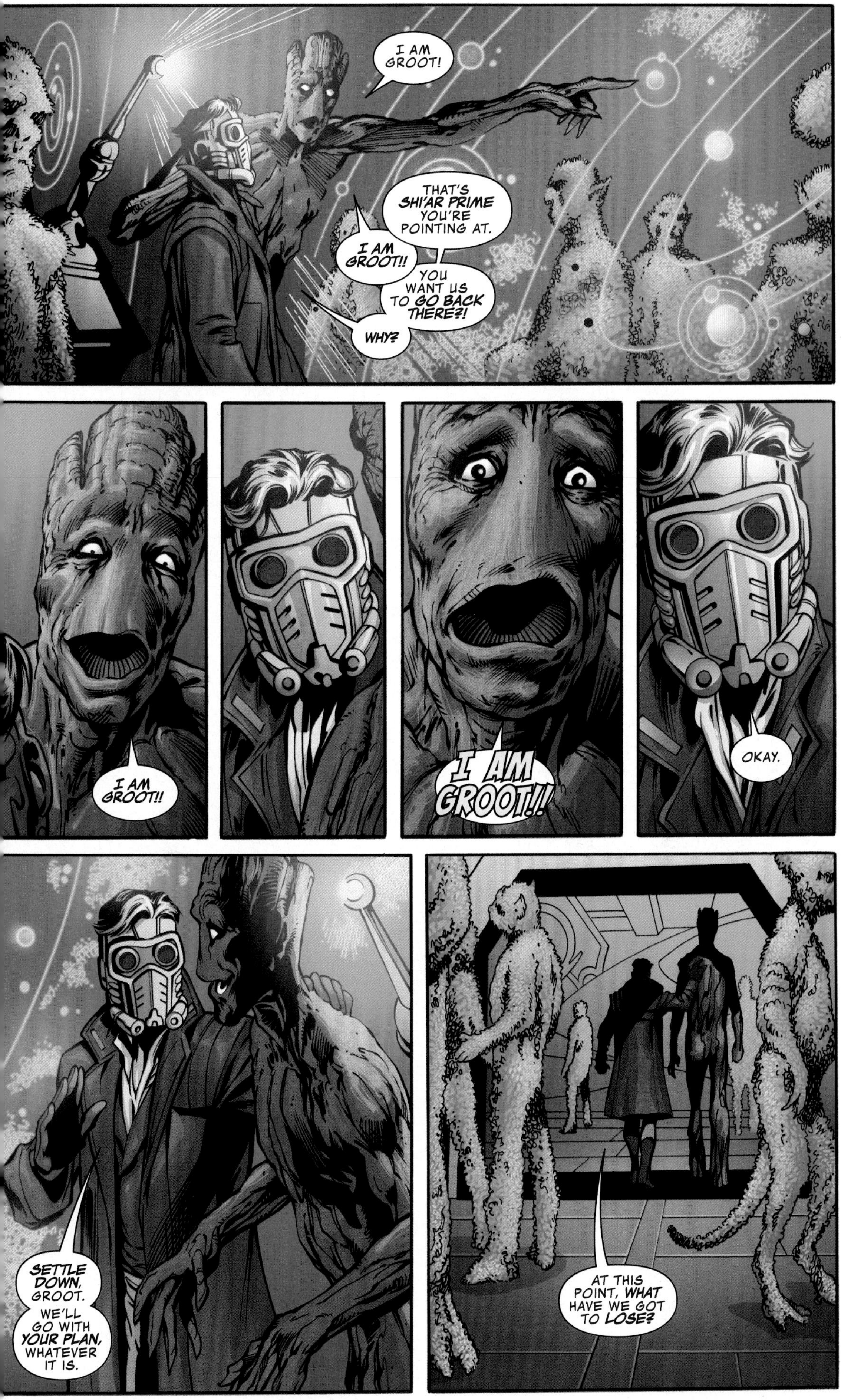
I AM GROOT!
THAT'S SHI'AR PRIME YOU'RE POINTING AT.
I AM GROOT!!
YOU WANT US TO GO BACK THERE?!
WHY?
I AM GROOT!!
I AM GROOT!!
OKAY.
SETTLE DOWN, GROOT.
WE'LL GO WITH YOUR PLAN, WHATEVER IT IS.
AT THIS POINT, WHAT HAVE WE GOT TO LOSE?

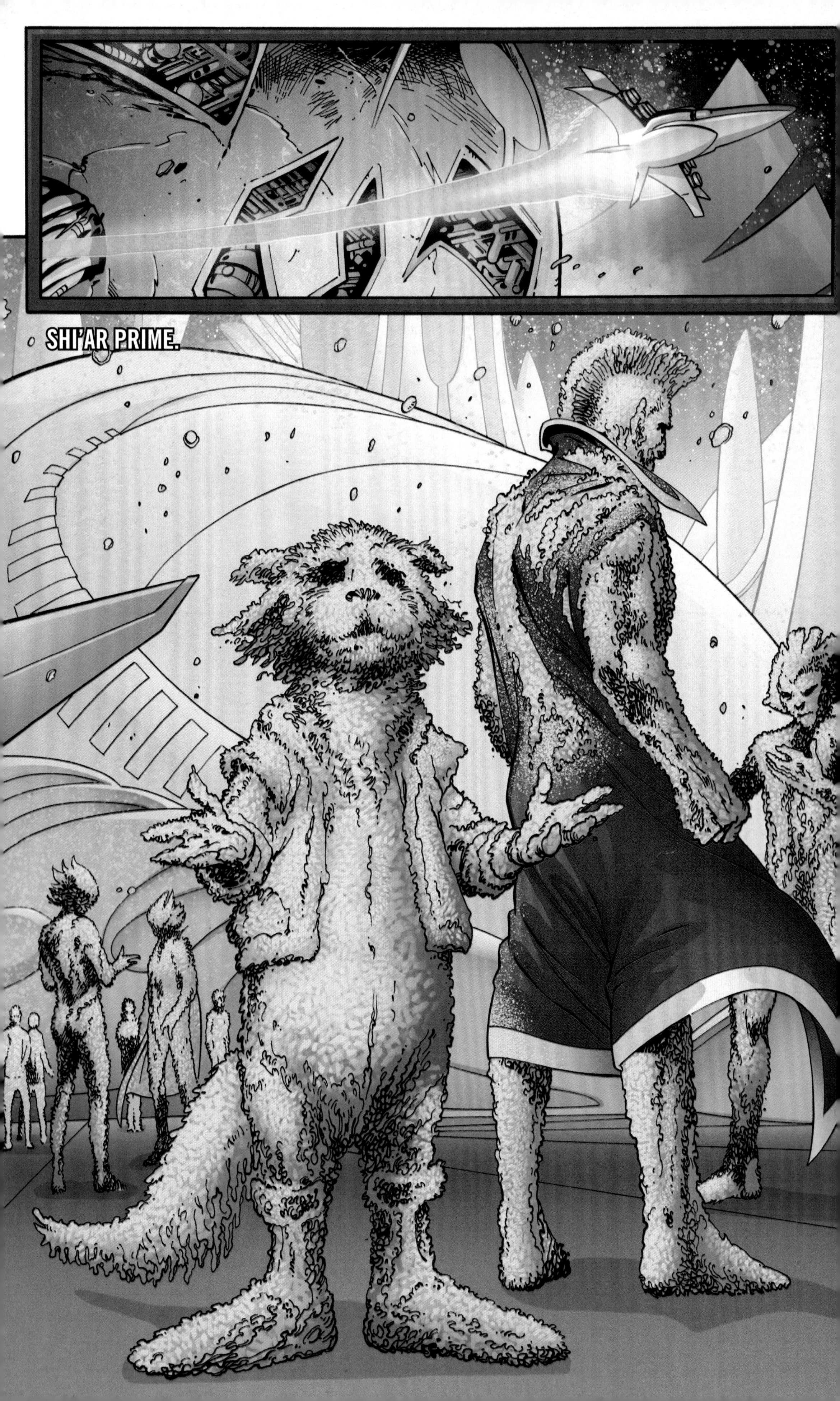
SHI'AR PRIME.

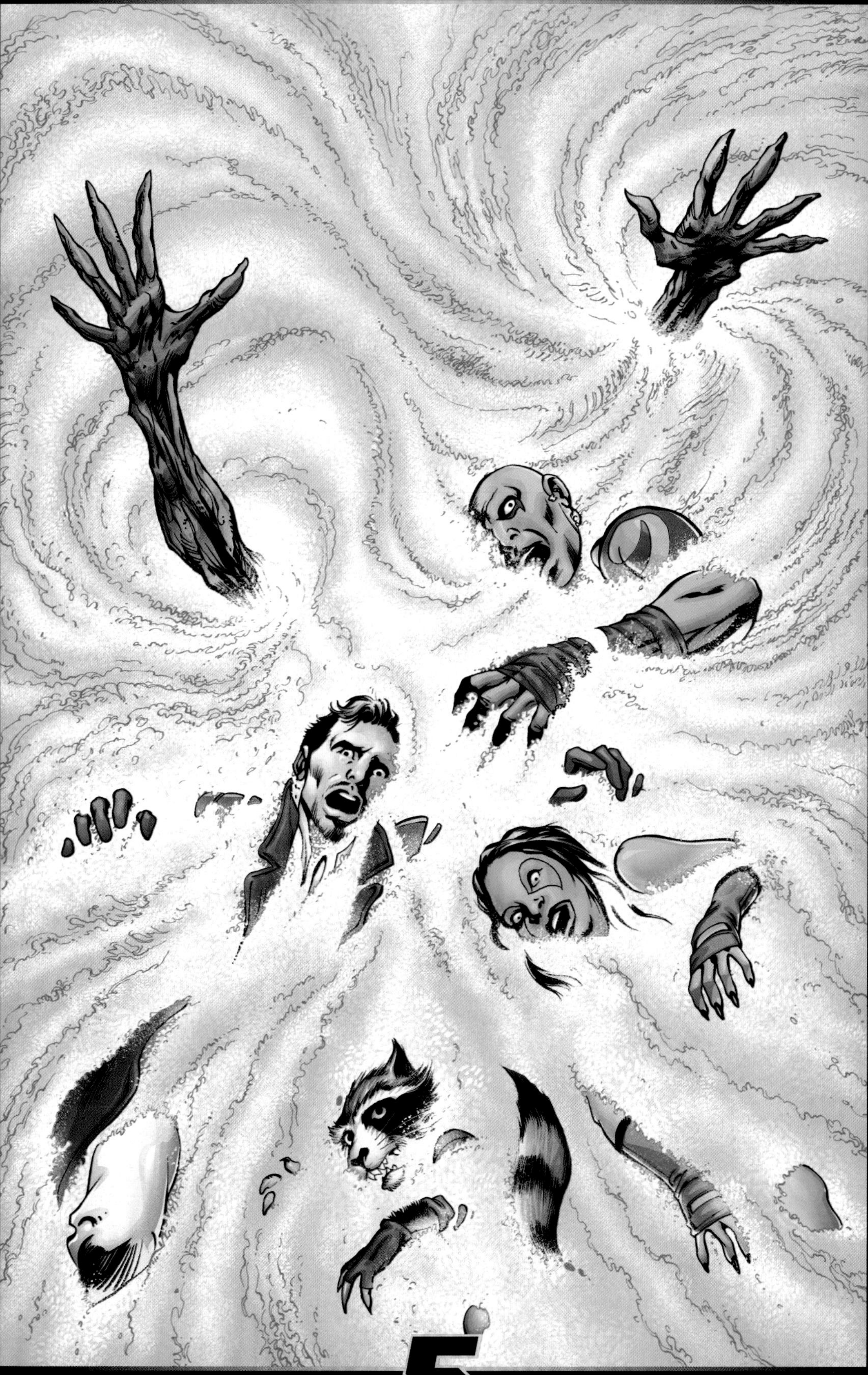

5

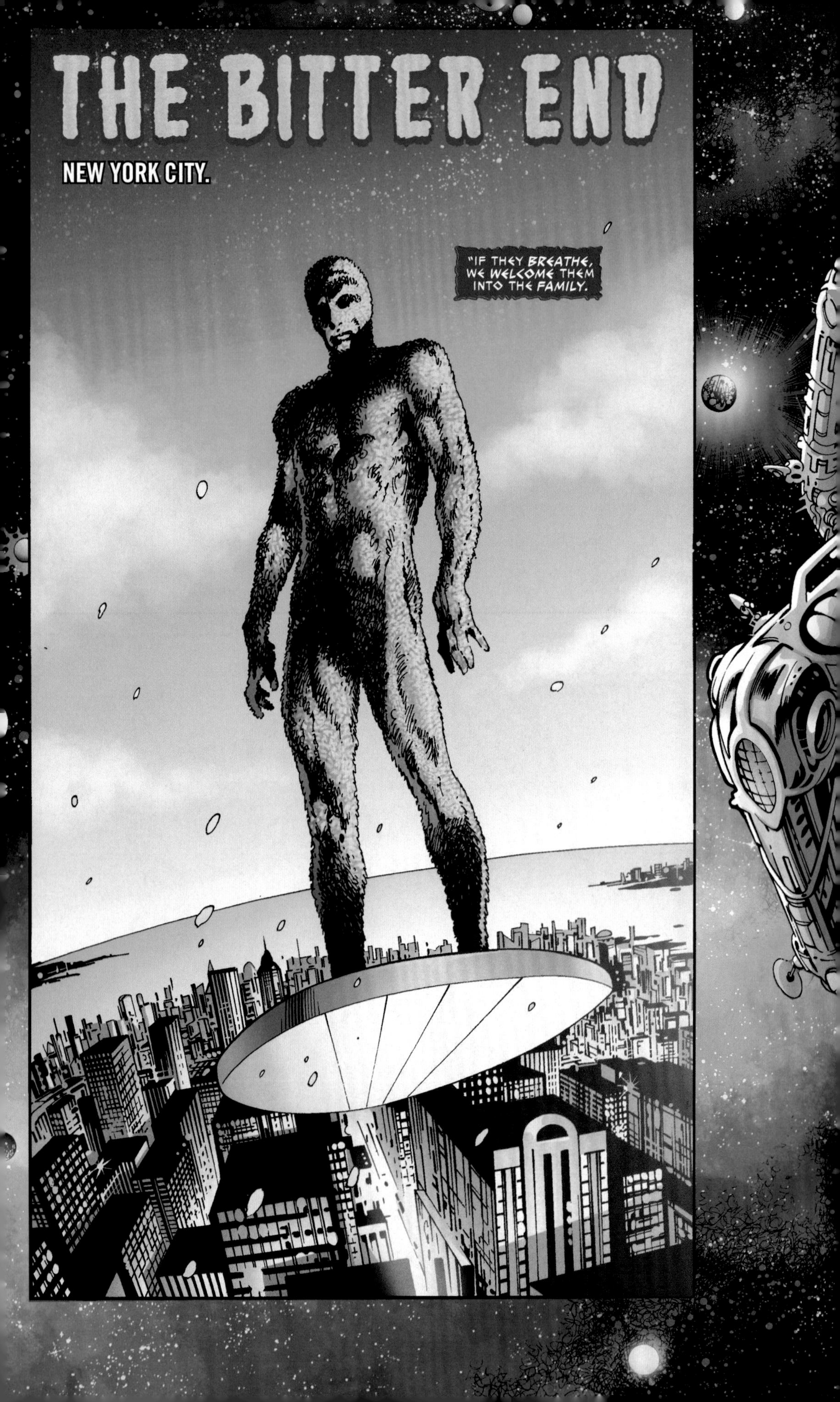
THE BITTER END
NEW YORK CITY.
"IF THEY BREATHE, WE WELCOME THEM INTO THE FAMILY.

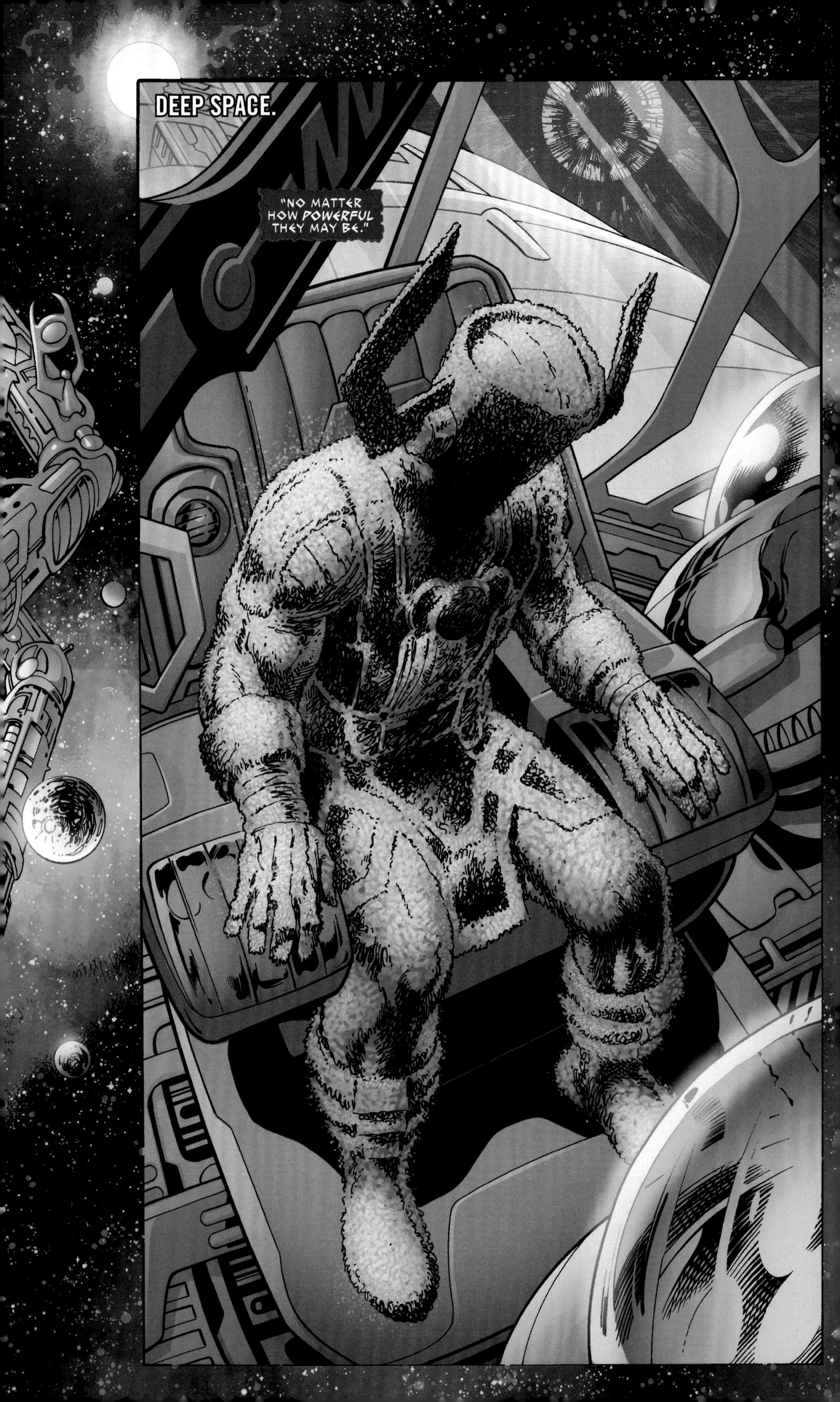
DEEP SPACE.
"NO MATTER HOW POWERFUL THEY MAY BE."

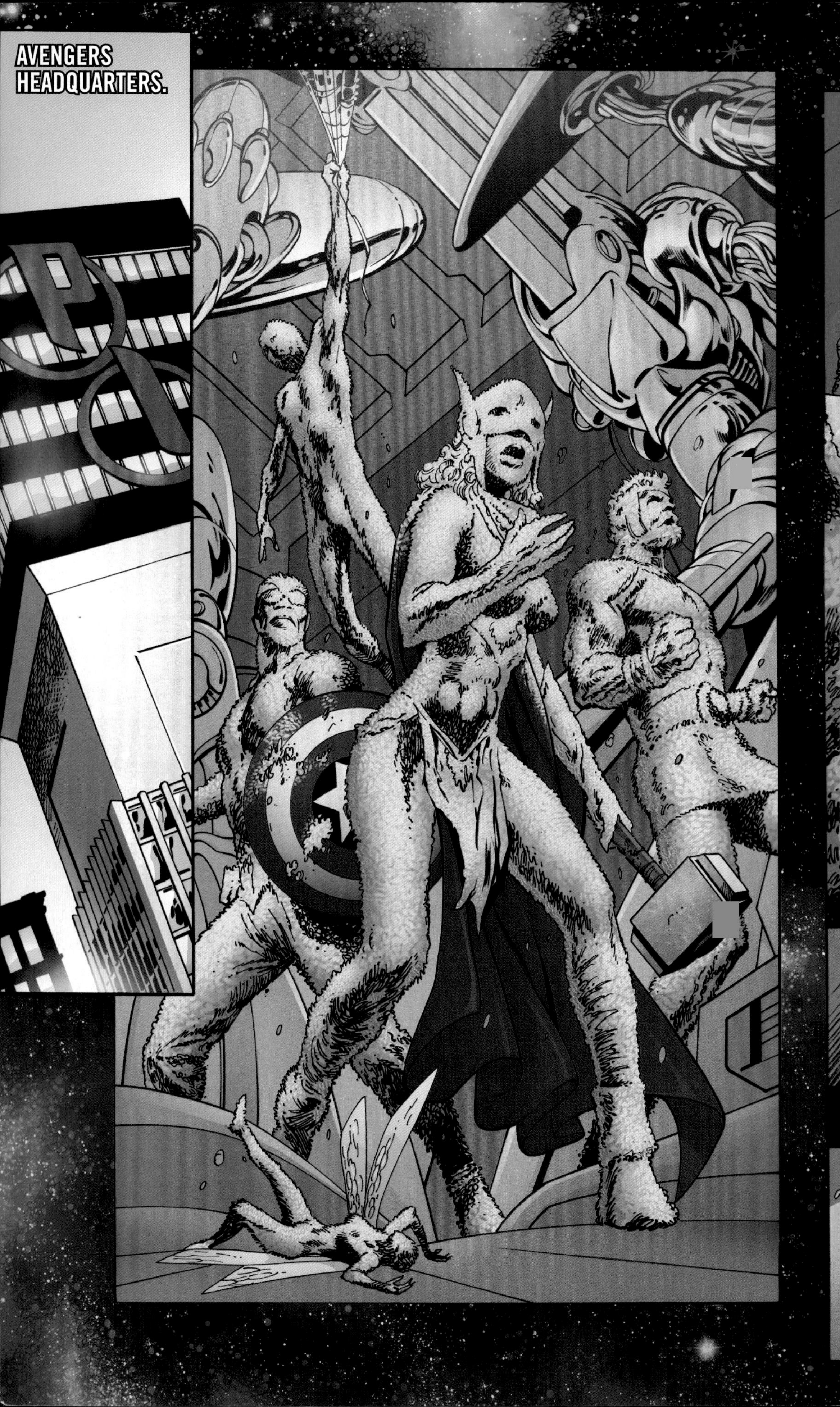
AVENGERS HEADQUARTERS.

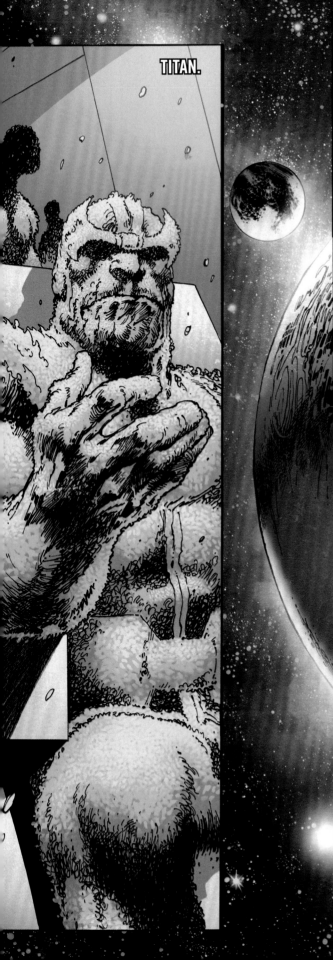

TITAN.

SHI'AR PRIME.

GUESS THERE MUST BE *SOME SENSE* TO WHAT *MOTHER ENTROPY* IS UP TO.

BUT I *DON'T* SEE IT.

WHAT *GOOD* DOES IT DO, HER TURNING EVERYONE IN THE UNIVERSE INTO *FUNGUS-COVERED ZOMBIES?*

MUST BE SOME KIND OF *PSYCHIC FEEDING-OFF-THEM* THING.

I AM GROOT.

YEAH, RIGHT.

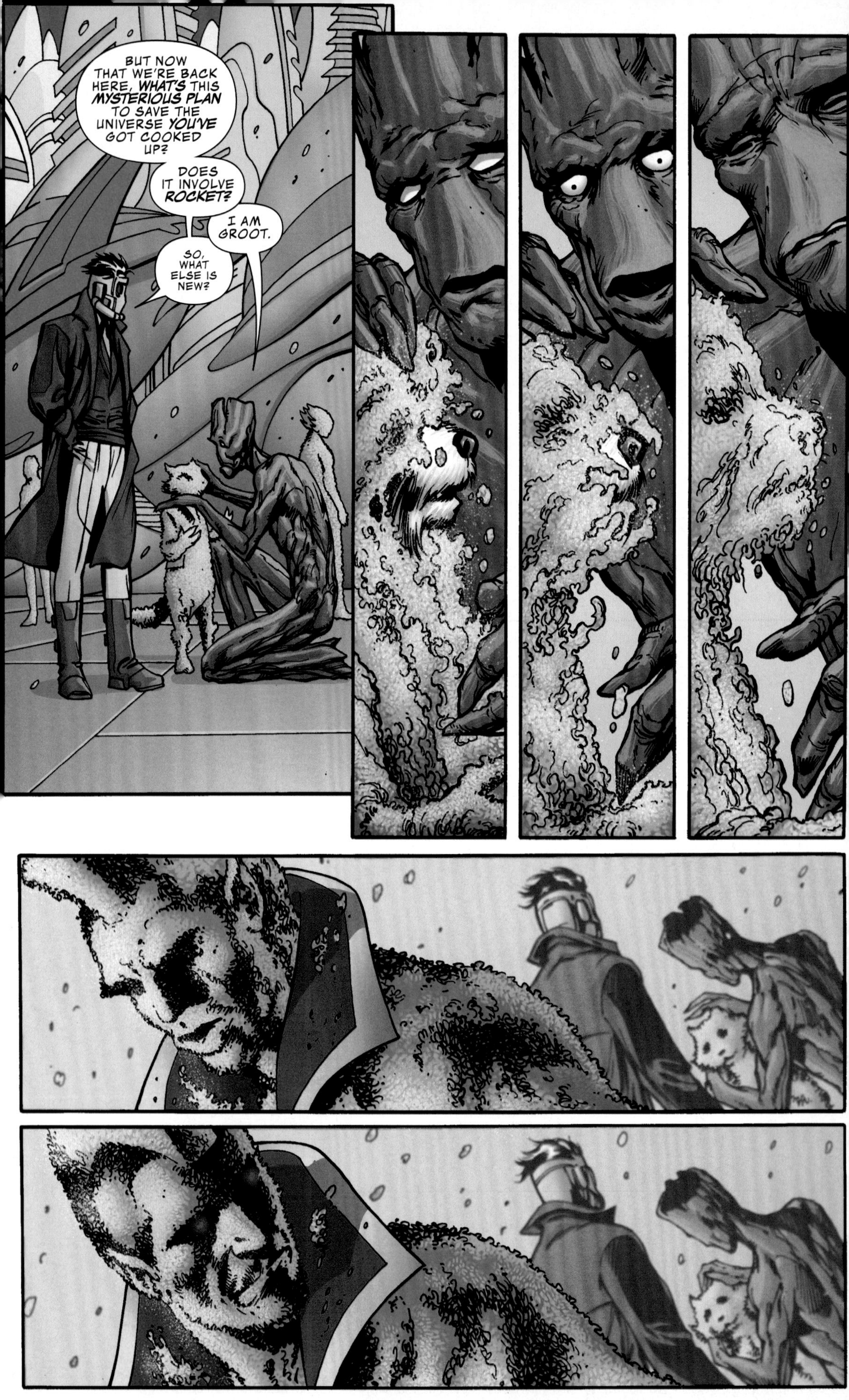
BUT NOW THAT WE'RE BACK HERE, WHAT'S THIS MYSTERIOUS PLAN TO SAVE THE UNIVERSE YOU'VE GOT COOKED UP?
DOES IT INVOLVE ROCKET?
I AM GROOT.
SO, WHAT ELSE IS NEW?

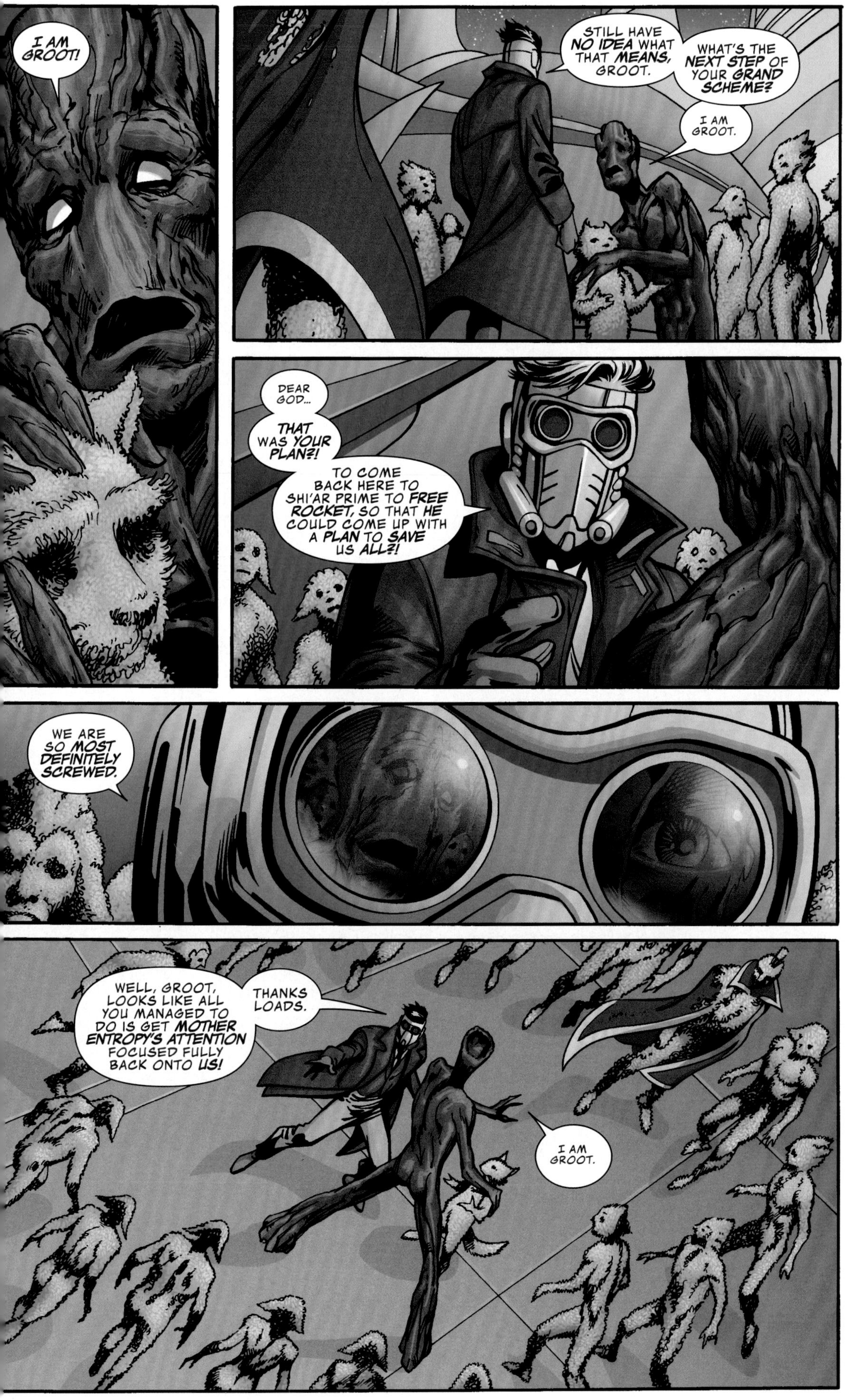
I AM GROOT!
STILL HAVE NO IDEA WHAT THAT MEANS, GROOT.
WHAT'S THE NEXT STEP OF YOUR GRAND SCHEME?
I AM GROOT.
DEAR GOD...
THAT WAS YOUR PLAN?!
TO COME BACK HERE TO SHI'AR PRIME TO FREE ROCKET, SO THAT HE COULD COME UP WITH A PLAN TO SAVE US ALL?!
WE ARE SO MOST DEFINITELY SCREWED.
WELL, GROOT, LOOKS LIKE ALL YOU MANAGED TO DO IS GET MOTHER ENTROPY'S ATTENTION FOCUSED FULLY BACK ONTO US!
THANKS LOADS.
I AM GROOT.

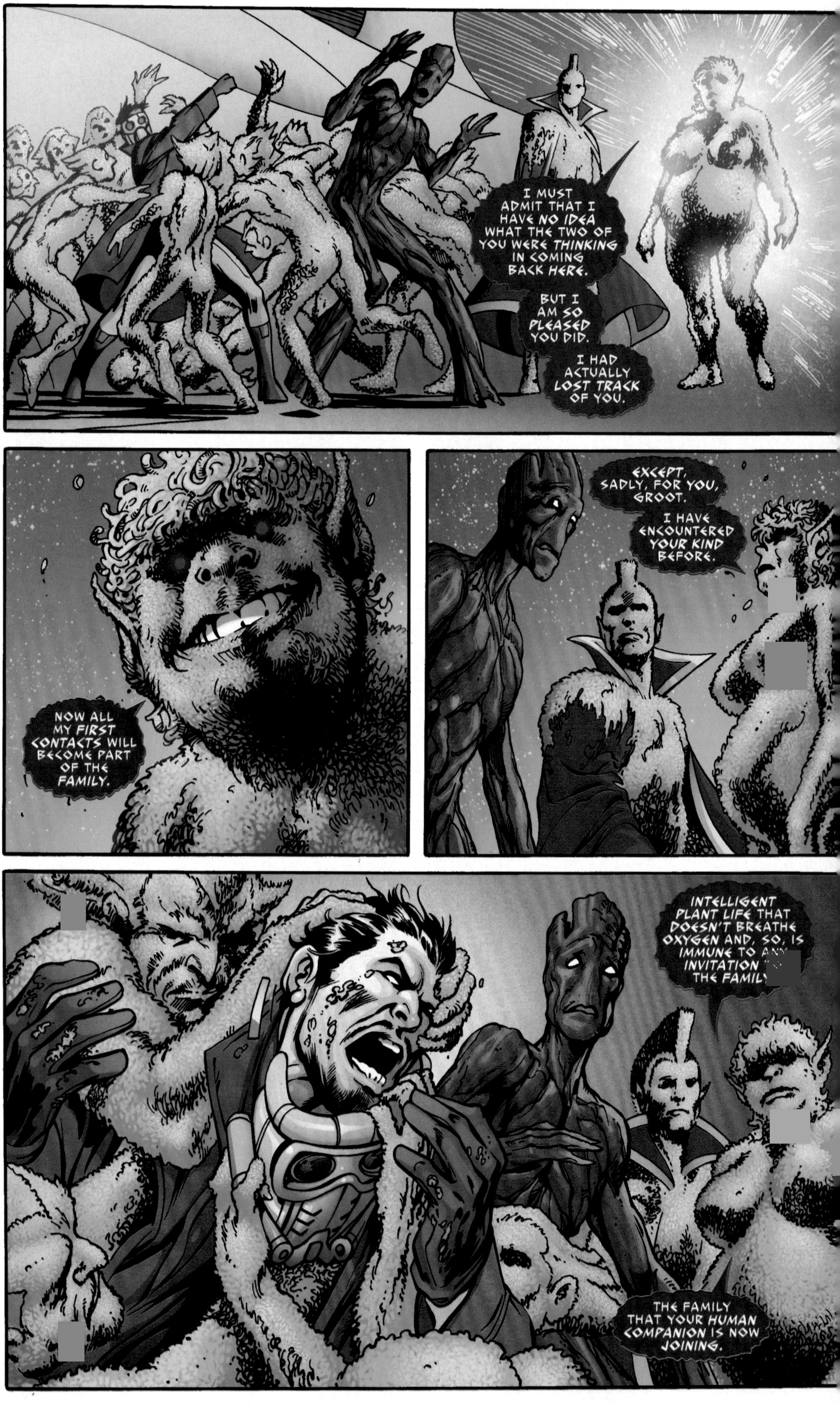
I MUST ADMIT THAT I HAVE NO IDEA WHAT THE TWO OF YOU WERE THINKING IN COMING BACK HERE.
BUT I AM SO PLEASED YOU DID.
I HAD ACTUALLY LOST TRACK OF YOU.
NOW ALL MY FIRST CONTACTS WILL BECOME PART OF THE FAMILY.
EXCEPT, SADLY, FOR YOU, GROOT.
I HAVE ENCOUNTERED YOUR KIND BEFORE.
INTELLIGENT PLANT LIFE THAT DOESN'T BREATHE OXYGEN AND, SO, IS IMMUNE TO AN INVITATION T THE FAMILY
THE FAMILY THAT YOUR HUMAN COMPANION IS NOW JOINING.

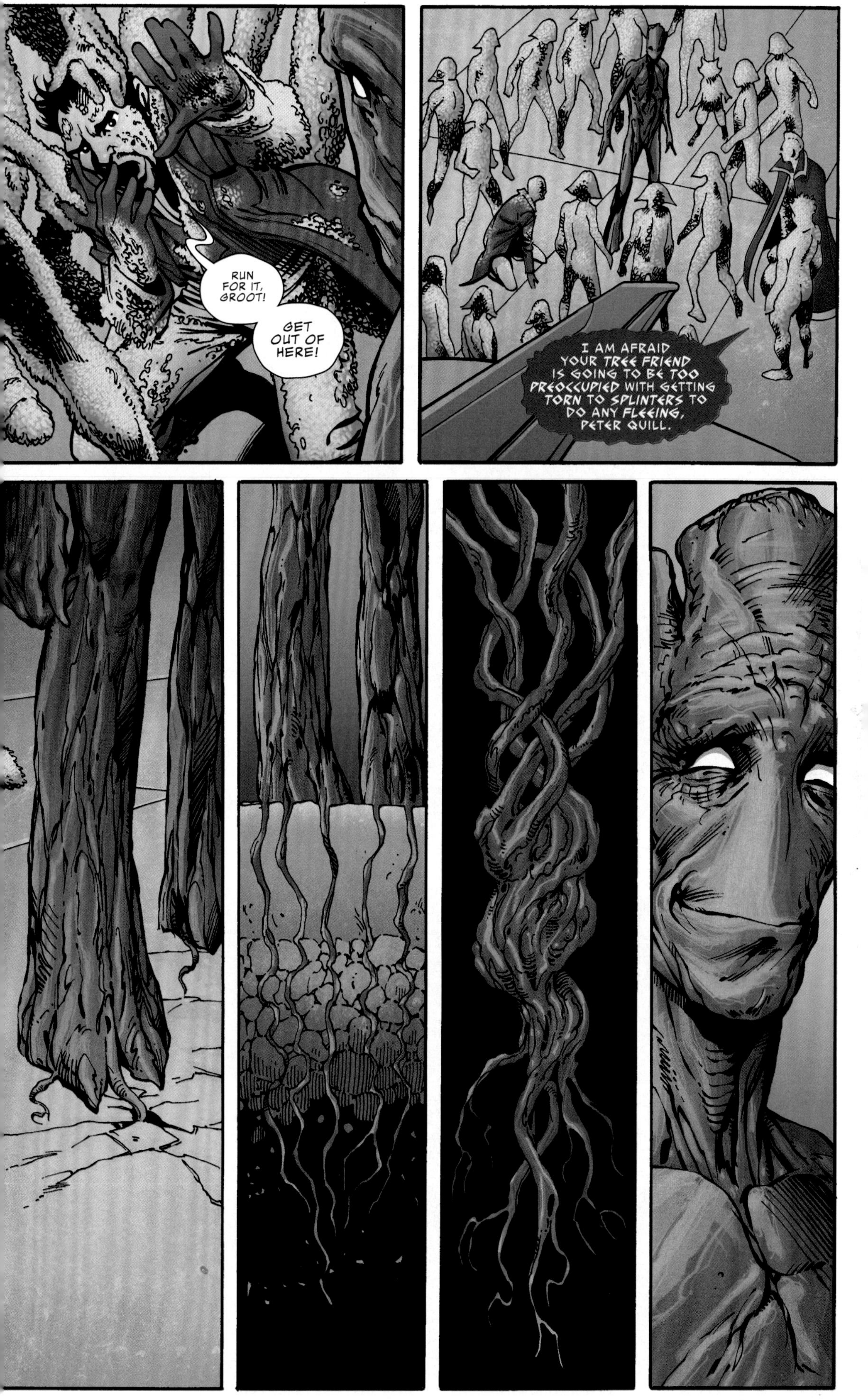
RUN FOR IT, GROOT!
GET OUT OF HERE!
I AM AFRAID YOUR TREE FRIEND IS GOING TO BE TOO PREOCCUPIED WITH GETTING TORN TO SPLINTERS TO DO ANY FLEEING, PETER QUILL.

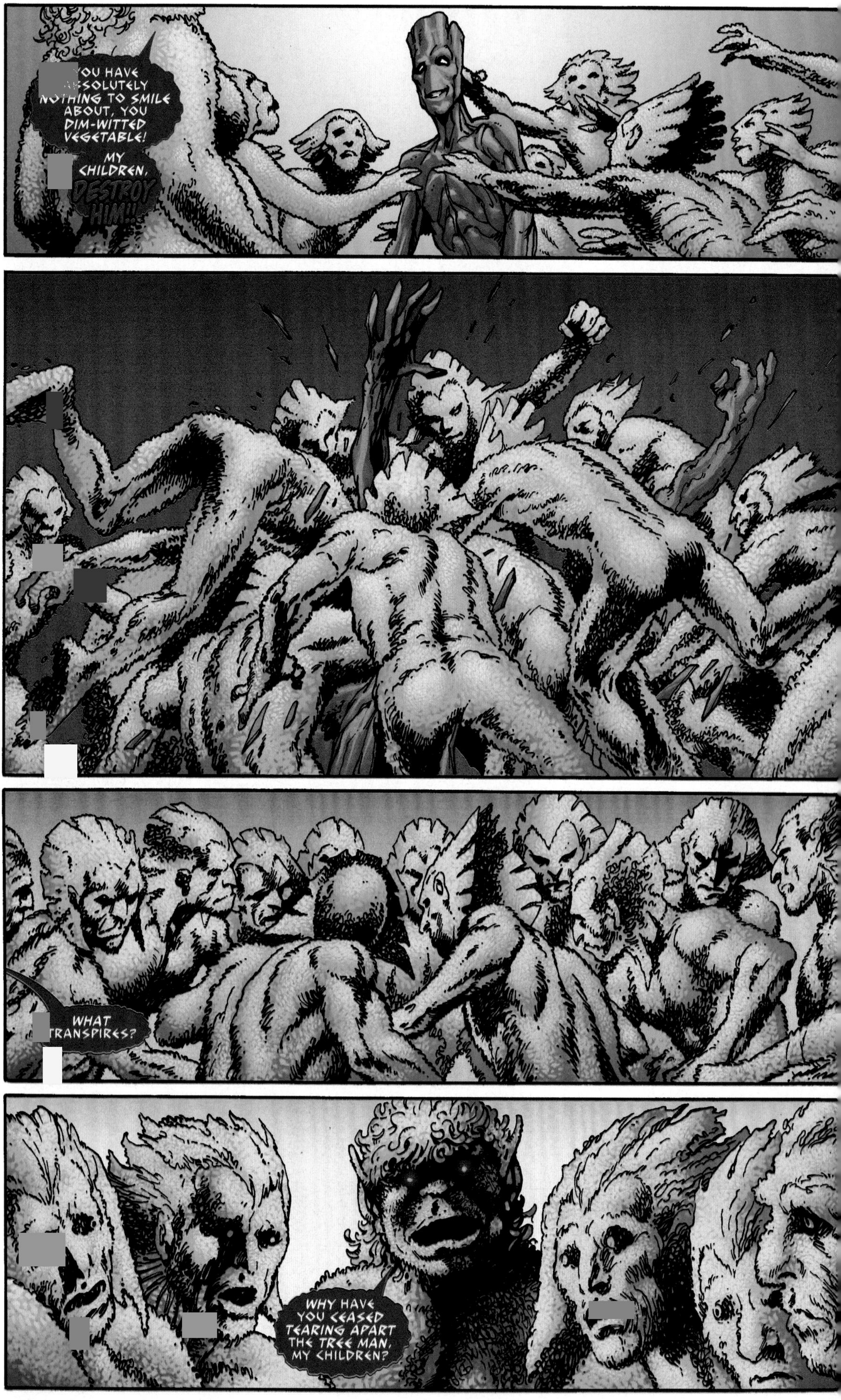
YOU HAVE ABSOLUTELY NOTHING TO SMILE ABOUT, YOU DIM-WITTED VEGETABLE!
MY CHILDREN, DESTROY HIM!!
WHAT TRANSPIRES?
WHY HAVE YOU CEASED TEARING APART THE TREE MAN, MY CHILDREN?

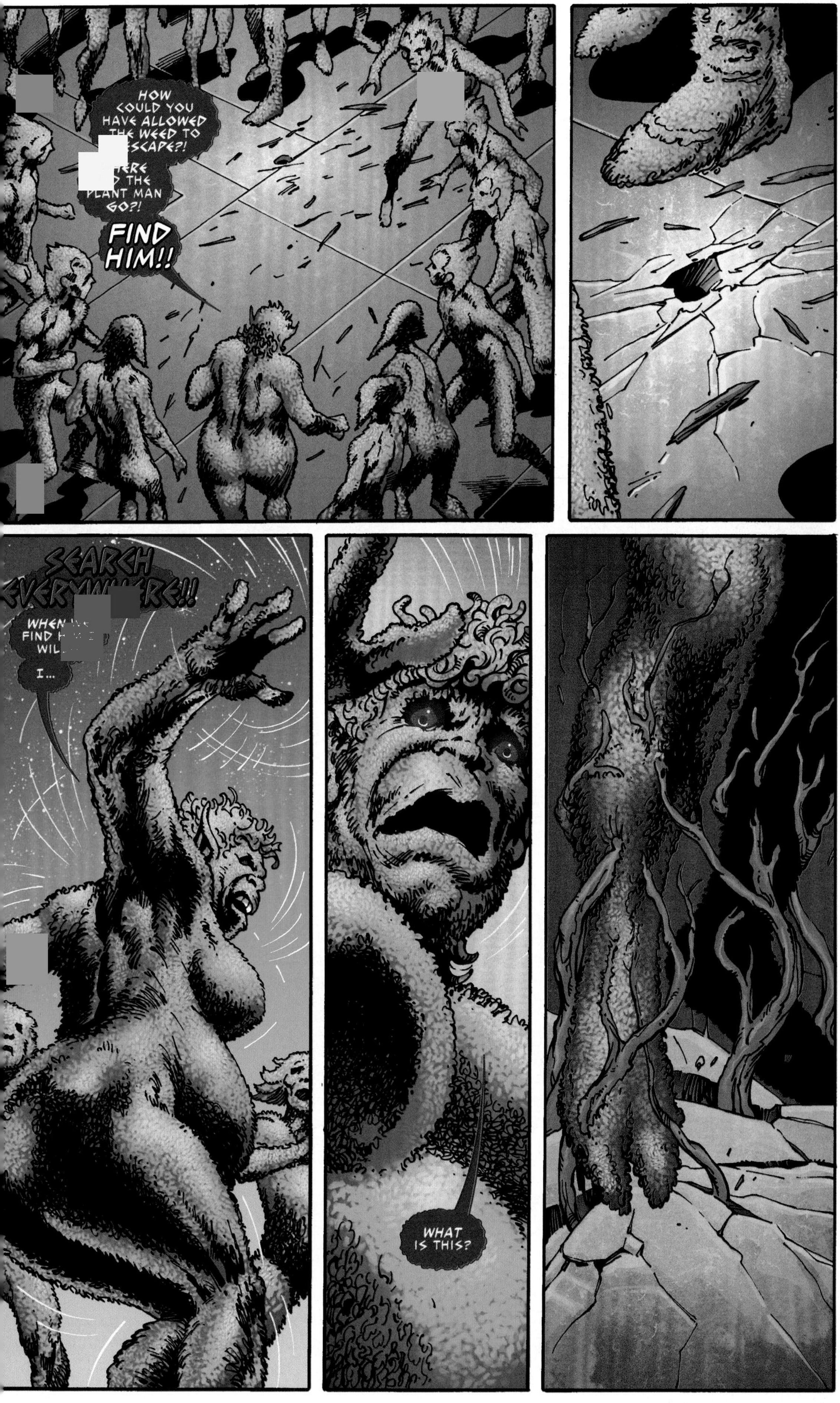
HOW COULD YOU HAVE ALLOWED THE WEED TO SCAPE?!
ERE D THE PLANT MAN GO?!
FIND HIM!!
SEARCH EVERYWHERE!!
WHEN FIND H WIL
I...
WHAT IS THIS?

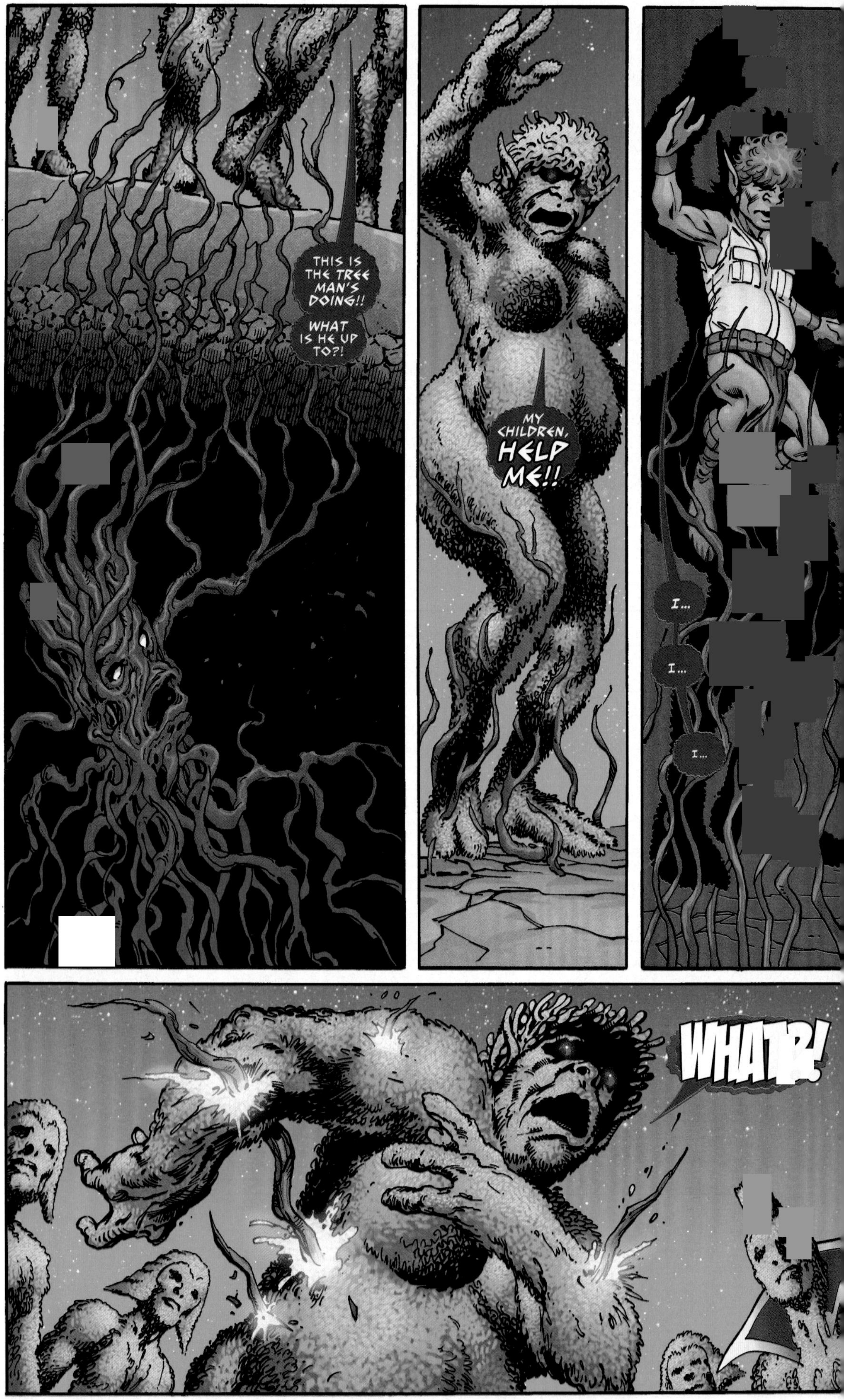
THIS IS THE TREE MAN'S DOING!!
WHAT IS HE UP TO?!
MY CHILDREN, HELP ME!!
I...
I...
I...
WHAT

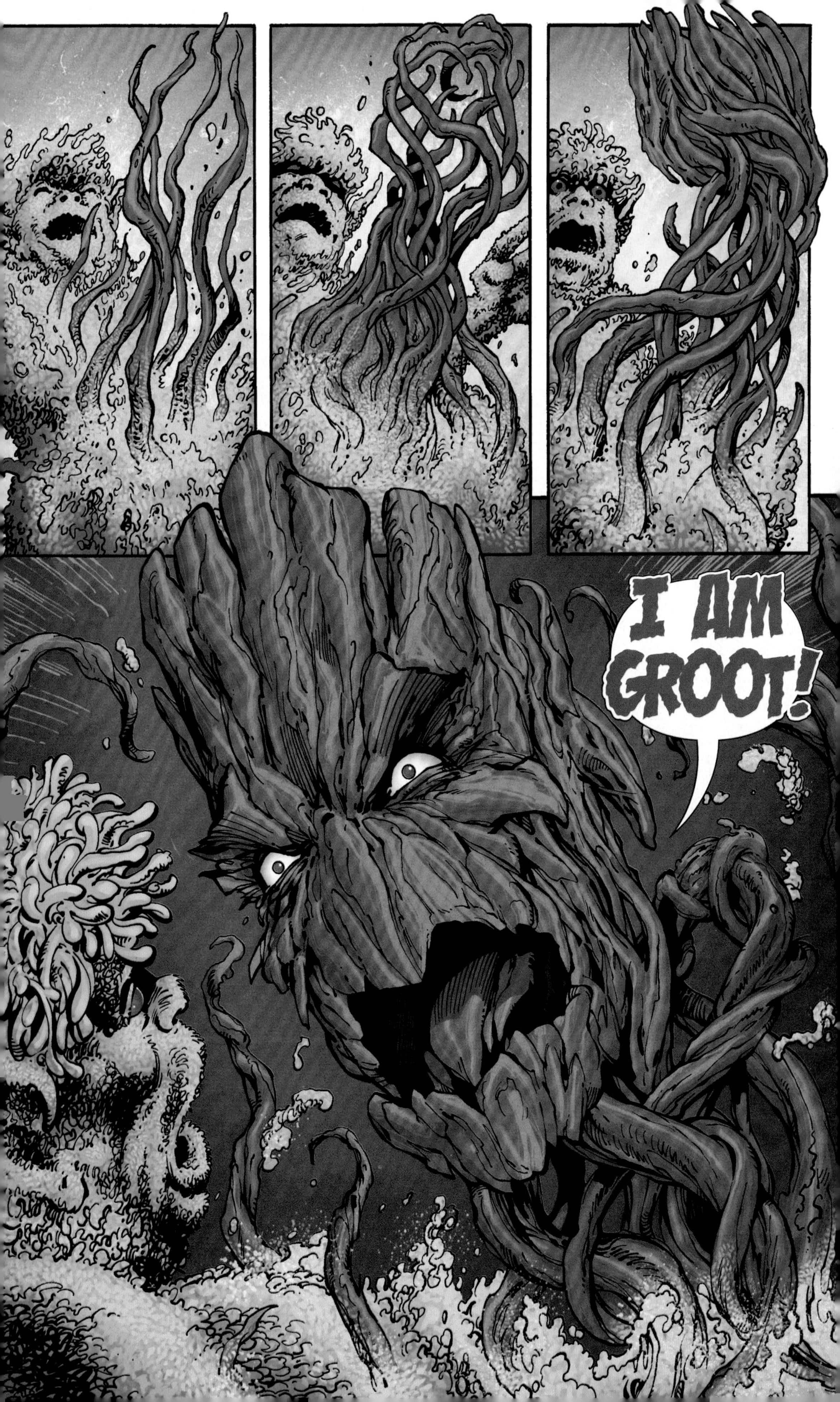
I AM GROOT!

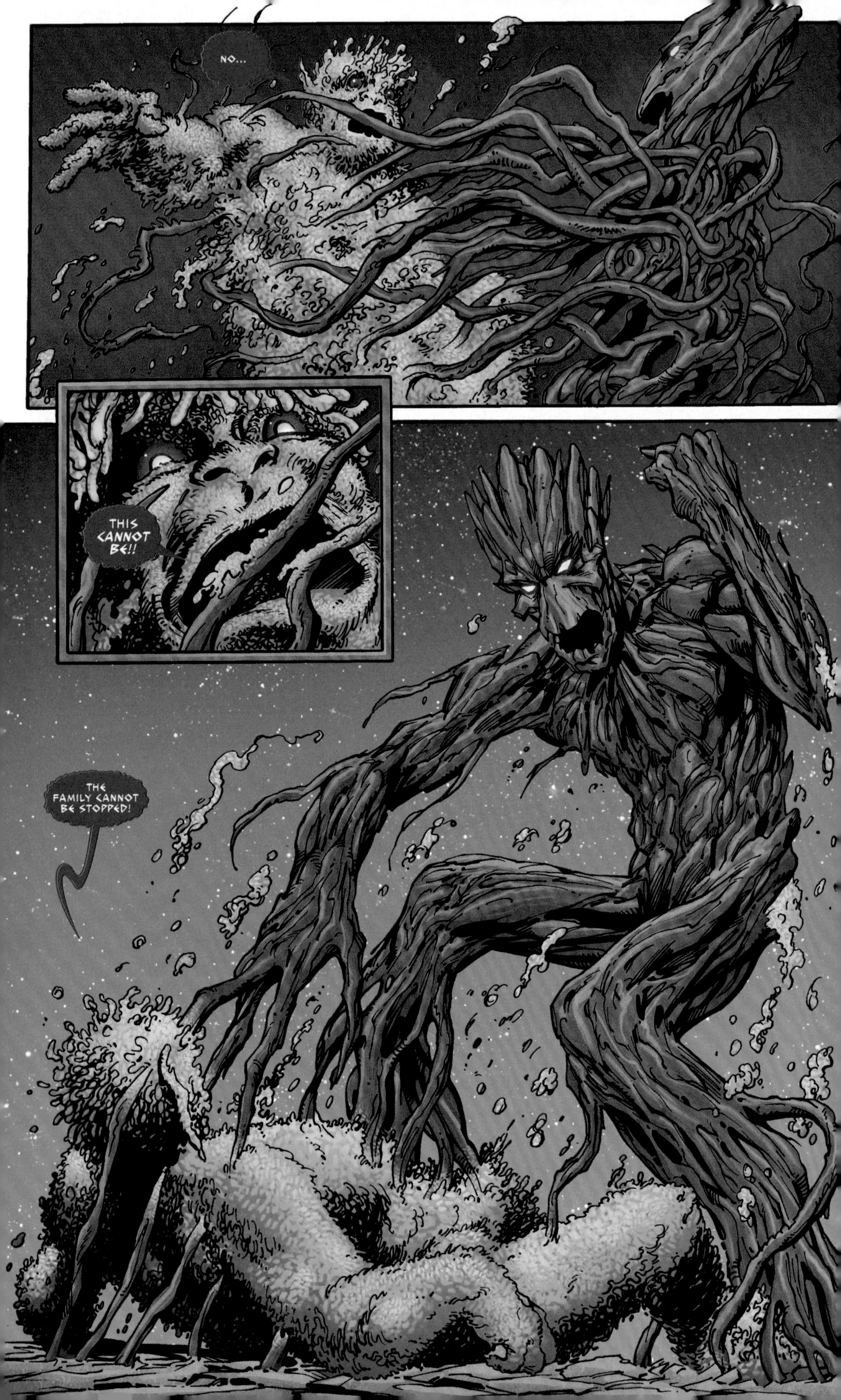
NO...
THIS CANNOT BE!!
THE FAMILY CANNOT BE STOPPED!

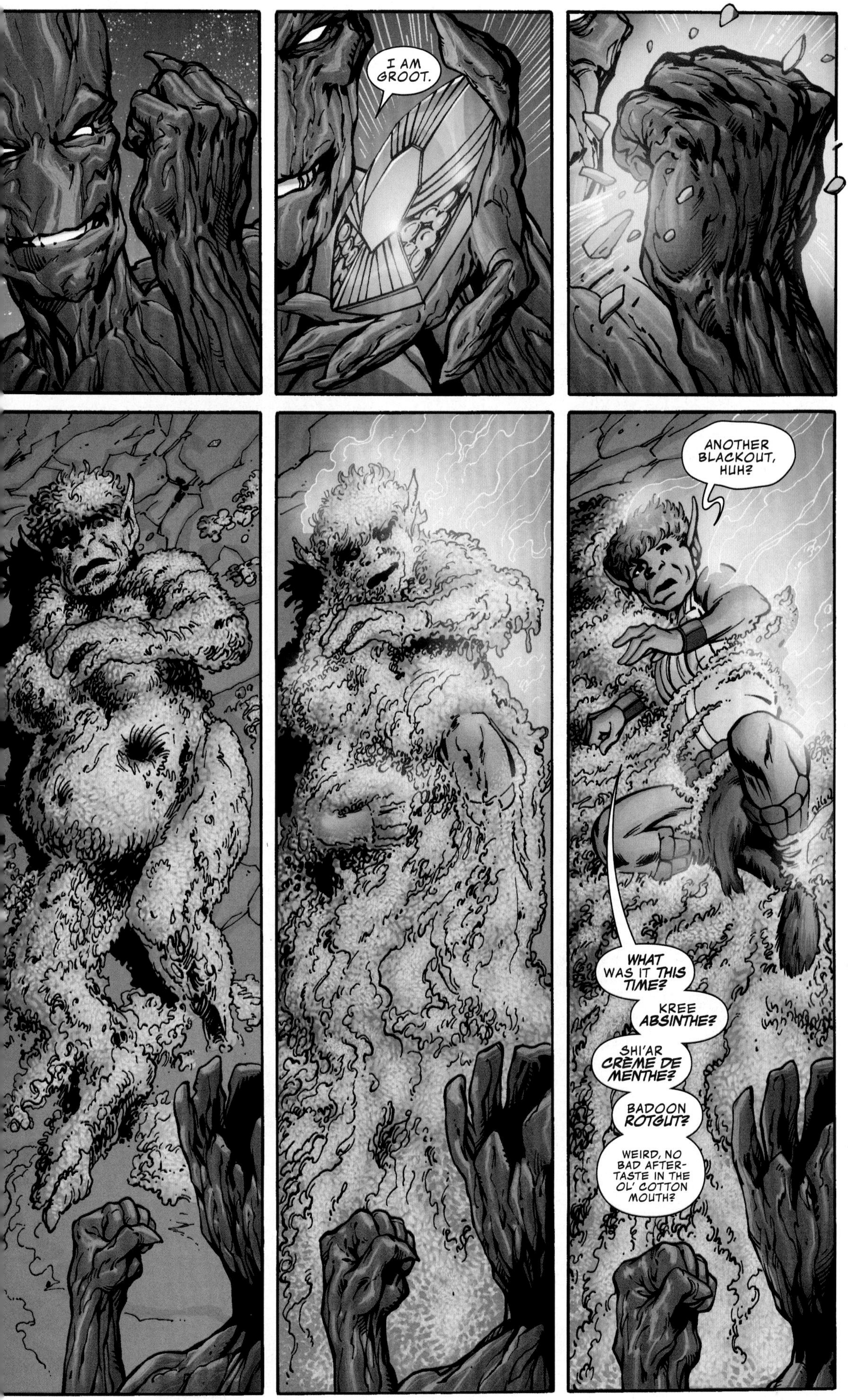
I AM GROOT.
ANOTHER BLACKOUT, HUH?
WHAT WAS IT THIS TIME?
KREE ABSINTHE?
SHI'AR CRÈME DE MENTHE?
BADOON ROTGUT?
WEIRD, NO BAD AFTER-TASTE IN THE OL' COTTON MOUTH?

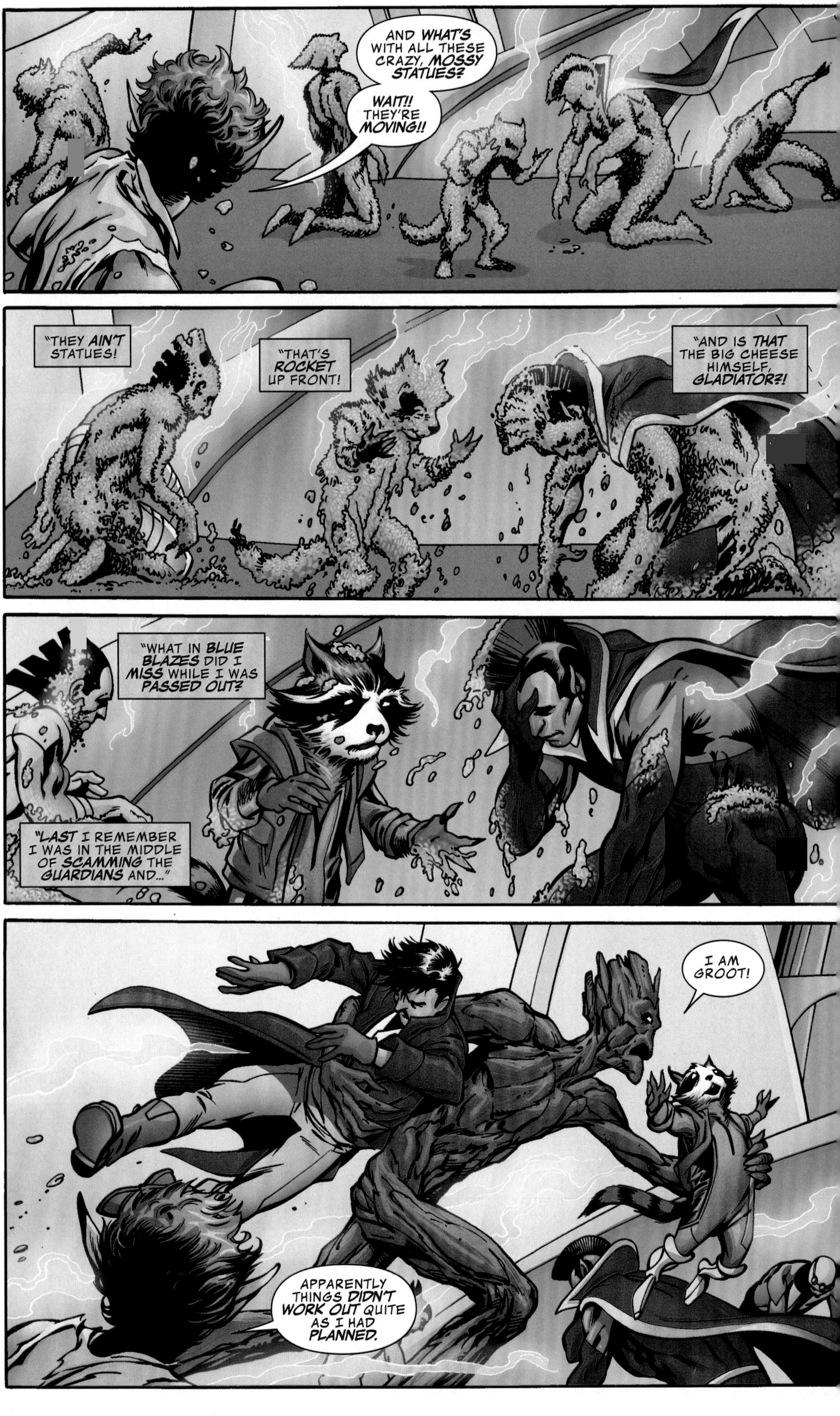
AND WHAT'S WITH ALL THESE CRAZY, MOSSY STATUES?
WAIT!! THEY'RE MOVING!!
"THEY AIN'T STATUES!
"THAT'S ROCKET UP FRONT!
"AND IS THAT THE BIG CHEESE HIMSELF, GLADIATOR?!
"WHAT IN BLUE BLAZES DID I MISS WHILE I WAS PASSED OUT?
"LAST I REMEMBER I WAS IN THE MIDDLE OF SCAMMING THE GUARDIANS AND..."
I AM GROOT!
APPARENTLY THINGS DIDN'T WORK OUT QUITE AS I HAD PLANNED.

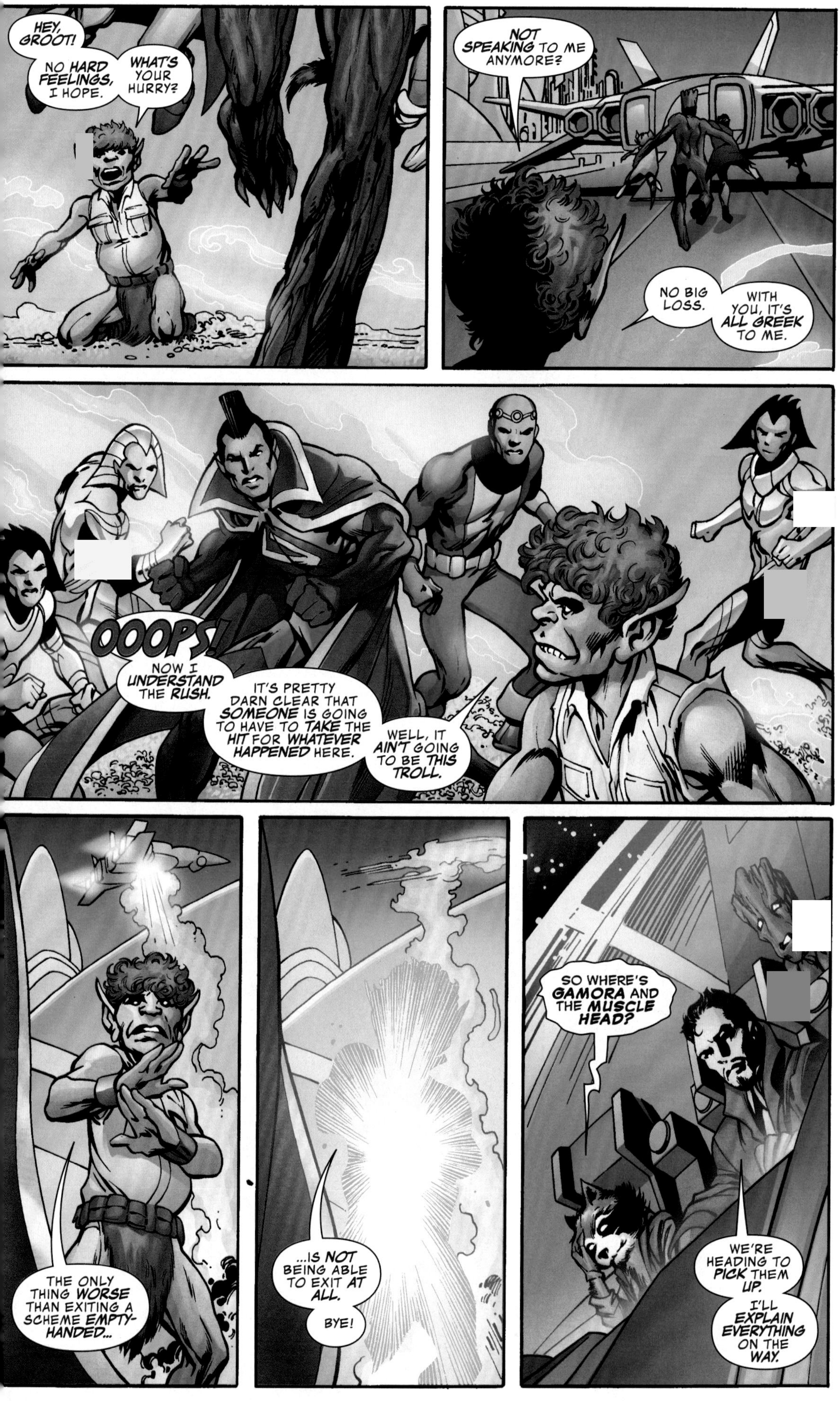
HEY, GROOT!
NO HARD FEELINGS, I HOPE.
WHAT'S YOUR HURRY?
NOT SPEAKING TO ME ANYMORE?
NO BIG LOSS.
WITH YOU, IT'S ALL GREEK TO ME.
OOOPS!
NOW I UNDERSTAND THE RUSH.
IT'S PRETTY DARN CLEAR THAT SOMEONE IS GOING TO HAVE TO TAKE THE HIT FOR WHATEVER HAPPENED HERE.
WELL, IT AIN'T GOING TO BE THIS TROLL.
THE ONLY THING WORSE THAN EXITING A SCHEME EMPTY-HANDED...
...IS NOT BEING ABLE TO EXIT AT ALL.
BYE!
SO WHERE'S GAMORA AND THE MUSCLE HEAD?
WE'RE HEADING TO PICK THEM UP.
I'LL EXPLAIN EVERYTHING ON THE WAY.

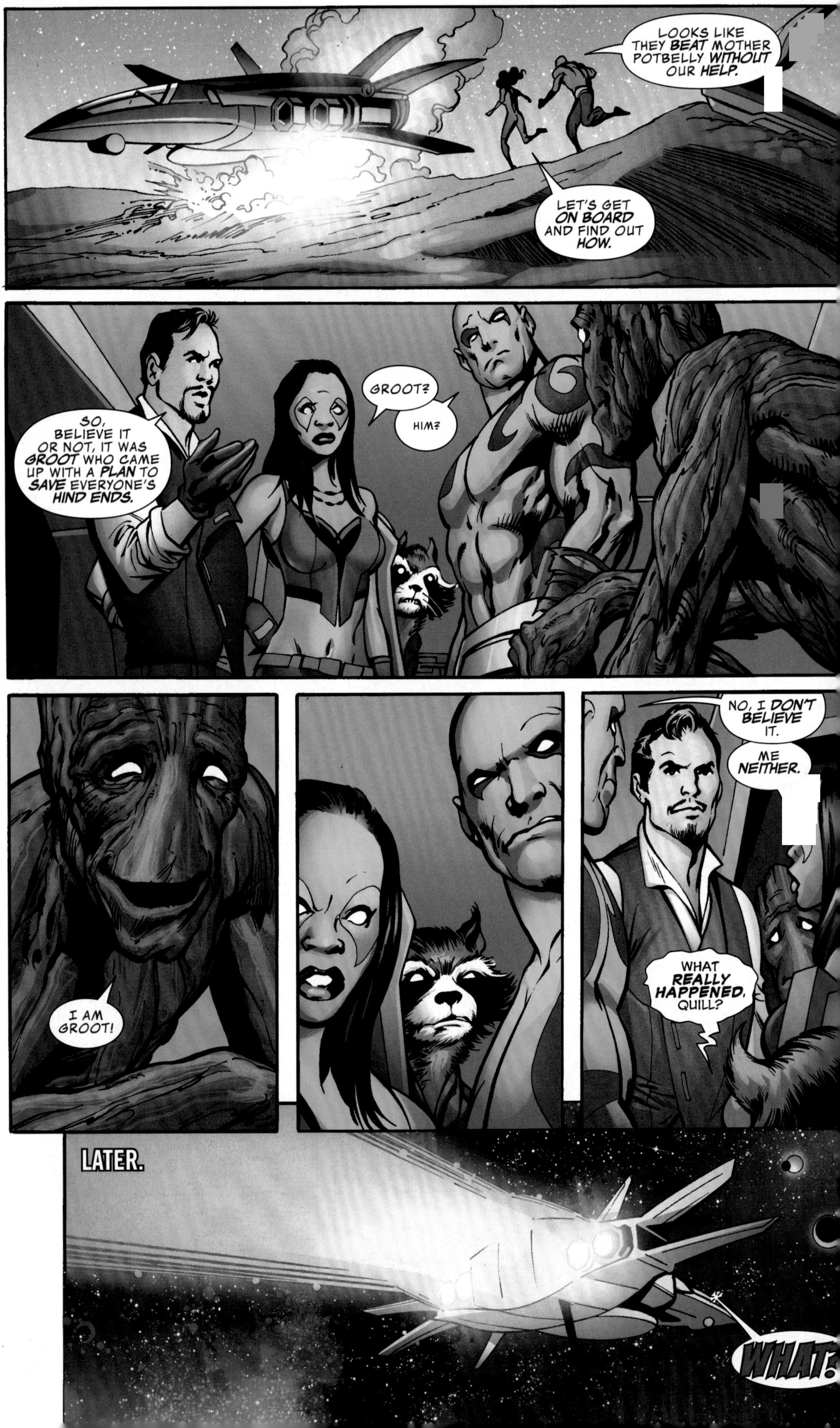
LOOKS LIKE THEY BEAT MOTHER POTBELLY WITHOUT OUR HELP.
LET'S GET ON BOARD AND FIND OUT HOW.
SO, BELIEVE IT OR NOT, IT WAS GROOT WHO CAME UP WITH A PLAN TO SAVE EVERYONE'S HIND ENDS.
GROOT?
HIM?
I AM GROOT!
NO, I DON'T BELIEVE IT.
ME NEITHER.
WHAT REALLY HAPPENED, QUILL?
LATER.
WHAT.

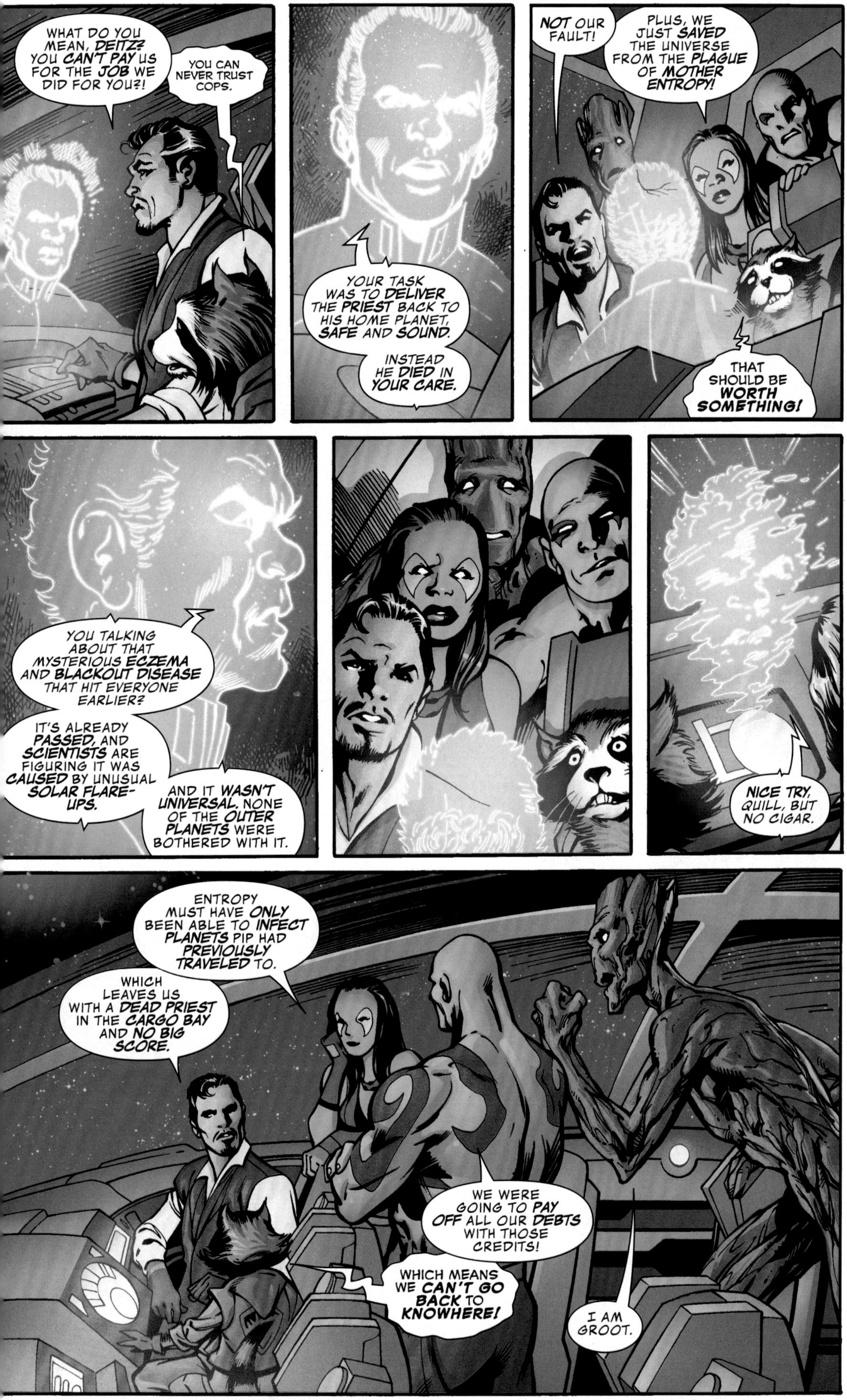

WHAT DO YOU MEAN, DEITZ? YOU CAN'T PAY US FOR THE JOB WE DID FOR YOU?!
YOU CAN NEVER TRUST COPS.
YOUR TASK WAS TO DELIVER THE PRIEST BACK TO HIS HOME PLANET, SAFE AND SOUND.
INSTEAD HE DIED IN YOUR CARE.
NOT OUR FAULT!
PLUS, WE JUST SAVED THE UNIVERSE FROM THE PLAGUE OF MOTHER ENTROPY!
THAT SHOULD BE WORTH SOMETHING!
YOU TALKING ABOUT THAT MYSTERIOUS ECZEMA AND BLACKOUT DISEASE THAT HIT EVERYONE EARLIER?
IT'S ALREADY PASSED, AND SCIENTISTS ARE FIGURING IT WAS CAUSED BY UNUSUAL SOLAR FLARE-UPS.
AND IT WASN'T UNIVERSAL. NONE OF THE OUTER PLANETS WERE BOTHERED WITH IT.
NICE TRY, QUILL, BUT NO CIGAR.
ENTROPY MUST HAVE ONLY BEEN ABLE TO INFECT PLANETS PIP HAD PREVIOUSLY TRAVELED TO.
WHICH LEAVES US WITH A DEAD PRIEST IN THE CARGO BAY AND NO BIG SCORE.
WE WERE GOING TO PAY OFF ALL OUR DEBTS WITH THOSE CREDITS!
WHICH MEANS WE CAN'T GO BACK TO KNOWHERE!
I AM GROOT.

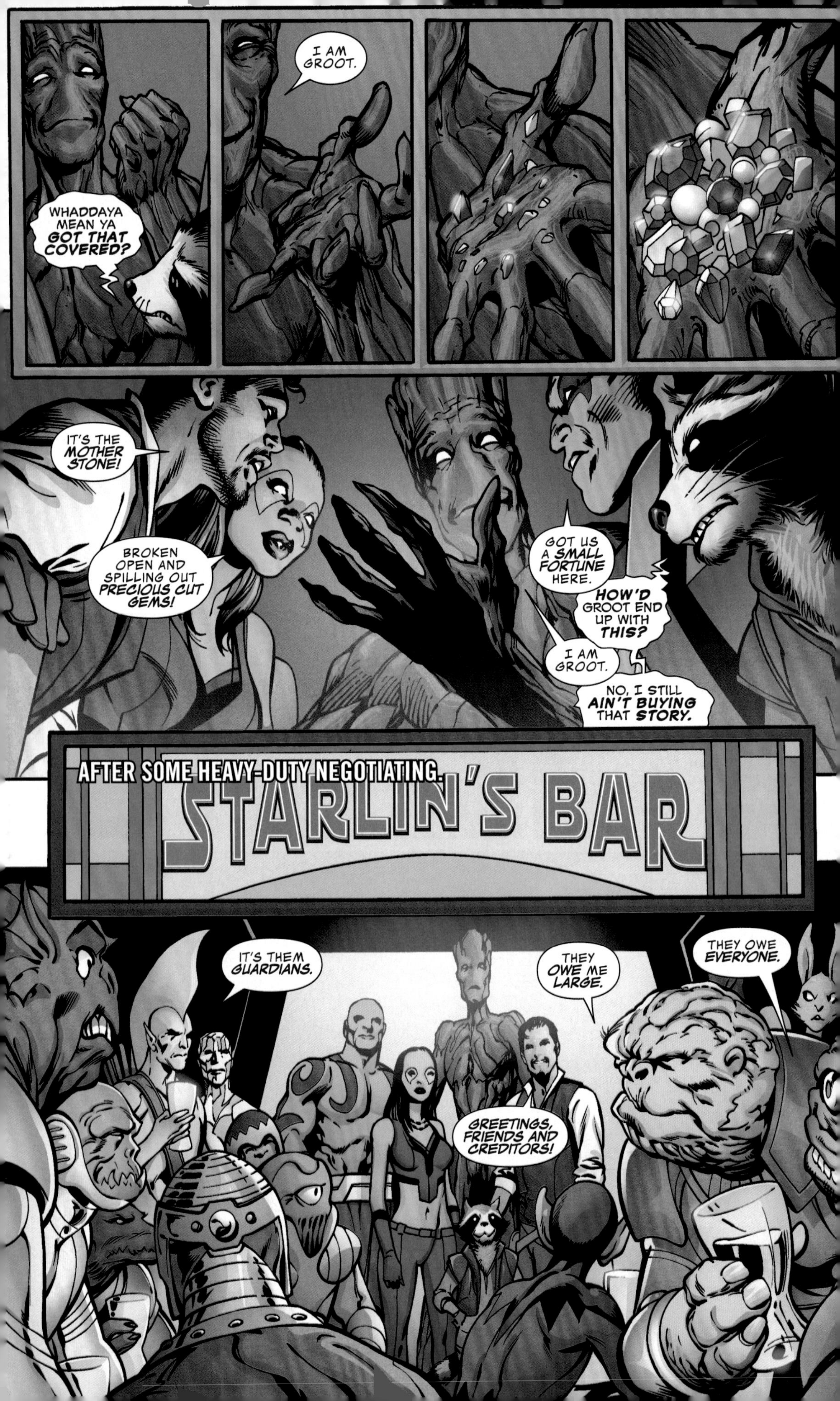
WHADDAYA MEAN YA GOT THAT COVERED?
I AM GROOT.
IT'S THE MOTHER STONE!
BROKEN OPEN AND SPILLING OUT PRECIOUS CUT GEMS!
GOT US A SMALL FORTUNE HERE.
HOW'D GROOT END UP WITH THIS?
I AM GROOT.
NO, I STILL AIN'T BUYING THAT STORY.
AFTER SOME HEAVY-DUTY NEGOTIATING.
STARLIN'S BAR
IT'S THEM GUARDIANS.
THEY OWE ME LARGE.
THEY OWE EVERYONE.
GREETINGS, FRIENDS AND CREDITORS!

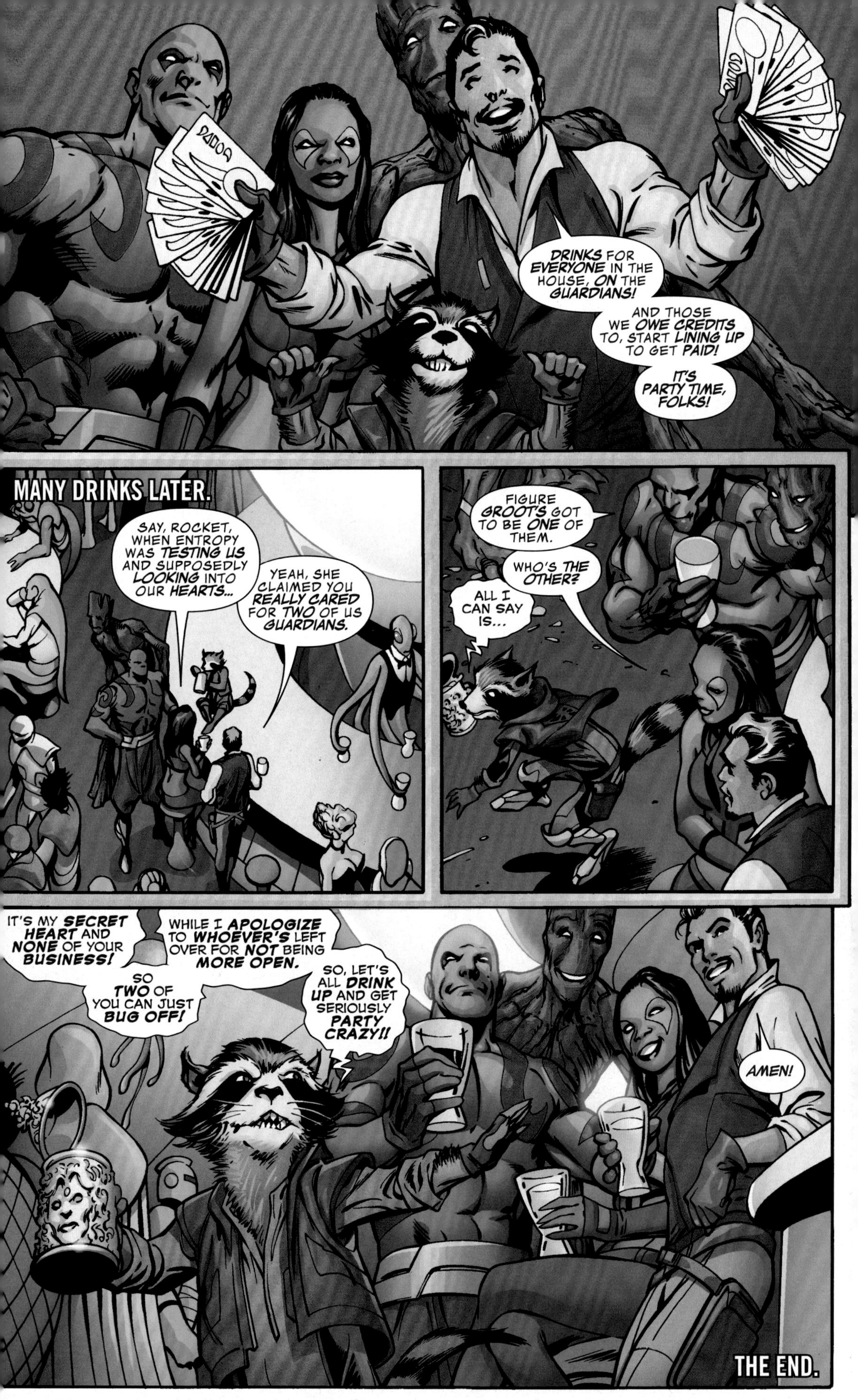

DRINKS FOR EVERYONE IN THE HOUSE, ON THE GUARDIANS!
AND THOSE WE OWE CREDITS TO, START LINING UP TO GET PAID!
IT'S PARTY TIME, FOLKS!
MANY DRINKS LATER.
SAY, ROCKET, WHEN ENTROPY WAS TESTING US AND SUPPOSEDLY LOOKING INTO OUR HEARTS...
YEAH, SHE CLAIMED YOU REALLY CARED FOR TWO OF US GUARDIANS.
FIGURE GROOT'S GOT TO BE ONE OF THEM.
WHO'S THE OTHER?
ALL I CAN SAY IS...
IT'S MY SECRET HEART AND NONE OF YOUR BUSINESS!
SO TWO OF YOU CAN JUST BUG OFF!
WHILE I APOLOGIZE TO WHOEVER'S LEFT OVER FOR NOT BEING MORE OPEN.
SO, LET'S ALL DRINK UP AND GET SERIOUSLY PARTY CRAZY!!
AMEN!
THE END.

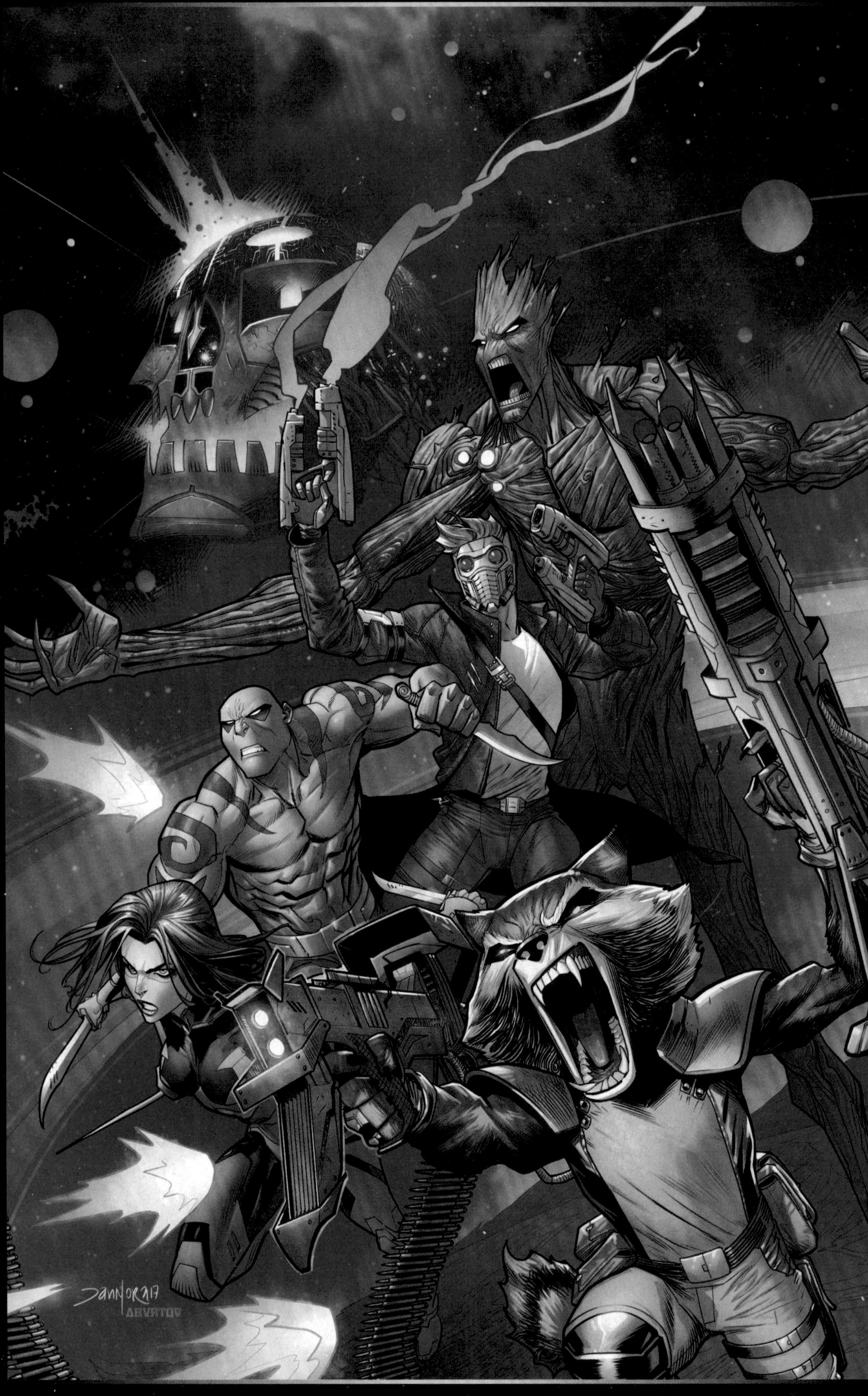

#1 VARIANT BY **DAN MORA** & **JESUS ABURTOV**